Work in the Soviet Union

MURRAY YANOWITCH

Work in the Soviet Union

Attitudes and Issues

M. E. SHARPE, INC.
Armonk, New York and London

Available in the United Kingdom and Europe from M. E. Sharpe Publishers, 3 Henrietta Street, London WC2E 8LU.

Published simultaneously as Vol. XIV, no. 3-4 of *International Journal of Politics.*

Library of Congress Cataloging in Publication Data

Yanowitch, Murray.
    Work in the Soviet Union.

    Bibliography: p.
    Includes index.
    1. Labor and laboring classes—Soviet Union—Attitudes. 2. Job satisfaction–Soviet Union. 3. Quality of work life—Soviet Union. 4. Industrial management—Soviet Union—Employee participation. I. Title.
HD8526.5.Y36 1985   306'.36'0947   84-27651
ISBN 0-87332-307-6

Printed in the United States of America.

Contents

To Rose

Acknowledgments

I would like to thank the National Council for Soviet and East European Research and Hofstra University for providing me with the opportunity to undertake the research which led to this volume. I am particularly grateful to my friend and colleague, Bertram Silverman, for his comments on the manuscript and for sharing with me his ideas on the problems of studying the work experience.

M. Y.

List of Tables

Work in the Soviet Union

Preface

How can we study, from a distance, the nature of the work experience and workers' perceptions of their lot in an alien society whose workers lack their own public "voice"—legally recognized, "independent" or "free" organizations and publications through which they can act and speak in defense of their own collective interests? We pose this question not to suggest that this situation is unusual in the modern world or that we have undertaken an inordinately difficult task—it is not—but to point to certain obvious difficulties involved in studying work and its discontents in this kind of society. It becomes necessary to rely on certain "proxies," as it were, for workers' expressions of their own attitudes and perceptions of their working lives. Thus we can never be quite certain whether the voices we hear are those of workers themselves or their constrained "proxies." More specifically, we have drawn heavily on two types of sources: (a) sociologists' studies of workers' job attitudes and (b) the growing Soviet literature on the need for work reform. Our impression is that Western students of Soviet society and economy have not yet adequately examined these materials for the light they can shed on the Soviet workplace and its problems. Since these sources are not likely to be very familiar, and may appear suspect to some readers, a few words on each seem in order here.

Since the early 1960s the study of work attitudes and motivations has been a principal concern of some of the Soviet Union's leading sociologists. Any such studies must obviously carry a certain ideological "load." Marxian visions of the transformation of work from "a means to existence" to an intrinsically rewarding and satisfying activity ("man's prime living need") continue to be invoked even if they have lost much of their credibility. But our judgment is that a sufficient number of these studies have been conducted with the kind of objectivity and scientific spirit that justifies a systematic and critical review of their findings. The best of them have been ready to admit that the

Marxian vision of communist work has been receding rather than approaching in recent years. At the very least we seek to demonstrate that they are worthy of closer attention than they have thus far received. The reader will have an opportunity to determine whether we have been "taken in." Our interest here is not only in overall levels of work satisfaction and discontent and their determinants, but in occupational and demographic differences in work attitudes, as well as the public discourse which the study of work has stimulated in the more "popular" and policy-oriented literature on labor problems. These are the issues which concern us in Chapters 1 through 3.

There is an abundant literature on Soviet attempts at economic reform and their failures. Much less attention has been paid to available evidence of pressures for work reform and enhanced opportunities for workers' participation in plant-level decision-making. It is a peculiarity of Soviet society that while it may be impossible to appeal (openly) for the democratization of political life, the urgency of "democratizing" and "enriching" working life has been voiced with increasing frequency in recent years. Reports of "experiments" in workplace democratization and appeals for more participatory forms of work organization have appeared in the writings of management specialists, sociologists and economists as well as in the "journalistic" media. Chapters 4 through 6 examine some illustrations of this work-reform current and the mechanisms used to subvert it "from within." It will become apparent that pressures for the kind of work-reform measures that we discuss here were no less alive during the brief Andropov interregnum, with its well-publicized campaign against "loafers" and "shirkers" and for heightened work efficiency, than they were in the closing years of the Brezhnev regime. Indeed, our impression is that Andropov's focus on workplace problems encouraged the adherents of work reform. Thus we find that some of the boldest appeals for "work democratization" were voiced in the immediate post-Brezhnev period (see, for example, our brief review of the recent writings of the sociologist Iadov and his colleagues in Chapter 6).

The materials we examine here reveal a striking contrast between the widespread recognition of the urgency of introducing work-reform measures on the one hand and the apparent incapacity or unwillingness of allegedly "all-powerful" central authorities to implement even relatively modest reformist policies on the other. How can we explain this "frozen" state of affairs at the Soviet workplace in the face of the increasing social and economic costs of inaction and in disregard of the persuasive "message" of work-reformers: that technological advance cannot be a palliative for problems rooted in the "social organization" of work? This is the issue we confront in our concluding Chapter 7, where we focus on some of the principal sources of resistance to changes in work organization.

Readers may notice that we have paid comparatively little attention to some topics that might be expected to play an important role in a study of Soviet workplace problems. There is little here, for example, on the theme of poor work discipline and the authorities' incessant appeals and efforts to "tighten" it. We take all this for granted, but it serves no purpose to elaborate on the familiar. Nor are there any but the most incidental references to the place of Soviet trade unions. This is not because we regard these as incidental matters unworthy of serious attention but rather that most of what needs to be said about them has already been adequately said by others.

We have been particularly concerned with the manner in which Soviet discussions of labor problems have become an arena of struggle between the forces of work reform and those groups which some participants in these discussions have labeled the "conservative forces." Since the views and practices of the latter are fairly well known, we have chosen to concentrate on some of the less familiar voices of the former. Although the work-reform current can hardly claim any major victories thus far (except perhaps that of being heard), the struggle seems to be continuing.

1
The Emergence of Soviet Studies of Work Attitudes

The first serious studies of work attitudes in the Soviet Union were initiated in the early 1960s shortly after the official recognition of sociology as a distinct and legitimate intellectual discipline. Since then such studies have multiplied and become a principal component of the Soviet version of "industrial sociology," with its focus on the "social problems of labor." By the late 1970s some of the initial investigations were already being replicated in their original setting, and new studies gradually encompassed an increasing range of occupational groups, technological environments and geographic locales. The quality of these studies is highly uneven. Some were obviously intended to serve primarily ideological rather than scientific ends. Others have been published in such bare summary form that it is impossible to assess their value. Nonetheless we are convinced that much can be learned about the nature of work and its discontents in the Soviet Union by a careful appraisal of these studies and the public discussion they have generated. This, of course, is the proposition which remains to be demonstrated below.

The economic and intellectual environment

Although the initial studies were made possible by the legitimation of sociology, a number of factors in the economic and intellectual environment of the 1960s and 1970s were particularly conducive to the burgeoning of interest in the study of attitudes toward work. Some familiar labor market problems appeared in a new setting, and some troublesome new ones emerged which had no obvious solutions—at least in the short run. But both the old and new problems made the period ripe for research on job attitudes.

a) Excessive labor turnover and unsatisfactory work discipline, for example, were certainly not new problems. Indeed the Soviet literature on the labor market during the prewar five-year plans is dominated by a concern with precisely these issues. Moreover the common explanation for the emergence of these problems during the early years of the industrialization drive seemed a fairly obvious matter. New recruits to the rapidly expanding industrial working class were drawn largely from peasants and their children. As a retrospective survey of that period by a group of Soviet sociologists recently put it, the problem of assimilating a mass inflow of peasants and former rural residents, "divorced from the foundations of their everyday life and incapable of adapting immediately to an urban mode of life, led to . . . a decline in the level of urban industrial culture."[1] By the 1960s and 1970s, of course, the situation had changed markedly. The process of "self-recruitment" of a "hereditary" working class was in full swing. In the midseventies the proportion of young workers (up to the age of 25) of peasant social origins was not more than 15% in such old industrial centers as Moscow, Leningrad and Kharkov. Although this share might reach 40% or more in new industrial centers and construction sites, surveys of young industrial workers' social origins in a variety of geographic locales revealed that a distinct majority were drawn from second- or third-generation working-class families.[2] Table 1.1 illustrates the dominance of "self-recruitment" of young workers in a range of industrial areas in the mid-1970s. In the words of the study cited above, these were youngsters whose "exposure to the peculiarities of the industrial organization of work . . . to the rhythm of urban life, to the norms and values of the working class begins long before their direct introduction to work activity."[3] Why, then, have the old problems of excessive labor turnover and poor work discipline reemerged in a form that seems just about as intractable—if not more so—as when workers were recruited largely from a peasant milieu? Why should it be necessary, some one-half century after the start of the great industrialization drive, to continually stress the need to develop the most elementary habits of an industrial culture (punctuality, precision, stability on the job)?

We are not concerned here with establishing the exact dimensions of these problems. Suffice it to say that recent studies of actual labor turnover commonly refer to it as being "considerably in excess of its normal level," and that poor work discipline (absenteeism, coming late to work or leaving early, intoxication on the job, refusal to follow

Table 1.1

Social Origins of Young Workers* Employed in Selected Geographic Areas, 1973–74 (in %)

| Social origins† | Geographic areas | | |
	Moscow Region	Urals	Bashkir ASSR
Workers	55.8	56.2	58.1
Peasants	15.2	18.7	36.4
Lower-level nonmanual employees	19.6	16.2	1.8
Specialists	5.4	8.3	3.3
Other	4.0	0.6	0.4
Total	100.0	100.0	100.0

Source: G. A. Slesarev, *Rastet rabochii klass*, Moscow, 1976, p. 27.
*This probably includes workers up to the age of 25.
†By occupational position of father.

superiors' orders) is acknowledged to be the source of "great losses" to the economy.[4] Nor are the answers to the questions posed above a complete mystery. Rather our point is that during a period when Soviet authorities have decided to mobilize the social sciences—including sociology—to aid in the "scientific management of society," problems like turnover and discipline have made the study of the values which Soviet citizens attach to their work activity, their perceptions of and orientations to work, and the sources of job satisfaction and dissatisfaction a matter of both "practical" and "scientific" interest.

b) The same is true of a relatively new problem which has attracted increasing attention since the mid-1960s—the alleged "gap" between workers' increasing educational attainments and the nature of the work tasks many are forced to perform. Among the first to anticipate that this could become an increasingly serious problem were the pioneers of Soviet studies of work attitudes, A. G. Zdravomyslov and V. A. Iadov. In a 1967 volume which reviewed the results of a 1962–64 survey of young Leningrad workers, they warned that a "disproportion" had already emerged between the expectations of young workers—fostered by prolonged schooling—for employment in "creative" or "high content" jobs and the still limited opportunities for such employment, given the relatively backward state of Soviet technology. Moreover the problem could be expected to intensify as an increasing proportion of youngsters entered the work force with a ''complete'' secondary education (normally ten or eleven years of schooling).[5] In the years since this early warning, the same theme has been frequently reiterated, and the idea that the rate of technological change since the early 1960s has lagged behind the rate of growth in educational attainments has been widely accepted in Soviet discussions of labor problems.[6]

Whether the problem should be formulated as an ''inflation'' of education, however, and what its consequences have been for work attitudes and work performance has stirred considerable controversy among Soviet economists and sociologists. We review this controversy in some detail in Chapter 3. What should be clear at this point is that there were solid grounds for concern about the difficulties of adapting a new breed of Soviet industrial workers to the kinds of jobs the economy was creating. The average years of schooling for a member of the work force increased by about 50% between 1959 and 1979, rising from approximately 6 years in 1959 to 7.5 in 1970, and to ''more than'' 9 in 1979.[7] By the late 1970s, with the government's campaign to ''universalize'' a complete secondary education in full swing, more than 90% of the youngsters graduating from the eighth grade continued their schooling in the upper grades of secondary school (see Table 1.2), with perhaps close to four-fifths or more attaining a complete secondary education, compared to distinctly less than half in the early 1960s.[8] If Soviet claims are anywhere near the truth, by the end of the 1970s the majority of workers in the 25-and-under age group in most industrial sectors had attained ten years of schooling.[9]

There is no simple way to compare these increases in educational attainments with changes in job characteristics and skill requirements. There is a crude measure, however, which both Western and Soviet economists have used as a rough indicator of the technological backwardness of Soviet industry and the continuing importance of ''unattractive and heavy labor''—the proportion of workers performing their jobs ''by hand, without the use of machinery and mechanisms.'' Although not all these jobs are unskilled, the relatively slow decline in such jobs (especially since the midsixties) is in striking contrast to the rapid increases in workers' educational attainments. The proportion of industrial workers employed in these strictly ''non-machine'' jobs changed as follows since the late 1950s (in %):

1959	45.5
1965	40.4
1969	38.2

1972   35.9
1975   34.6
1979   32.8

If we add to these purely manual workers those whose jobs were only incidentally aided by "machines and mechanisms," the percentage of manual workers (as distinct from those whose jobs may be regarded as essentially mechanized) rises to some 40–50% of the total. A similar order of magnitude is also suggested by V. A. Iadov's remark at the end of the 1970s that "no less than 40% of workers in basic production perform low-skilled manual and heavy physical work which does not provide any particular scope for creativity."[10]

Table 1.2

Proportions of Eighth-Grade Graduates Continuing Their Schooling in Educational Institutions Providing a "Complete" Secondary Education (in %)

Type of secondary educational institution	Eighth-grade graduates continuing their schooling (in %)		
	1970	1975	1978
Daytime general education school (ninth grade)	54.9	61.7	60.1
Evening general education school (ninth grade)	10.8	16.5	14.6
Specialized secondary school*	11.1	9.5	8.6
Secondary vocational-technical school†	1.7	8.8	15.5
All forms of secondary schooling	78.5	96.5	98.8

Source: F. R. Filippov, "Children in the Country of Developed Socialism," *Sotsiologicheskie issledovaniia*, 1979, no. 4, p. 61.

*These schools provide training leading to semiprofessional occupational status (technician, accountant, agronomist, nurse).

†These schools provide training for semiskilled and skilled workers' occupations.

The problem here is not simply the relatively rapid increase in young workers' educational levels in the face of a slow decline in the proportion of "low-content" jobs. It also involves the frustrations associated with the change in the traditional occupational destinations of secondary school graduates. Until the early 1960s the customary path followed by most youngsters with ten years of schooling was admission to a higher educational institution (*VUZ*) followed by attainment of intelligentsia ("specialist") occupational status upon graduation. This was made possible by the small contingent of youngsters receiving a full secondary education. Even in the early 1960s Soviet *VUZy* were able to absorb between one-third and one-half of secondary school graduates. With the explosion of upper-level secondary schooling later in the decade and throughout the 1970s, the situation changed markedly. By the latter half of the 1970s only some one-fifth of general-secondary school graduates could expect admission to full-time study at a *VUZ* (see Table 1.3). For the great majority completion of secondary school was followed by entry into the labor force and employment in workers' jobs (sometimes following a brief stint at a vocational school offering training in workers' trades) or in lower-level nonmanual occupations.

But the process of transforming—more accurately, "deflating"—the traditional educational and career expectations of this group of Soviet youth was by no means a painless one. Abundant evidence drawn from studies of youngsters' "career plans" (or "vocational

Table 1.3

Number of Students Admitted to Daytime Study in Higher Educational Institutions (VUZy) in % of Number of Graduates of General-Secondary Schools

	Daytime VUZ admissions	
	in % of daytime secondary school graduates	in % of total secondary school graduates
1950–53	77	61
1960–63	57	32
1970–73	24	19
1975	22	17
1976	21	16
1977	20	15
1978	21	15
1979	23	16
1980	23	16

Sources: Calculated from figures in S. L. Seniavskii and V. B. Tel'pukhovskii, *Rabochii klass SSSR (1938–1965)*, p. 153; Tsentral'noe statisticheskoe upravlenie SSSR, *Narodnoe khoziaistvo SSSR v 1974 g.*, Moscow, 1975, p. 693; *Narodnoe obrazovanie, nauka i kultura v SSSR*, Moscow, 1977, pp. 93, 247; *Narodnoe khoziaistvo SSSR v 1977 g.*, Moscow, 1978, pp. 490, 501; *Narodnoe khoziaistvo SSSR v 1980 g.* Moscow, 1981, pp. 458–68.

orientations'') in the 1960s and early 1970s showed that a substantial majority of those reaching the graduating classes of secondary schools hoped to continue a full-time schooling, usually at a *VUZ*, as a means of attaining ''specialists''' occupational and social status.[11] The fact that most were destined to be disappointed did not ease the task of adapting them to ''careers'' in working-class occupations. Some accounts of this process have not hesitated to stress its demoralizing impact on a section of Soviet youth. The ''shattering'' of career plans was accompanied by the growth of ''attitudes of skepticism, a weakening of belief in ideals. . . .'' Youngsters ''roamed'' from one lower-level job to another, jobs which they regarded as ''temporary evils'' which had to be borne pending admission to a *VUZ*—which usually failed to materialize.[12] By the late 1970s, however, a process we might loosely call ''consciousness lowering'' had apparently begun to take effect. Surveys of graduating secondary school students began to report some moderation in the overambitious career and job expectations of Soviet youth.[13] We may question, however, whether this process of submission to necessity has been wholly positive in its impact on job attitudes and work morale. For the moment our point is simply that the historical ''descent'' of secondary school graduates into workers' jobs is part of an economic setting which has been conducive to—and has provided raw materials for—the serious study of the values and attitudes associated with work activity.

c) We referred above to the slow decline in the proportion of jobs performed ''by hand, without the use of machinery and mechanisms.'' But what about those subject to the continuing process of ''mechanization and automation''? One of the endlessly repeated dogmas in the popular—and sometimes in the more ''academic''—literature is the notion that technological advance, with its reduction of heavy physical labor, is the ultimate solution to the economic and social problems associated with the prevalence of low-skilled manual jobs. But a more serious current in the Soviet literature on labor problems has recognized the ''contradictory'' or ''dual'' consequences of new technology for the work process:

> . . . in and of itself the acceleration of rates of mechanization and automation under present circumstances does not solve the whole problem of unskilled and low-skilled labor. . . . New technology lightens labor, but in the course of doing so it frequently leads to the simplification of work operations and to a reduction in their intellectual content.[14]

The view that ''scientific-technical progress'' is not an unmixed blessing has been most clearly expressed in connection with the extension of assembly-line operations in Soviet factories. In language that is highly reminiscent of earlier Western descriptions of this production technology, Soviet observers have portrayed it as subdividing the work process into highly fragmented, routine, and repetitive operations, as increasing the monotony of work and as requiring workers whose training for their "elementary operations" can be accomplished in a matter of days. In a word, technological change in the form of "conveyorization" often impoverishes the work experience.[15] Hence the difficulty which some of the most technologically advanced Soviet auto assembly plants, including the much heralded Volga Automobile Plant, had in the early 1970s in recruiting and retaining "stable cadres" of workers.[16] Nor is this simply a shorthand, stylized description of auto-assembly work. Similar accounts of the impact of productivity-increasing technological innovations in machine building, watch manufacture, and oil drilling have also pointed to the reduction in "the richness of work content," i.e., in workers' skill requirements, that has sometimes accompanied this process.[17]

Even the promise of automated technology—although typically proclaimed in glowing colors—is now recognized as having ambiguous consequences for the content of work and hence presumably for work attitudes. Not only does it create a new type of "worker-intellectual," it also produces "button-pushers" whose work "does not require any intellectual powers."[18] Some sociologists engaged in research on the new technology have warned that at least in the near future, automated technology will increase rather than reduce the number of monotonous types of jobs.[19] The comparatively recent concern for the problem of monotony at work has been extended to "routine mental labor," which some observers now regard as no less harmful in its consequences than monotonous manual labor:

> The operator sitting at a control panel does not directly see the results of his activity. He is separated from his colleagues and has very limited opportunity for communication. The more complicated the control panel, the greater is the emotional strain which the work requires of the individual. The negative consequences of routine mental work are more profound than the similar consequences of monotonous physical work.[20]

It is hard to believe that a large proportion of the Soviet work force will soon confront the fate of the employee at this control panel, or that if they did, they would reject it in favor of their present jobs. But the increasingly common acknowledgment that progress in "mechanization and automation" may have problematic consequences for the workers affected represents a move away from the simplistic technological optimism that for so long dominated Soviet visions of the future of work. It can hardly be accidental that studies of workers' reactions to their jobs have been encouraged, or at the very least tolerated, as this optimism has begun to wane.

d) One familiar but overriding feature of the Soviet labor market deserves at least brief mention at this point. Both the Soviet and Western literature suggest that since at least the early 1970s, it would be appropriate to characterize this market as a "seller's market." Although there is abundant evidence of padded employment rosters and underemployment of hired staffs, the overwhelming impression is one of widespread labor scarcity. As Holland Hunter puts it, "It is therefore literally true that apart from seasonal difficulties, unemployment scarcely exists in the Soviet economy."[21] Moreover there is the expectation, also shared by Western specialists, that recent labor shortages will probably intensify as new additions to the labor force decline sharply in the 1980s.[22] The relevance of this to our theme is that under such conditions, the prospects for economic growth have become increasingly dependent on the growth of labor productivity. While none of the sociologists engaged in work attitude studies has claimed a simple functional relationship between work satisfaction and labor productivity, the urgency of increasing the latter under conditions of labor scarcity has been explicitly invoked to justify close attention to workers' job attitudes. Such attention seems all the more justified in light of the decline in annual productivity growth in industry from 6% in 1971–75 to 3.4% in 1976–79 according to Soviet sources (or from 4.4% in 1971–75 to 1.8% in 1976–80 according to CIA estimates).[23]

The concept of "social planning"

The "practical" issues briefly outlined above have had their counterpart in the emergence of the concept of "social planning."[24] Essentially the same concept has appeared under a variety of rubrics, all stressing the urgency of planning the enterprise's "social development," its "social processes," its "social effectiveness." Emerging in the late 1960s, the Soviet literature on social planning as a supplement to economic planning has now reached sizable proportions and warrants a separate study. Our interest, however, is confined mainly to the manner in which social planning has served as a vehicle to promote the study of work attitudes and the factors which affect them. It has become part of the intellectual environment in which permissible public discourse on the problem of mobilizing work effort now proceeds.

It is not at all clear that social planning embodies a distinct institutional mechanism designed to implement a set of specific targets, or that it has made much difference in the actual functioning of Soviet economic enterprises. At the very least, however, it has introduced and popularized a new vocabulary in Soviet discussions of labor problems. At the most, it has introduced some new ideas which an optimist might regard as auguring institutional changes designed to better adapt individuals to their work roles, to improve their work performance and indeed to create a heightened sense of participation in enterprise decision-making—in a word, to increase work satisfaction.

In the popular and not altogether precise language that often accompanies expositions of social planning, it is represented as focusing on the "human factor" in production, as seeking to improve the social-psychological climate of the enterprise and as having the "humanization of work" as a principal objective. In the more traditional Marxian terminology, while economic planning has largely meant planning the development of the "productive forces," with changes in the "relations of production" emerging as unplanned consequences, social planning seeks to directly affect the "relations of production."[25] In more operational and modest terms, this has meant the formulation of a set of "social indicators" of enterprise activity. A partial list of these indicators includes the following: (a) an improvement in the skill mix of available jobs; (b) the provision of retraining facilities when required by the introduction of new technology; (c) increased outlays on occupational health and safety measures; (d) the specification of allocations from enterprise funds for housing, child-care, and recreational facilities; (e) a rise in the level of workers' job satisfaction.

Although some of the literature on social planning has gone so far as to argue that its goals should be regarded as equivalent in "rank" to those of economic planning, and some leading sociologists-economists (T. Zaslavskaia, for example) have even affirmed that socialist development should be regarded as "not only, and perhaps not so much, an economic as a social process,"[26] it is difficult to believe that managerial personnel pressed to meet production, sales and profit targets have fully assimilated these views. Whether these social indicators are taken seriously or not at the enterprise level must depend heavily on the extent to which they seem necessary to enhance work morale and job performance. And if they are taken seriously, their translation into realizable targets requires access to resources which have competing uses and which may be beyond the powers of an individual enterprise to acquire. What is of interest for our purposes, however, is not so much the still dubious reality of social planning as some of the ideas that have emerged in connection with this concept.

The work of N. I. Lapin and his colleagues may serve as an illustration. For this group of sociologists the discussion of social planning becomes the occasion for exposition of a particular version of "organization theory" with a distinct role for studies of work attitudes. In highly compressed form the links in the argument are as follows.[27] The problem of social planning requires analysis of the interaction between the individual and the organization. The production organization (economic enterprise) imposes certain demands on the behavior and abilities of individuals. These demands flow from the goals or objectives of the organization as a producing enterprise. The individual's "conformity" or "fit" to the requirements of the organization is expressed in his contribution to the realization of the organization's goals. This contribution is indicated by his labor productivity, the quality of his output, his work discipline—essentially by his work performance. These "parameters of individual behavior" depend partly on the "objective conditions" established at the enterprise—the extent of mechanization of production processes, the pleasantness of working conditions, the system of work incentives. But the individual's contribution to the organization's goals also depend significantly on "subjective factors"—the extent to which he has accepted the "values and norms" of the organization and has a sense of being "included" or "integrated" in it.

By analogy the individual confronts the organization with certain requirements of his own. The individual's goal in the organization is both the direct satisfaction of certain needs (for "work activity, prestige, communication with others, self-actualization") as well as obtaining the resources necessary for their satisfaction. Thus the "effectiveness of the organization with respect to the individual may be defined as the magnitude of the organization's contribution to the satisfaction of the individual's needs." The latter are distinguished in accordance with Maslow's theory of a "hierarchy of needs," with higher-level needs (for recognition, esteem, creativity) coming to the fore after lower-level physical and security needs are met. In this context the state of work discontent at the enterprise may serve as an important "parameter of social planning." It yields information signaling required changes in the organization's "working conditions, managerial style, incentive system.'' The study of work attitudes thus becomes an instrument for improving the functioning of the organization.

Other industrial sociologists have stressed a somewhat different but related use for information on individuals' reaction to their work roles. For N. A. Aitov a principal problem is the need for "the social regulation of technological progress."[28] Although the precise institutional mechanism for implementing this "social regulation" is not specified, Aitov's general point seems clear. The choice of technology should not be based on productivity considerations alone, without regard to its impact on workers' skills and job attitudes. In particular, "social regulation" is required to avoid the multiplication of low-skilled jobs for an increasingly educated work force. Recognizing that his proposal may require "more than one five-year plan" to implement, Aitov has urged that studies of work attitudes be used to design "a model of an optimal structure of implements of labor" geared to increasing workers' job satisfaction.[29]

These discussions in the social planning literature, with their appeal for sensitivity to the "human factor" in production, may be regarded as an expression of a particular variant of Soviet managerial ideology. Information on work attitudes and the source of work dissatisfaction is to be made available to "formulators of plans,"[30] to those who make decisions on the introduction of new technology, perhaps even to those who design it. The information itself is to be gathered by sociologists working jointly with the enterprise's "social organizations" (the Party, Komsomol and local trade union). There are no obvious signs of any recognition that workers may need distinctive institutional channels of their own for the formulation of their attitudes to the workplace and their own interests in "humanizing" it. Thus social planning and its acceptance of the need for monitoring job attitudes seem designed mainly to serve the purpose of a kind of enlightened managerialism grappling with the problems of improving work performance.

The Marxian heritage

Thus far we have considered mainly those sources of Soviet interest in work attitudes which are rooted in recent labor market problems. What role, if any, has the Marxian vision of work activity played in Soviet studies of the work experience? Although a fuller answer will emerge as we review the Soviet studies in some detail below, for the moment we wish to do little more than pose the question and suggest some broad outlines of an answer.

But even to raise the question may strike some as an idle or, at best, naïve exercise. Isn't the main function of Marxism in the Soviet Union essentially to justify whatever policies the ruling authorities have decided to pursue and to provide a kind of compulsory vocabulary in which to clothe intellectual discourse, especially in the social sciences? There is no need to dispute this widely shared view at this point except to note that it does not exhaust the uses of Marxism in the Soviet Union, particularly in studies of the meaning of work. What we should not ignore is the possibility that Marxian categories may lend themselves to research on work attitudes and may even operate as a stimulus to such research—even in the Soviet Union.

In the West, of course, Marxian concepts have had a noticeable impact on studies of the work process and its psychological consequences. This is certainly the case in the United States, where the Marxian tradition has rarely been a major intellectual influence. We refer in particular to those studies which have taken the Marxian category of alienated labor seriously and have attempted to apply it in empirical investigations of the meaning of work. Starting from Marx's basic concept of alienation as the individual's loss of control over both the product and process of his work activity, these studies have sought to make it a more precise and operational concept by specifying a number of dimensions or indices of alienation—for example, powerlessness, meaninglessness, isolation, self-estrangement. They have then examined the relationship between work in different technological settings (Robert Blauner) or work differing in scope for initiative, thought and independent judgment (Melvin L. Kohn), on the one hand, and the subjective experience of alienation on the other.[31]

It would be strange indeed if Soviet sociologists did not draw in some way on this intellectual heritage in their own studies of the work process. In fact the applicability of the concept of alienated labor to Soviet conditions has been explicitly acknowledged since the early 1960s.[32] In its minimalist or "apologetic" version, this acknowledgment takes the form of admitting that the socialization of productive property eliminates only the "economic foundations" of alienation, that "survivals" of alienated labor continue to exist and are rooted in the "immaturity" of the productive forces. The latter still require the kind of division of labor which confines workers to narrow specialties for a lifetime and generates substantial inequalities in rewards for work. The objective indicator of alienation appears in "the problem of dissatisfaction with work," which is confined largely to workers unaided by machinery or engaged in routine assembly-line operations.[33]

The hallmark of this position is the identification of alienation with underdeveloped technology in the Soviet Union (but with private ownership of property in capitalist societies).

A more sophisticated and fruitful utilization of the Marxian framework appears in the major Soviet studies of the work process. The concept of alienation itself is only rarely explicitly invoked in these studies, but some of the ideas traditionally associated with it are elaborated. Thus Zdravomyslov and Iadov distinguish between two basic orientations to work: (a) work activity as externally imposed necessity, as a means of satisfying needs external to the work process, and (b) work activity as an "inner need," an "end in itself" (*samotsel'*). The empirical question then becomes not simply establishing the levels of satisfaction or dissatisfaction with work but determining the values attached to work activity. Attitudes toward work which are governed mainly by the material rewards associated with it point to the dominance of the first orientation. When work derives its meaning mainly from the content of the work process itself, or as Zdravomyslov and Iadov put it, from the opportunity it provides for initiative and creativity, the second orientation dominates. Thus the overcoming of alienated labor is not simply a matter of increased work satisfaction but of the perception of work as an inherently rewarding, self-fulfilling activity.[34] Progress toward "communist labor" would therefore be signaled by the increasing relative importance of "creative" work content (relative to money earnings) as the principal source of work satisfaction. Anticipating somewhat an interesting issue that will arise when we review the Soviet findings below, this way of projecting the vision of "communist labor" leaves open the possibility that this vision may either recede or come closer to realization with the passage of time.

This highly compressed and perhaps oversimplified summary of a Soviet effort to formulate the problem of work attitudes in Marxian terms should not obscure the possibilities inherent in the Marxian heritage for the serious study of the work experience. Whether the final product turns out to be mainly empty rhetoric, findings of scientific value or some combination of both should remain an open question.

The Soviet studies to which we now turn are, of course, mainly a response to immediate labor problems, not to a Marxian vision of unalienated work. But their findings have necessarily been "filtered" through some version of what has become an "official" state philosophy. How much can such studies reveal?

2
Work Attitudes: Conceptual Issues and Principal Findings

One of our principal objectives here is a systematic review of the available evidence on Soviet work attitudes. But we are also interested in the intellectual discourse which has accompanied Soviet studies in this area, particularly the elements of controversy that have emerged. How have Soviet sociologists responded to their own findings? To what extent have these findings been used as vehicles for proposing changes in the organization of work? How has Soviet thought on the significance of work attitudes and the techniques for assessing them evolved since the early 1960s? Thus our concern throughout is not only with the perception of the work experience as revealed in Soviet studies of job attitudes but in the impact of these studies on the public discussion of problems of work morale and performance. Obviously we refer only to the kind of discussion that surfaces in published form.

The conceptual apparatus

The initial investigation of Leningrad workers' job attitudes by Iadov and Zdravomyslov in the early 1960s has had a profound impact on all subsequent Soviet studies of the work experience. In some cases these later efforts have sought to replicate, in whole or in part, the approach of the Leningrad study in other geographic locales. In other cases, where the analytical categories and general approach have departed somewhat from those used in the early Leningrad study, the sociologists involved nevertheless seemed to be "building on" and responding to this pioneering work. Thus even if its findings are necessarily dated by now, a brief examination of the conceptual apparatus and structure of the Iadov and Zdravomyslov study may serve as a useful introduction to our review of the larger body of Soviet work in this area.

The Leningrad study developed four indicators of work attitudes. One of them was an "objective" indicator in the sense that it was based on an assessment of the repondents' work performance rather than their "subjective" reactions to their work roles. The assumption was that "real attitudes" would be reflected in workers' behavior in production activity. Performance ratings supplied by supervisors included information on workers' productivity (norm fulfillment) and quality of work, "discipline and conscientiousness," and "initiative." These ratings were combined to derive a typology of work-performance groups ranging from "best" to "worst."[1] This method of gauging work attitudes has not played a significant role in most subsequent Soviet studies, possibly because the association between "objective" and "subjective" indicators was a rather tenuous one, and interest was focused chiefly on the latter indicators. We mention it here to suggest something of the wide range of the Leningrad study, but also because Iadov and Zdravomyslov drew on the "objective" indicator to formulate a conception of "communist work." One of the elements in this "objective" indicator of work attitudes, it will be recalled, was the degree of initiative exercised by the worker. For these Leningrad sociologists, ". . . the most characteristic trait of the communist attitude toward work is the initiative of the worker expressed in his active participation in the rationalization of production, in his readiness to propose ways of improving work organization . . . ." Initiative means a readiness to ". . . act against routine in the organization of work, against outmoded technology."[2] This formulation will be worth recalling when we turn later to the policy implications of Soviet work attitude studies.

More important for our purpose at present and for their influence on subsequent studies of work attitudes were some of the "subjective" indicators developed by Iadov and Zdravomyslov. There were three such indicators: (a) satisfaction with work, (b) satisfaction with "specialty" (occupation), and (c) workers' evaluations of the "social value" of work. In contrast to the "objective" indicator, responses here were obtained directly from the sampled workers by means of questionnaires administered by the team of sociologists.

Of the two satisfaction indicators, satisfaction with work has played the larger role in Soviet studies, and we may focus our attention on this measure. Workers' responses in the Leningrad study could range from "highly satisfied" to "highly dissatisfied." They could also choose the option "I am indifferent to my work"; and as we shall see, a fair number did so. There were additional "control questions" designed to eliminate from the "satisfied" category those workers who expressed satisfaction with work but also indicated that they wanted to change jobs or would not return to their current jobs if for some reason they were temporarily absent from work. Such workers were classified as having given "contradictory answers" rather than as being satisfied with work. In addition to these general (or "facet-free," in the language of similar American studies) work satisfaction questions, the worker-repondents were asked to rate more than a dozen specific facets of their work situation. The objective here was to isolate the particular job characteristics which contributed to overall work satisfaction or discontent, with special stress on the relative importance of "work content" versus "material rewards." The attempt to assess the relative impact of these factors on work attitudes became an abiding theme in future studies. It should be apparent from this brief summary that the Leningrad project was a carefully conceived and executed piece of research. Little wonder that the studies which followed should have regarded it as a model to emulate, although relatively few—if any—seem to have matched its standards.

The last of the "subjective" indicators—perceptions of the "social value" of work—was something of a misnomer. What Iadov and Zdravomyslov had in mind here was essentially the worker's conception of a "good job" rather than an explicit evaluation of his current one. The questions were formulated in such a way that the possible answers could fall somewhere between the two extremes of (a) "a good job is any job that pays well" and (b) "a good job is one where you are most useful and needed." This was an attempt to identify the values which workers bring to their jobs or which they develop on the job. Clearly, the answers had implications for assessing the prevalence of "communist attitudes" toward work. However these were to be defined, they obviously would not be characterized by the identification of a good job as "any job that pays well." In more recent years the study of values associated with work activity has moved beyond the rather narrow formulation found in the Leningrad study, but it was the latter which initially posed this issue as an appropriate one for empirical investigation.

Since much of the discussion which follows focuses on various aspects of the work satisfaction studies, it is important to ask how "work satisfaction" is conceptualized in the Soviet literature. Assuming it can be properly measured, what does it reveal? How important a measure is it? Why should it be studied? Directly or indirectly, all of these questions have been confronted in the Soviet literature, but the answers have not always been the same.

Given the long-standing Soviet concern with improving workers' job performance, it should come as no surprise that some of this literature has stressed a "productionist" justification for job satisfaction studies. In its clearest form this approach regards information on work satisfaction (dissatisfaction) as primarily a means of ascertaining available "reserves for increasing labor productivity."[3] While a concern with productivity is never entirely absent in Soviet job attitude studies, this formulation would undoubtedly be regarded as simplistic by the more sophisticated Soviet investigators. For Iadov and Zdravomyslov, to identify the study of work attitudes with the search for sources of increased labor productivity represented a kind of narrow "utilitarianism" unworthy of a socialist society. Even in their earliest writings these sociologists stressed that the significance of work satisfaction "goes far beyond the limits of purely production problems." It impinges on the "psychic health" of the population, on the whole moral tone of the society.[4] As for its direct impact on worker productivity, their own studies, as well as those of American researchers (here they cited the work of Frederick Herzberg), had found that job satisfaction is "quite weakly correlated with the results of work."[5] This rejection of the simple "productionist" approach simultaneously restricted and enlarged the significance of work satisfaction.

Perhaps the most common Soviet formulation of the general concept of work satisfaction regards it as reflecting the prevailing "balance" between workers' needs associated with laboring activity on the one hand and the opportunities for their realization on the other.[6] Viewed in this way, a high level of job satisfaction among a particular group of workers is not necessarily an unambiguous blessing. To be satisfied with unskilled or monotonous work bespeaks an impoverishment of the individual's needs and interests. Similarly, the existence of a certain amount of work dissatisfaction is not invariably an unhealthy state of affairs. When it reflects a high level of unfulfilled "claims" which people make on their work, it may generate a kind of creative tension leading to desirable changes at the workplace. Thus the degree of satisfaction or discontent should never be assessed in isolation but always in relation to workers' "claims," "needs," "interests."[7] Where the Soviet literature specifies the needs whose satisfaction may be either blocked or realized at the workplace, the list is a wide-ranging one: from "physiological (elementary) needs" to "social and spiritual needs," with the latter category including—in part—"friendship, prestige and recognition, autonomy . . . creativity, cognitive and esthetic experience."[8] Once the qualifications indicated above are recognized, most Soviet students of work attitudes would probably agree with the authors of a recent handbook on industrial sociology that an increase in job satisfaction over time signifies "progressive changes" in the position of the worker and the organization of production.[9]

One of the ideas recognized by some Soviet investigators, particularly N. F. Naumova, is that the level of job satisfaction not only is a response of the individual to his own work situation (given the "richness" or "poverty" of his needs and interests) but also reflects his evaluation of his relative position in the work organization or even in the society at large. Why is it that the job satisfaction of a group may remain essentially unchanged although its conditions of work and pay have improved? Partly because there may have been parallel changes in "neighboring" occupational groups. "An individual's conviction that he has less of something than others is much more important for him than the fact that he has more of it than he had yesterday or ten years ago."[10] Similarly, a process of reliance on traditional "group norms" or "criteria of normalcy" may explain a somewhat different phenomenon: a group's unexpectedly high level of job satisfaction in jobs characterized by "objectively" poor working conditions. Occupational groups in which women predominate—Naumova cites agricultural laborers as an example—may serve as an illustration of this mechanism.[11] The pressure of conventional "group norms" operates to predispose them to accept as "normal" their current work roles. Essentially the same point is made by sociologists who invoke workers' limited knowledge of alternative employment opportunities (or the incapacity to imagine them) as a source of satisfaction with (or at least acceptance of) low-ranking jobs.[12]

Perhaps the most direct challenge to any simplistic interpretation of work satisfaction—whether in the form of the "productionist" fallacy or the view that "the more satisfied the better"—has appeared in some of the later writings of V. A. Iadov. He has sought to redirect the concern of attitude studies to the characteristics of the employing organization, for "the level of satisfaction reveals only the level of adaptation of the worker to the given organization, nothing more." Adaptation, in turn, signifies the worker's assimilation of the "occupational and organizational requirements associated with his work activity. . . ." What requires study and evaluation, therefore, is the nature of organizational arrangements and the kinds of demands they make on employees.[13] High levels of satisfaction can be expected when there is a close "fit" between workers' needs ("dispositions" in Iadov's more recent work) and the organization's demands. Thus a critical question is whether the latter provide scope for "initiative and creativity," or do they call largely for the mere "execution of tasks (*ispolnitel'nost'*) and punctuality"? At the risk of reading more into this formulation than was intended, we are inclined to emphasize its special importance under Soviet circumstances. By stressing the responsibility of the employing "organization" for both workers' job satisfaction and their productive performance, it leaves the door open for a wider range of policy responses than the more traditional reliance on technological advance. Opportunities for more satisfying and more productive work need not wait only on the promise of further "mechanization and automation."

It would obviously be an exaggeration to claim that Soviet sociologists have developed a comprehensive "theory" of job satisfaction. Enough has been said, however, to suggest that their studies of work attitudes have gone well beyond the mere tallying of "do you like your job or not" responses. But what about the general reliability of responses to work-attitude questions under Soviet conditions? Can they be taken seriously? Investigators in Western settings have long been sensitive to the pitfalls of relying on self-reporting of job attitudes. Mechanisms of self-deception, ego defense and social pressure tend to bias responses in favor of job satisfaction. As a recent study for the OECD by Jack Barbash puts it:

> Job satisfaction is so closely tied in with one's self-esteem that the respondent may not be really answering the question as to whether or not he is satisfied with his job so much as whether or not he feels his life has been worthwhile. . . . What is being measured in part may not be satisfaction in work but a deep need in the worker to say that he has found some acceptable accommodation with his environment.[14]

Are not these problems of reliability likely to be magnified in the Soviet environment? Quite apart from pressures on respondents, are not the pressures on the sociologist-investigator to stress the prevalence of "positive" work attitudes so overwhelming that any substantial evidence of work discontent is likely to be concealed?

Although a more complete response to these objections will emerge as our study proceeds, some preliminary remarks are in order here. What Soviet studies are or are not permitted to reveal is not something to be decided a priori. There are institutionalized channels through which Soviet workers regularly express their attitudes toward their jobs. They change them, and do so with a frequency that has long disturbed Soviet authorities. But at least in recent years those authorities have not imposed serious obstacles to free movement in the labor market. Under such conditions it would be surprising if workers felt unduly inhibited in the self-reporting of job attitudes. Moreover our interest is not primarily in determing "absolute" levels of work satisfaction—which would be a problematic undertaking under any conditions—but in a whole range of related questions: occupational and demographic differences in perceptions of work, the role of specific job characteristics in explaining variations in work attitudes, the use of work-attitude surveys in public discourse and policy discussions. None of this is meant to deny that the sources of distortion which Western investigators have pointed to in their own studies also exist in a Soviet setting, or that Soviet investigators rarely ask certain important types of questions (for example, questions relating to possible conflicts of interests between workers and managers), or that sociologists must be politically sensitive in reporting their findings. The major problem of relying on the Soviet data, however, lies elsewhere—the limited availability of experienced, professionally competent Soviet investigators with the technical expertise to design and execute work-attitude surveys in a manner that approaches "scientific" standards. We can do little more at this point than indicate our awareness of all these problems and urge the reader to postpone deciding whether we have been "taken in" until the uses made of Soviet data in this study become apparent.

Some initial findings

We may begin at the most general level, with indicators of overall work satisfaction and dissatisfaction. There is no need to burden the reader with excessive detail on Soviet data problems, but a word on the available sources and their limitations may be useful. We are unaware of any Soviet "macro" studies based on national samples. All the available surveys apply to particular localities, in some cases to individual plants. The respondents in most surveys are confined to the "workers" (*rabochie*) occupational category. In some cases only engineering-technical personnel were surveyed, and in a few others representatives of all major occupational groups (from common laborers to higher-level managers) were included. We confine our attention here to nonagricultural jobs. In addition to "satisfied" or "dissatisfied" responses, most surveys include an "other" option which may encompass one or a combination of the following: "indifferent," "can't answer," "indeterminate," "contradictory answer."

The results of more than a dozen such surveys are brought together in Table 2.1 (derived from the "raw" data in Appendix Table A-1). Although these findings exhibit considerable variation at the extremes, there is a readily observable clustering of responses in most surveys.[15] Among worker-respondents—barring a couple of extreme cases—approximately one-half to two-thirds normally reported satisfaction with their jobs, with the more typical satisfied proportion falling closer to the lower end of this range. In those studies which included nonmanual occupational categories, the proportion of satisfied respondents was usually somewhat higher—on the order of 60% to 80% in eight out of nine surveys. In none of the cases summarized in Table 2.1 was the proportion of respondents indicating satisfaction with work in excess of 80%. Where the "highly satisfied" could be distinguished from the total satisfied, the former category generally accounted for some one-fifth to one-third of all respondents, reaching 50% in only one case (see Appendix Table A-1). What about the dissatisfied? Aside from one unusually blissful sample of automobile industry workers in a 1974 study reporting a dissatisfaction rate of less than 5%, and another in the Gorky region in 1979 in which 5–6% were dissatisfied, the proportion of respondents dissatisfied with their jobs ranged from one-tenth to one-third of those questioned. A dissatisfaction rate of close to 20% or more was not unusual.

What are we to make of these initial findings? It would be foolish, of course, to attach much significance to any comparison of this scattering of local Soviet studies—representing the early stages of Soviet efforts to measure work attitudes—with the results of the carefully designed national surveys conducted in the United States by organizations with a tradition of attitude surveys. But even the crudest of such comparisons cannot help but confront one striking point: Soviet respondents seem somewhat more restrained in expressing satisfaction with work and at least as willing to report job dissatisfaction as their American counterparts.

In a review of national surveys conducted in the United States through the early 1970s, George Strauss summarized their findings as follows: "In the typical study, only 10–20% of those who reply report that they are dissatisfied with their jobs."[16] Essentially the same result is suggested by the recent studies of the University of Michigan's Survey Research Center (Table 2.2), which reported rates of job

Table 2.1

Summary of Responses in Soviet Job Satisfaction Surveys

Occupational category	Year	Scope of sample	Response categories (in %)		
			satisfied	dissatisfied	other
Workers	1962–64	2,665 workers up to age 30, Leningrad industrial enterprises	40.9	16.1	43.3
	1966	833 workers, Perm industrial enterprises	51.2	13.2	34.7
	1971–72	approximately 3,000 workers, Kishinev Tractor Plant	48.7	21.3	30.0
	1972	878 workers, Volga Auto Plant	48.7	22.3	29.0
	1972	37% of workers up to age 28, Angarsk Oil-Chemical Combine	46.1	29.5	24.4
	1972	workers in Kazakhstan industrial enterprises:			
		mining metallurgical combine	63.7	13.0	23.4
		cotton-textile combine	56.9	16.7	26.4
		meat-packing combine	59.3	22.6	18.1
	1972–74	workers in oil industry:			
		Glavtiumenneftgaz association	70.7	22.3	7.0
		Sakhalinneft association	56.9	32.9	10.2
	1973	workers in three building-materials plants in Uzbekistan	58.0	13.2	28.7
	1974	385 workers in 4 auto plants*	76.8	3.4	19.8
	1976	1,534 workers up to age 30, Leningrad industrial enterprises	40.2	22.0	37.8
	1979	workers in enterprises of Gorky region	71.6	5.9	22.5

Occupational category	Year	Scope of sample	Response categories (in %)		
			satisfied	dissatisfied	other
Engineering-technical personnel	1965	2,083 engineering-technical personnel Bashkir republic industrial enterprises and design bureaus	73.2	26.8	
	1965–70	2,696 engineering-technical personnel, Leningrad industrial enterprises and research organizations	62.8	27.3	9.9
	1970	218 engineers, Leningrad design and research organizations	79.4	13.2	7.4
	1973	engineering-technical personnel in three building-materials plants in Uzbekistan†	70.3	9.5	20.2
	1979	engineering-technical personnel, Gorky region	66.0	6.4	27.6
Mixed occupational groups	1965–66	5,000 workers and nonmanual employees to age 28, auto and tractor industry	49	29	22
	1970–74	workers and nonmanual employees, Odessa ship repair plant and port	59.1	10.2	29.5
	1975	4,000 workers and nonmanual employees, urban residents in Moldavia	63.5	14	22.5
	1977	1,500 workers, engineers, technicians, teachers, medical and film personnel in three Latvian cities, to age 30	67	33	

*These figures are derived by taking a simple average of those shown separately for automated and nonautomated work in Appendix Table A-1.

†An undetermined number of nonmanual "employees" (*sluzhashchie*) were included here along with engineering-technical personnel.

Note: For detail on sources and notes, see Appendix Table A-1.

satisfacation on the order of 85 to 90%. Unlike most American studies the Soviet surveys have a sizable "other" category in addition to "satisfied" and "dissatisfied." Removing it from the percentage base would obviously raise the proportion of "satisfied" Soviet respondents (although it would leave this proportion at less than 80% in most cases), but it would do the same to the "dissatisfied"; and we have seen that the latter already approximates or exceeds the corresponding proportion typically found in American studies.

Table 2.2

Job Satisfaction Responses in Survey Research Center's Quality of Employment Surveys, 1969, 1973, 1977

		Response categories, in %			
Year	N	very satisfied	somewhat satisfied	not too satisfied	not at all satisfied
1969	1,528	46.4	39.1	11.3	3.2
1973	2,088	52.0	38.0	7.6	2.4
1977	2,281	46.7	41.7	8.9	2.7

Source: Robert P. Quinn and Graham L. Staines, *The 1977 Quality of Employment Survey* (The University of Michigan, Ann Arbor, Survey Research Center), 1978, p. 210.

Whatever the limited representativeness of the available Soviet studies (younger age groups are clearly overrepresented), whatever the intercountry differences in techniques of measurement, would it be naïve to suggest: (a) that the relatively high rates of job dissatisfaction reported in the Soviet studies represent a "real" rather than accidental phenomenon, and (b) that they are in part related to the chronically "tight" state of the Soviet labor market and the widespread consciousness of alternative job opportunities engendered by relatively full employment?

What is clear, in any case, is that the percentage of Soviet respondents reporting explicit dissatisfaction with work tends to understate the frequency of what might reasonably be regarded as "negative" work attitudes—at least by Soviet standards. A "truer" measure of such attitudes may be derived by combining the overtly dissatisfied and the "indifferent." If the former includes mainly those who are poorly adapted to their employing organization, the latter embraces those whose adaptation takes the form of apathy or passivity. A society which proclaims work activity as the "decisive" sphere of life, as "the highest moral value," cannot easily regard open expressions of indifference to work with equanimity. For the more vigilant Soviet interpreters, such attitudes represent "survivals of alienation of labor in pure form," a "characteristic sign of the psychology of individualism" and more disturbing evidence of survivals of "old attitudes toward work" than overt job dissatisfaction.[17] All the more significant, therefore, that a few surveys of job attitudes have included "indifferent" as an option for respondents. Where this has been done, it has not been unusual for the combination of "dissatisfied" and "indifferent" responses to reach some 35–40% of the total (see Table 2.3).[18] In all of the six locales shown here, the sum of "dissatisfied" and "indifferent" respondents exceeded one-fifth of the total sample. There are good reasons for Soviet investigators to couple the dissatisfied and the indifferent. Compared to the satisfied, both groups are less likely to take on "social assignments" (to participate in the work of Party, Komsomol and trade union organizations), to attend political education lectures, to read newspapers regularly.[19] Apparently indifference to work (and work dissatisfaction) "spills over" to other indicators of social integration.

Western studies of work attitudes have sometimes utilized indirect measures of job satisfaction to supplement the more direct indicators of "satisfied" and "dissatisfied." Such indirect measures may include the respondent's readiness to seek alternative employment or to recommend his own work to a friend or his children. Some Soviet studies have done the same, and not surprisingly, the indirect measures reveal more widespread dissatisfaction (or less "adaptation") than the direct. Here, for example, is a Soviet report on work attitudes in two building material plants in Estonia in which less than one-fifth of the employees voiced overt "dissatisfaction" with their jobs (the coupled figures in each case refer to the two separate plants):

> . . . to the question "Would you return to the same job if you were far from your factory and could choose your place of work with complete freedom?" 38.2% and 41.6% of the respondents answered negatively. A large part of the respondents, 45% and 47.4% respectively, wanted to change their place of work in the future . . . 75% and 76.7% . . . of the respondents did not want to see their son (daughter) in their own jobs, and 52.7% and 48.2% did not want him (her) to work at their plant. This does not mean direct dissatisfaction with one's work or plant, but it does suggest that the latter have not become close (*blizkami*) for a large proportion of the respondents.[20]

Indirect measures of job dissatisfaction (or the degree of "distance"

Table 2.3

Proportion of Respondents Reporting Dissatisfaction or Indifference in Soviet Job Satisfaction Surveys

		Response categories, in %		
Year	Location and type of sample	dis-satisfied	in-different	total, dis-satisfied and in-different
1962–64	workers in Leningrad industrial enterprises	16.1	26.0	42.1
1965–66	varied occupational groups in auto and tractor industry	29	22	51
1966	workers in Perm industrial enterprises	13.2	9.6	22.8
1972	workers at Volga Auto Plant	22.3	15.3	37.6
1972	workers in Kazakhstan industrial enterprises:			
	mining-metallurgi-cal combine	13	23.4	36.4
	cotton-textile combine	16.7	26.4	43.1
	meat-packing combine	22.6	18.1	40.7
1973	workers in building enterprises in three Uzbekistan cities	13.2	10.0	23.2

Note: For sources and notes, see Appendix Table A-1.

between oneself and one's current job) in other available studies point in the same direction—namely, they are considerably in excess of direct measures.[21] There is much that Soviet respondents and the sociologists who report their perceptions of work may conceal, but neither group seems particularly inhibited in reporting negative job attitudes. Perhaps this augurs well for our further examination of Soviet perceptions of the work experience.

Occupational differences

Whatever the ambiguities in the concept, most Soviet and American observers would probably agree with the view that job satisfaction is a "desired, valued, and unequally distributed outcome of work."[22] In the United States some students of the subject have sought to assess the extent of class and occupational differences in job satisfaction.[23] Nothing quite so ambitious can be attempted on the basis of the available Soviet materials. But it is clear that in addition to somewhat higher rates of work satisfaction among most nonmanual strata than among typical working-class occupations, there are also substantial inequalities in job satisfaction within the broad engineering-technical category and within workers' occupations. Some of the available evidence is brought together in Table 2.4.

Engineering-technical personnel encompass a highly diversified group of jobs ranging from shop foremen to higher-level managerial positions. Rates of job satisfaction within this group increase markedly as we move up the hierarchy from foreman (with less than one-half reporting job satisfaction in a Leningrad study in the late 1960s) to researcher (66% satisfied) and "group chief" (81%). A roughly similar picture of marked inequalities emerges in Iadov's 1970 study of Leningrad design and research organizations, in which more than one-fifth of engineers reported job dissatisfaction while less than 5% of "chief engineers" did so. Some of these classifications, of course, are really job titles rather than distinct occupational groups, but the data clearly point to substantial differences between "higher" and "lower" positions in the occupational hierarchy. Among the lower positions in the engineering-technical category—foreman, for example, or even engineer—job satisfaction rates do not appear to differ much from those of the more skilled working-class occupations.[24]

Perhaps the most consistent finding in this area is that unskilled laborers and assembly line workers exhibit the lowest satisfaction ratings among working-class occupations, well below those for skilled manual workers and workers employed in the maintenance and repair of machinery, and of course much lower than those of such intelligentsia occupations as medical and "cultural" personnel, teachers and industrial designers (see figures for Latvia in Table 2.4). Unskilled laborers are the only occupational group in which the proportion of respondents expressing overt dissatisfaction with work typically exceeds the proportion satisfied. These results are hardly surprising, but they have played an important role in Soviet discussions of the sources of job satisfaction and discontent. One reason for this was the finding that the most dissatisfied occupational groups were not always the lowest paid. Iadov and Zdravomyslov were particularly impressed by the fact that the relatively highly paid low-skilled laborers in their sample of young Leningrad workers exhibited the lowest indicators of job satisfaction among six occupational groups.[25] Similarly, the study of the Kishinev Tractor Plant some years later found that assembly line

Table 2.4

Job Satisfaction Indicators for Selected Occupational Groups

Year	Occupational groups	% satisfied	% dissatisfied	Index of satisfaction *
1965–70	Engineering-technical personnel, Leningrad industrial enterprises and research organizations			
	group chiefs	81.3		
	researchers	65.7		
	technologists	40.6		
	foremen	38.9		
1970	Engineers, Leningrad design and research organizations			
	chief engineers		3.9	
	group chiefs		11.2	
	engineers		21.8	
1962–64	Workers to age 30, Leningrad industrial enterprises			
	skilled manual workers	51.2	7.3	.34
	workers combining operation and adjustment of automatic equipment	45.7	13.0	.22
	assembly line workers	35.7	18.2	.15
	unskilled and low-skilled laborers	19.7	32.1	–.12
1972	Kishinev Tractor Plant			
	control panel operators			.33
	skilled manual workers			.23
	low-skilled laborers			.08
	assembly line workers			.05
1972	Volga Auto Plant			
	skilled manual workers			.40
	assembly line workers			.05

Table 2.4 (continued)

Year	Occupational groups	% satisfied	% dissatisfied	Index of satisfaction *
1972	Alma-Ata Cotton Textile Combine			
	workers on maintenance and repairs of machinery	71.8	4.6	
	unskilled laborers	26.5	47.1	
1973	Building materials plants, Uzbekistan			
	skilled workers	60.6	13.2	
	engineering-technical personnel and employees	70.3	9.5	
1973–76	State farms, Kazakhstan			
	production intelligentsia ("specialists")			.61
	construction workers			.53
	skilled workers on agricultural machinery			.46
	unskilled laborers			.06
1977	Three cities, Latvia			
	teachers, "cultural" and medical personnel, engineer-designers	73–76		
	technicians and adjusters	65		
	workers and conveyer	32		
1979	Industrial enterprises, Gorky region			
	workers	71.6	5.9	
	engineering-technical personnel	66.0	6.4	

Sources: 1962–64 study of Leningrad workers from Zdravomyslov and Iadov, *Chelovek,* p. 386; figures for state farm personnel in Kazakhstan from Akademiia nauk Kazakhskoi SSR, Institut filosofii i prava, *Nauchno-tekhnicheskaia revoliutsiia i dukhovnoi mir cheloveka,* Alma-Ata, 1979, p. 297; all others from sources indicated in Appendix Table A-1.

* 1 = highest possible score and − 1 = lowest possible score; derived by assigning a value of + 1.0 to the highly satisfied, + .5 to the somewhat satisfied, 0 to the indifferent, − .5 to the somewhat dissatisfied, − 1.0 to the highly dissatisfied, and dividing the resulting sum by the number of respondents.

workers, the most dissatisfied with their jobs among five occupational groups, were among the highest paid workers at the plant.[26] Such findings clearly had a bearing on Soviet discussions of the important issue of intrinsic versus extrinsic sources of work satisfaction, to which we now turn.

The receding vision of "communist work"

What job attributes make work satisfying or dissatisfying in the Soviet work environment? The problem of distinguishing the separate effects of different job characteristics on overall work attitudes is a difficult one under any conditions, but it assumes special importance under Soviet circumstances. Knowledge of workers' reactions to specific facets of the job environment is not only a "management tool," a means of better adapting them to their current work roles. It is also a way of gauging the extent to which the underlying meaning of work has changed, if at all, in the direction of "communist labor." Does work continue to be perceived primarily as a "means to life," with workers oriented mainly to the material rewards associated with their work activity? To what extent has it become an "inner need," an "end in itself," with workers oriented mainly to job content, to the work process itself as a rewarding activity? Thus there are good reasons, rooted both in management practice and in ideology, for Soviet investigators to have moved beyond merely establishing general levels of job satisfaction to inquire into their specifc sources in the work environment. As noted earlier, our concern is not only with the findings of Soviet studies but with the elements of controversy and changing views which have emerged.

As in almost everything else, most Soviet investigators of workers' reactions to particular facets of their jobs have been guided by the procedures used in the Leningrad study of the early 1960s. Given the extensive reliance on these procedures, a brief review of the Leningrad methods will be helpful here. Iadov and Zdravomyslov asked their young worker-respondents to rate a variety of "elements of the work situation." These elements or job attributes included such matters as wages, relations with co-workers, work content, opportunities for skill advancement, management's attitude toward workers and sanitary and hygienic conditions on the job. The possible ratings for each element were confined to "positive," "negative," or "neutral" (no answer). Quantitative ratings or scores for each job attribute were derived by deducting the number of negative responses from the positive and dividing the result by the total number of workers questioned. Thus the numerical ratings could range from $+1$ to -1. The ratings were derived separately for workers who had expressed overall job satisfaction and those who reported dissatisfaction, and the differences between the ratings of each element by these two groups were then obtained. Table 2.5 shows the ratings of the 14 job attributes used in the Leningrad study.

Table 2.5

Ratings of Various Elements of the Work Situation by Leningrad Workers Satisfied and Dissatisfied with Their Jobs, 1962–64

Elements of work situation	Satisfied with job	Dissatisfied with job	Divergence in ratings
The work requires mental effort or doesn't require one to think	.40	−.32	.72
Good or bad pay	.31	−.30	.61
Opportunity for raising one's skill or not	.25	−.33	.58
Variety or monotony in work	.33	−.15	.48
Good or poor work organization	.16	−.22	.38
Management's attitude is attentive or not	.24	−.11	.35
Importance of final product an attractive feature or not	.42	.07	.35
Work is physically overtiring or not	.15	−.19	.34
Equipment in good shape or not	.10	−.22	.32
Good or poor safety equipment	.32	.01	.31
Good or bad sanitary and hygienic conditions	.02	−.29	.31
Convenient or inconvenient shift	.42	.13	.29
Regular or irregular flow of work	.01	−.20	.21
Good or poor relations with co-workers	.70	.60	.10

Source: Zdravomyslov and Iadov, *Chelovek*, p. 177.

The principal objective of this procedure was to identify those specific factors in the work experience (the "elements of the work situation") which most sharply differentiated the satisfied from the dissatisfied, i.e., those elements whose ratings by these two groups exhibited the greatest divergences. The differences in the ratings of a particular job attribute showed the connection "between job satisfaction (or dissatisfaction) as a whole and the particular element of the work situation." These differential ratings were regarded as indicators of the "motivational significance" of the various job attributes.[27]

A factor like "relations with co-workers," since it was rated positively by the dissatisfied as well as the satisfied, could not be expected to have a sizable differentiating effect on the overall work attitudes of the two groups. The same was true of workers' perception of "sanitary and hygienic conditions," but for a different reason. This factor received a relatively low rating by the satisfied (in some Soviet studies a negative rating) as well as by the dissatisfied. The set of work characteristics exhibiting the most clear-cut differential ratings by the satisfied and dissatisfied included wages, work content ("does the job require mental effort?"), opportunities for skill advancement and variety in work. These were the job attributes Iadov and Zdravomyslov had in mind when they noted that "satisfaction with certain elements of the work situation corresponds here to satisfaction with work as a whole, and . . . dissatisfaction with these elements signifies dissatisfaction with work."[28] Of these elements, work content ranked at the top. Hence the conclusion of Iadov and Zdravomyslov that "the most important feature influencing the degree of work satisfaction (and correspondingly the most important motive of labor) is the content of work activity."[29]

We are not concerned for the moment with the somewhat shaky grounds for this conclusion—particularly the reliance on "mental effort" required by the job as the principal indicator of work content. After all, wages ranked ahead of "variety in work," surely another indicator of work content. What does seem important is that the primacy of work content over "material rewards" became a leading theme in much of the sociological literature on job satisfaction. In part this reflected the high prestige of the Leningrad study. But it also seemed to be reinforced by the results obtained in several other studies which followed the procedures used in Leningrad. We show the findings of two such studies together with those for Leningrad in Table 2.6. In all three cases, as well as in several others,[30] the "motivational significance" of wages for overall job satisfaction ranked lower than work content. In fact, it was usually further below the top position than in Leningrad.

How were these findings to be reconciled with the traditional stress on "material incentives" in Soviet discussions of labor problems? Unlike some commentators who seemed prepared to remove material rewards from the status of a "leading factor" in job satisfaction, the authors of the Leningrad study interpreted the apparent primacy of workers' orientations to the functional content of work with some care. The Leningrad findings needed verification by means of more representative studies in other regions. The Leningrad respondents,

Table 2.6

Ranking of Main Elements of Work Situation According to Their Influence on Overall Job Satisfaction, Three Studies

Leningrad, 1962–64	Rank	Volga Auto Plant, 1972	Rank	Odessa ship repair plant and port, 1970–74	Rank
Work requires mental effort	1	Work requires mental effort	1	Interesting work	1
Satisfactory wages	2	Is work overtiring	2	Organization of work	2
Opportunity for raising skill	3	Opportunity for raising skill	3	Relations with management	3
Variety in work	4	Variety in work	4	Satisfactory wages	4
Organization of work	5	Management's attitude toward workers	5	Fairness in distribution of work assignments	5
Management's attitude toward workers	6	Satisfactory wages	6	Correspondence of job to worker's skill	6
Is work overtiring	7				
Condition of equipment	8				

Sources:

Leningrad: Zdravomyslov and Iadov, *Chelovek*, p. 181. The respondents were workers up to age 30.

Volga Auto Plant: I. E. Stoliarova in *Sotsiologicheskie issledovaniia*, 1975, No. 2, p. 154.

Odessa: I. M. Popova, *Stimulirovania trudovoi deiatel'nosti kak sposob upravleniia*, Kiev, 1976, p. 171. The respondents were workers and employees up to age 30. The results shown for older respondents were essentially the same.

after all, had been relatively young workers, the more educated portion of the working class, whose aspirations for "creative" work content were not necessarily shared by their older colleagues. Indeed, Iadov noted that for older workers, job content and opportunities for advancement lagged behind wages and sanitary-hygienic conditions in the "scale of motives." As for the younger workers on whom the Leningrad study had concentrated, their primary orientation to creative job content only suggested that the attitude toward work as an "inner need" was in the process of "becoming" (not "had become") dominant. Moreover the orientation to wages as the second major "motive of work activity" meant that the attitude to work as a means of satisfying needs outside the labor process itself retained its "competitive position" relative to the orientation to creative work content. The latter, together with "material rewards" and the worker's perception of his opportunities for skill advancement, constituted the "kernel" of the whole motivational structure of work activity. The dominant position of work content within this kernel signified that having attained a certain minimally adequate living standard (*prozhitochnogo minimuma*), the worker's need for creative job opportunities was coming to the fore in the hierarchy of work motives.[31]

Whatever the limitations in the empirical support for these conclusions, they seemed a healthy departure from the long established habit of equating work incentives with "material incentives." But even in the relatively restrained form just described, these conclusions were received with skepticism by some sociologists—and not only by those who might be regarded as political guardians of the "official" line on material incentives. For one thing, not all the empirical studies pointed in the same direction. The authors of a study of industrial workers' job attitudes in Perm (N. F. Naumova and M. A. Sliusarianskii) made a point of stressing that for their subjects, the relationship between wages and job satisfaction was "no less strong" than that between work content and job satisfaction. When workers were asked, "What needs to be done in order to make people work willingly?" (*s okhotoi*), the two main factors in the hierarchy of motives turned out to be improved wages and work organization. Similarly, a study of engineers and technicians found that the desire for increased wages ranked well ahead of "interesting, creative work" when the subjects were asked what was required to make them work "with greater willingness and satisfaction." According to the author (M. I. Zaitseva), "For most engineers, technicians and foremen, creativity was not a factor in satisfaction when it was present in work nor a factor in dissatisfaction when it was absent in work."[32] It was difficult to imagine a result at greater variance with the Leningrad study than this. The conflict seems even more striking when we recall that the respondents in Leningrad were workers while those in Zaitseva's study were engineers and technicians.

Some sociologists who were skeptical of the Leningrad study's finding of the primacy of job content over wages in work satisfaction did not deny that job content occupied a leading role in workers' "value orientations." But the latter were not identical with workers' "motivating needs" (or "real needs"). The problem was that workers' real needs and interests tended to be verbalized in socially approved ways. "Needs and interests in verbally expressed ratings are to a considerable degree corrected by the value concepts of society and of different groups."[33] In effect the argument of the skeptics was that workers often found it easier to openly express their job dissatisfaction (or satisfaction)—or to justify their decision to change jobs—by invoking work content rather than wage levels. To the extent that this was the case, an important conclusion followed. The primacy of job content in workers' ratings of the sources of work satisfaction (dissatisfaction) could not be easily regarded as an indicator of the approach of "communist work"—the transformation of work from a "means of existence to an 'inner need.' "

Clearly this was not an issue that could readily be resolved by the kinds of job attitude surveys we have reviewed here. The suggestion that the importance of "material factors" in job satisfaction was partly concealed ("corrected") by workers' habits of responding in a socially sanctioned manner sounded a useful cautionary note against accepting workers' ratings of job attributes at face value. But it is not at all obvious that Soviet workers have been particularly reticent in acknowledging the importance of "material rewards" in work activity. For example, when asked about their conception of a "good job," close to one-half or more of sampled workers have regularly expressed the view that adequate wages are the most important attribute of such a job (see the first two rows of Table 2.7).[34] It seems difficult, therefore, to accept the view that pressures on workers to exhibit their conformity to socially dominant value orientation lead them to substantially understate the role of material factors in job satisfaction.

In our view a more effective challenge to the Leningrad study and to others which pointed in the same direction (the dominance of job content over wages in work satisfaction and motivation) came from one of the sociologists whose findings appeared to support these studies. This challenge was directed not at their empirical findings as such but at the conclusions which some had drawn from them. For I. M. Popova the subordinate role of wages in work motivation had "an altogether real basis" in current economic policies. For example, certain consumption needs were met not out of wages but via communal consumption (presumably medical care, education, subsidized rents). But the more substantial argument followed. In the casual and somewhat indirect manner often reserved for making an important point on a sensitive issue, Popova remarked: "It is also possible that a certain significance should be attached to the fact that the range of goods which can be acquired in exchange for wages is insufficiently broad."[35] In somewhat more direct terms this meant that (a) workers' ratings of job attributes which pointed to the subordinate role of money wages in work satisfaction and motivation were, at least on occasion, quite believable; but (b) rather than providing empirical evidence of new work attitudes and

Table 2.7

Respondents' Conceptions of a "Good Job" in Three Surveys of Work Attitudes

	Distribution of responses, in %			
			Kishinev Tractor Plant, workers and employees, 1972 with:	
Conceptions of a "good job"	Leningrad workers to age 30, 1962–64	Tallin workers, 1965*	7 years education	8–9 years education
Any work is good if it pays well	15.0	11.2	33.3	32.5
Pay is the main thing, but the meaning of the work is also important	30.7	38.8	19.0	19.6
The meaning of the work is the main thing, but you can't forget the pay	31.1	31.7	14.3	19.0
A good job is one where you are needed and useful	23.2	15.2	25.4	23.3
No answer	—	3.1	8.0	5.6
Total	100.0	100.0	100.0	100.0

Sources:

Leningrad: Zdravomyslov and Iadov, *Opyt*, p. 162.

Tallin: M. Lepp, "The Attitude toward Work in the Light of Sociological Studies," *Kommunist Estonii*, 1966, No. 6, p. 48.

Kishinev: Akademiia nauk Moldavskoi SSR, p. 68.

*The exact year of this study is uncertain, but the results were reported in a 1966 publication. They were based on a sample of 1,495 workers in three industrial enterprises in the city of Tallin.

progress toward "communist labor" (the interpretation offered by the authors of the Leningrad study), such ratings reflected the limited effectiveness of money wage differentials under conditions of widespread scarcities of consumer goods and the narrow range of choice in this market.

Perhaps the most interesting aspect of this discussion was the way in which the essential validity of Popova's views was implicitly acknowledged in the late 1970s on the basis of new findings by one of the co-authors of the original Leningrad study. In 1976 V. A. Iadov replicated the Leningrad study of some fifteen years earlier. The objective was to determine how "the great changes which have occurred over the past fifteen years have affected the character of needs and work motivation."[36] From the standpoint of the issue we have been reviewing here, the salient finding of the new study was that the motivational significance of the wage factor and of conditions of work (essentially "sanitary-hygienic conditions," safety, "comfort" on the job) had increased with the passage of time, i.e., they now had a distinctly greater impact on work attitudes than fifteen years earlier. These latter two elements of the work situation now ranked on a par with work content (scope for "creativity," opportunity for "mental effort"). This is how Iadov summed up his new findings in this area:

> It was found that the amount of wages has a much greater effect on the young worker's attitude toward work than was the case fifteen years earlier. The role of this factor was comparable to the role of work content. . . . If the significance of work content is taken as equivalent to one (in both 1962 and 1976—M. Y.), the significance of wages in 1962 was equal to 0.8, while in 1976 it was equal to one. The third factor, which is no less important than the preceding two, is working conditions.[37]

These relative values for the motivational significance of various job characteristics were presumably derived in the manner described earlier and illustrated in our Tables 2.5 and 2.6 above. The magnitude of the change, at least for the wage factor, was hardly overwhelming; but it was the direction of change that counted. That direction (implying a decline in the relative importance of work content) was certainly not in accord with the expectations which had prevailed at the time of the initial Leningrad study of the early 1960s.

Young workers in the late 1970s were characterized by a somewhat different distribution of "life interests" than their predecessors. They exhibited an "increased importance of family and household orientations and a turn toward the sphere of active leisure, together with a stabilization or some weakening of social-production interests and orientations."[38] In other words, the principal explanation for the observed changes in work motivation—particularly the higher ranking of wages among the various elements of the work situation—was to be found in the changes which had affected nonwork life (*byt*), or more accurately, the interplay between the latter and the relative stability of conditions at the workplace. The changes in the nonwork environment (in the "mode of life") which Iadov had in mind included workers' increased absorption in growing consumption opportunities, the shift from communal and dormitory housing to private apartments and the greater availability and range of leisure time activities. The new world of consumption and household amenities, rather than the familiar world of work, was becoming the sphere through which increasing numbers of workers could "find themselves." These changes in the general "mode of life" outside the workplace helped account not only for the increased role of material rewards in work motivation but also for the heightened motivational significance of working conditions. "The young worker, having become accustomed to everyday material comforts, naturally makes higher demands on the level of comfort in the sphere of working conditions."[39]

But the principal change observed in the 1976 study was appropriately characterized by Iadov as signifying a heightening of the "instrumental value" of work, its function as a means to ends extrinsic to the work process itself. This obviously placed in question the dominant interpretation offered earlier for the primacy of work content over material rewards revealed in earlier studies—that it demonstrated the approach of "communist work," a "tendency to the full overcoming of alienated labor." It demonstrated nothing of the kind. That primacy, to the extent that it described a real rather than imagined situation, had been substantially affected by widespread scarcities of elementary consumption opportunities. Now—in the late 1970s and early 1980s—that such scarcities were beginning to be overcome, some serious social commentators even began to observe the emergence of an unhealthy "consumerism," an absorption in the "cult of things," attitudes of "money-grubbing,"[40] all of which were some of the more extreme manifestations of the displacement of workers' interests from the production problems of the workplace.

No less important than the observed increase in instrumental orientations toward work was something notable for its absence in Iadov's review of his recent findings—the failure to claim any increase in overall levels of work satisfaction for comparable samples of young workers between the early 1960s and late 1970s. The reason for Iadov's reticence on this score is clear. The fragmentary information released on the 1976 study pointed to essential stability or—more likely—a moderate decline in job satisfaction rates among young Leningrad workers since the early 1960s (see Table 2.8).[41] All this, together with Iadov's explicit admission that work discipline had declined in the interim and that many workers were simply "indifferent" to their work (regarding themselves as "temporary" or "alien" members of their work collectives), clearly justified Iadov's observation that the "path to communist labor as a prime inner need was not simple and unilinear."[42] The prospects of "communist work" as a self-rewarding activity obviously seemed more distant in the late 1970s than they had in the early 1960s.

We shall return later (Chapter 6) to the important role which Iadov's

Table 2.8

Job Satisfaction Responses of Young Workers (up to age 30) in Leningrad Surveys, 1962 and 1976

		Response categories (in %)		
Year	N	satisfied	neutral[†]	dissatisfied
1962[*]	1,476	42.8	35.4	21.8
1976	1,534	40.2	37.8	22.0

Source: Calculated from figures for five occupational gorups in A. A. Kissel', "The Value-Normative Aspect of Work Attitudes," *Sotsiologicheskie issledovannia*, 1984, No. 1, p. 53.

[*]The figures shown here for 1962 differ somewhat from those shown in Table 2.1. The source we rely on here apparently adjusted the original 1962 findings for comparability with the occupational groups included in the 1976 survey.

[†]This appears to be a combination of the "indifferent" and those whose attitudes were "indeterminate."

more recent study has played in Soviet discussions of the urgency of work reform. For the moment what should be recognized is that his implicit admission of the faulty interpretation of earlier finding on job attitudes reflects a relatively "open" quality in Soviet discussions of the work experience. It suggests that concepts and findings which break new ground can be expected to appear as the study of the labor process unfolds. An additional illustration of this quality deserves brief consideration at this point.

A new direction?

The study of work, both in its "objective" dimensions and in its impact on workers' perception of their job experience, is obviously at an early stage in the Soviet Union. Although we have concentrated thus far largely on a review of Soviet findings on job attitudes, no less important is the process by which new concepts and a new vocabulary have been assimilated into the professional discourse on problems of work. Until the late 1970s the conceptual apparatus developed by Iadov and Zdravomyslov in the early 1960s served as the accepted framework for organizing the study of work attitudes. This was particularly apparent in their concept of "elements of the work situation" as the set of job attributes having a significant impact on work attitudes and (depending on the ranking of these attributes) revealing the currently prevailing hierarchy of work motives. Even when some sociologists' findings differed from those of the Leningrad study, or when they questioned the meaning which Iadov and Zdravomyslov attached to their results, the discussion remained within the confines of the job attributes (shown in Table 2.5) specified by the Leningrad sociologists. Whether these attributes were sufficiently comprehensive to capture the major elements of the work experience was not questioned.[43]

The dominance of the conceptual apparatus formulated in the original Leningrad study was also evident in the meaning commonly assigned to the concept of "work content." The latter referred to the extent of "creative opportunities" offered by a job. But the important point here is that such opportunities were regarded as mainly a function of technological advance. Thus when Iadov and Zdravomyslov classified occupations according to the "richness" of their work content, the classification was based on the "different steps along the ladder of technological progress."[44] When they found that job satisfaction rates increased and work motives changed as one moved along the spectrum of occupational groups (from unskilled manual laborers to assembly-line workers to operators and adjusters of automated equipment), the results were interpreted as reflecting the impact on work attitudes of "the characteristics of equipment, the degree and character of mechanization of the work process." In this perspective progress toward "communist labor" as indicated by the primacy of work content in the hierarchy of work motives necessarily depended largely on the rate of technological modernization.

This is the view which was challenged by the introduction of the concept of "work autonomy" or "on-the-job independence" (*proizvodstvennaia samostoiatel'nost'*) into Soviet discussions of the work experience. In the words of the sociologist who initially posed the issue (A. V. Tikhonov), the traditional meaning assigned to job content confined its attention to the "horizontal" dimension of the work process, the distribution of functions within the 'man-machine system.' " Such an approach ignored the "vertical component, the distribution of functions between the execution of work and the control and management of work."[45]

More specifically, work autonomy refers to the degree to which "the planning of the job assignment, the organization of work performance and the monitoring and recording" of its results all inhere in the worker's job functions.[46] In this sense it reflects the degree to which the functions of "conception" and "execution" of work are joined in the individual's work activity. On-the-job independence, therefore, necessarily depends not only on the worker's "technical" functions imposed

by the state of productive equipment but on the social and organizational arrangements at the enterprise, i.e., the degree to which the organization delegates managerial tasks to workers.

Tikhonov had introduced the concept of work autonomy in the context of a discussion of work attitudes. His study of a sample of workers
in oil-drilling operations suggested that job autonomy (in the sense
defined above) had at least as strong an impact on work attitudes as
work content (in the "technological" sense defined by Iadov and
Zdravomyslov). Work attitudes here referred to such "objective
indicators" as workers' initiative, quality of output and productivity
rather than job satisfaction. But work autonomy was not simply being
suggested as one more job attribute to be added to the traditional set of
"elements of the work situation." The failure to consider it as a distinct
and strategic facet of the work experience had represented a serious
impoverishment of the whole conceptual apparatus used in previous
studies of the labor process. The point of Tikhonov's discussion was
the need to recognize that the extension of job autonomy was a key
element in enhancing work commitment and performance, not to speak
of developing a communist attitude toward work, and that such an
extension was being impeded by "social and organizational
constraints" rather than simply by technological backwardness.

> The selection of work autonomy as a distinct object of study is of
> both current and long-term significance. In historical perspective we
> cannot regard the process of enriching work and broadening its cre-
> ative potential as merely the direct result of scientific and technical
> progress. One of the major advantages of socialism is the planned
> improvement of social relations, particularly managerial relations,
> which substantially determine the creative opportunities offered by
> the functional content of work, and which also play an important
> independent role in enriching work and in achieving a high level of
> work performance.[47]

By the late 1970s and early 1980s job autonomy was in the process of
being assimilated into the vocabulary of Soviet discussions of work
attitudes and work organization.[48] Among those who accepted and
helped to legitimate the new concept was V. A. Iadov, the co-author of
the initial Leningrad survey which had paved the way for all subsequent studies in this field. The emergence of the theme of work autonomy was only one expression of a "participatory current" in the Soviet
literature on problems of work, but this is a separate matter which deserves its own extended discussion. We return to it in Chapters 5 and 6.

3
Demographic Variables and Work Attitudes

What do Soviet materials reveal about the impact of sex differences, age and education on the perception of the work experience? Once again our concern is not only to review the statistical findings but to examine the variety of ways in which these issues have generated changing interpretations, policy recommendations and public discussions of problems of work. In particular, we are interested in the way in which the interaction of sociologists' findings and the more "popular" discourse on problems of work have set the stage for consideration of the need for "work reform" in the Soviet Union.

Sex differences in work attitudes

One of the more obvious issues to emerge from Soviet studies of work attitudes is the striking contrast between the markedly unequal work roles of men and women on the one hand and the relatively moderate differences in their reported rates of job satisfaction on the other. Since it seems so appropriate to Soviet circumstances, we may take as our point of departure the implicit question posed in a U.S. department of Labor summary of sex differences in work attitudes in the United States:

> Considering the large wage gap between men and women and the overrepresentation of women in lower status occupations, it is surprising that sex differences in overall job satisfaction have not been consistently observed. Moreover, even the few differences that have been observed are small.[1]

The inferior job status of Soviet females relative to males in working-class occupations has been abundantly documented in both the Soviet and Western literature and requires little elaboration at this point.[2] We may take it as established that Soviet women are substantially underrepresented in the more skilled workers' occupations, those commonly referred to as involving "high content" jobs. The same is true, if to a somewhat lesser extent, when nonmanual occupations are considered. Since some of the principal Soviet studies of work attitudes apply to younger age groups, it is worth noting that sex-linked inequalities in occupational status and wage levels are already quite marked early in the work careers of men and women and almost certainly increase with age. Table 3.1 summarizes the male-female skill and wage gap for a national sample of young industrial workers (up to age 30) in the early 1970s. (Anticipating an issue to be discussed below, this table also provides evidence of the superior educational attainment that

Table 3.1

Sex Differences in Skill, Wage Levels and Years of Schooling, Industrial Workers to Age 30, 1972

Skill, wage levels and schooling	Men (in %)	Women (in %)
Skill groups		
low-skilled	7.0	11.4
semiskilled	35.3	58.8
skilled	57.7	29.8
Total	100.0	100.0
Wage levels		
low-paid (60–90 rubles per month)	10.7	41.8
medium-paid (91–150 rubles per month)	53.5	53.6
high-paid (more than 150 rubles per month)	35.8	4.6
Total	100.0	100.0
Average years of schooling	9.3	9.5

Source: Calculated from material in Akademiia nauk SSSR, Institut istorii SSSR, *Sotsial'nyi oblik rabochei molodezhi*, Moscow, 1980, pp. 30, 64, 66, 78–79, 253, 262.

Note: The study from which these figures are drawn was based on a sample of approximately 5,200 young workers drawn from the machine-building, ferrous metallurgy, coal and textile industries. Of the respondents, 52.2% were male and 47.8% female. The figures shown above for skill groups were calculated by including unskilled and low-skilled manual workers and assembly-line workers in the "low-skilled" group; workers with "average occupational training" on machines and mechanisms and workers operating automatic and semiautomatic equipment in the "semiskilled" group; and skilled manual workers and workers operating and adjusting automatic and semiautomatic equipment in the "skilled" group.

accompanies the subordinate job status of young women workers.) The proportion of young male workers employed in relatively skilled jobs (57.7%) was almost double that of young females (29.8%); fewer than 5% of young women workers were in "highly paid" jobs (more than 150 rubles per month) compared to more than one-third of young males. More recent local studies (in the industrial center of Taganrog in 1978, for example) make it clear that the inferior occupational and wage status of female workers remained in effect throughout the decade of the 1970s.[3]

Whatever the full range of factors generating the early emergence of these inequalities, one such factor is surely what Alastair McAuley has described as the pressure on women "to choose jobs that are convenient rather than satisfying."[4] The greater constraints on occupational choice for women are reflected in their answers to the question "How did you choose your occupation?" More frequently than men, the females responded, "Circumstances were such that there was no other choice." More frequently than women, the males responded, "The specialty seemed interesting." The reasonable interpretation which Soviet sociologists attach to the "circumstances" cited by women is that the latter are more likely to be guided by such considerations as the proximity of the job to the place of residence and the convenience of working hours—in a word, by the possibility which the particular job offers of combining "household responsibilities" with work in social production. To the extent that any real choice is available, women, more so than men, select a "place" of work rather than a "type" of work. These findings, initially disclosed in the original Leningrad study of the early 1960s, have been essentially duplicated in more recent investigations.[5]

It seems all the more significant, therefore, that reported rates of work satisfaction fail to reveal the kinds of clear-cut and persistent inequalities we have just observed in the job status, wage levels and occupational choices of men and women. Table 3.2 summarizes the results of seven Soviet studies of work satisfaction among women conducted between the late 1960s and late 1970s. In all cases the proportion of women respondents reporting satisfaction with their work ("fully" and "more satisfied than not") ranges from 62% to 80%. We do not suggest that a weighty conclusion can be drawn from this scattering of figures, but it does seem of some importance that these rates of job satisfaction are of approximately the same order of magnitude as those observed earlier in Table 2.1 for men and women combined. Indeed, the responses of women fall somewhat closer to the

Table 3.2

Responses of Women Workers in Soviet Job Satisfaction Surveys

Year and coverage of study	Response categories (in %)					
	fully satisfied	more satisfied than not	more satisfied than dissatisfied	dissatisfied	indifferent	don't know
1966, Moscow confectionary factory, Penza watch factory, Leningrad industrial enterprises (N = 427)*	68.8	9.3	10.1	7.6		4.2
1966, Leningrad textile, tobacco, electrical equipment and machinery plants (N = 540)	44.0	28.5	18.1	9.4		
1968, Kostroma textile plants (N = 480)	55.1	23.5	11.9	9.5		
1969–70 Voronezh textile and machine-building plants	6.2	(58)†	(16)†	9.4	(10)†	
1972, Semipalatinsk Meat-Packing Combine‡	62.4		11.8		21.6	4.2
1973, Uzbekistan building materials plants§	62.8		10.4		5.5	21.3
1978, Taganrog industrial enterprises	80		10			10

Sources:

Moscow and Penza: Osipov and Shchepanskii, p. 422.

Leningrad and Kostroma: A. G. Kharchev and S. I. Golod, *Professional'naia rabota zhenshchin i sem'ia*, Leningrad, 1971, p. 45.

Voronezh: N. V. Nastavshev. "The Attitude toward Work and Some Characteristics of the Personality," in V. S. Rakhmanin et al., eds., *Lichnost' i problemy kommunisticheskogo vospitaniia*, Voronezh, 1973, p. 89.

Semipalatinsk: Akademiia nauk Kazakhskoi SSR, Institut ekonomiki, *Upravlenie sotsial'nym razvitiem proizvodstvennykh kollektivov*, Alma-Ata, 1975, p. 154.

Uzbekistan: V. I. Soldatova and A. S. Chamkin, *Proizvodstvennyi kollektiv i voprosy kommunisticheskogo vospitaniia*, Tashkent, 1979, p. 131.

Taganrog: E. B. Gruzdeva and E. S. Chertikhina, "Soviet Women: Problems of Work and Everyday Life," *Rabochii klass i sovremennyi mir*, 1982, No. 6, p. 113.

*About 7% of this sample included engineering-technical personnel and nonmanual employees.

†These figures were read from a graph and should be regarded as rough estimates.

‡These figures refer to attitudes toward "ocupation" rather than to "job."

§Engineering-technical personnel and employees are included here along with workers.

upper range of job satisfaction rates for respondents undifferentiated by sex. There is an important limitation, of course, associated with any such comparison. Most of the figures for women in Table 3.2 are drawn from different enterprises and locales than those for men and women combined in Table 2.1. It is conceivable, but unlikely, that the relatively high job satisfaction rates of women (high, that is, relative to their typical occupational status and wage level) reflect the unusually favorable local circumstances in which these studies were conducted.

But the picture does not change substantially when we examine the few cases in which separate male and female job satisfaction rates have been derived within the same locales and enterprises. The dominant impression remains one of fairly close proximity rather than consistent and marked inequalities in these rates. Thus in the Leningrad study of young workers in the early 1960s, "sex shows an insignificant correlation with work satisfaction in favor of women . . . ." In a Kazakhstan study of a decade later, sex differences in job satisfaction rates were again reported as "insignificant," but this time in favor of men.[6] In most of the remaining studies which distinguish these rates by sex, job satisfaction seems to be somewhat higher for men than for women, but in no case do these differences approach the magnitude of typical sex inequalities in job status and earnings.[7] Hence the bulk of the available evidence appears to lend support to N. F. Naumova's generalization: "Other things being equal [presumably occupational and wage levels— M. Y.], work satisfaction is generally higher among women than among men . . . ."[8]

How were these findings to be explained? Until the late 1970s Soviet discussions of sex-related differences in perceptions of work consisted largely of variations on a few basic themes. Before considering these discussions it is well to recall that the great majority of women respondents in Soviet studies were employed in low-skilled and semiskilled working-class occupations. Perhaps the most common theme in these discussions was that women's "demands" or "claims" on the richness of work content, on the "creative opportunities" of work, tend to be lower than those of men. Women were also more satisfied than men at given wage levels and were less concerned than men with opportunities for increasing their work skills. On the other hand they were particularly sensitive to the "psychological atmosphere" of the workplace—the "socioemotional" climate of the job—and the comfort aspects of work (sanitary-hygienic conditions, availability of rest periods). On the whole they were more adaptable than men to assembly-line jobs, partly because of their limited aspirations for intrinsically satisfying work and partly because a psychologically healthy "collectivism" compensates to some degree for the "negative aspects of monotonous work."

All of these characterizations are drawn from Iadov and Zdravomyslov's study of young Leningrad workers.[9] They will undoubtedly strike some readers as conforming to the stereotypes of women's work attitudes common in the United States until recently, and perhaps still accepted in some quarters. Stereotypes or not, it is interesting to see how essentially similar portrayals of women workers' job attitudes have generated varying degrees of acceptance and rationalization among Soviet sociologists. For Slesarev and Iankova, investigating a sample of working mothers confined largely to low-level, routine industrial jobs in the late 1960s, the limited involvement of such women in their work—whatever its problematic aspects—also served a positive function:

> . . . we must keep in mind that the absence of creativity in work activity often corresponds to the demands which women workers make on their labor. At the current stage of development, the opportunity for performing primarily repetitive work which does not require large expenditures of nervous energy corresponds to the work aspirations of a considerable proportion of women, particularly those of low skills and cultural levels. The activity of many of them, as the study of assembly-line work has shown, is basically oriented to the family which requires a great deal of additional work from women. . . . The repetitive character of a job . . . not calling for the need to think about work operations, is fully satisfying to many women precisely because it is less fatiguing.[10]

In Kharchev and Golod's study of women workers in Kostroma and Leningrad, we find the same theme of women's perceptions and evaluations of their jobs as being dominated by their primary roles as wives and mothers. Thus they exhibit little interest in "opportunities for initiative and creativity," in prospects for job advancement, in continuing their formal education and raising their skills. Their chief job-related concerns—in addition to supplementing family income—are the proximity of the workplace to their homes, the availability of child-care facilities and the opportunity to work convenient shifts. Their reactions to their work roles are "always refracted in the last analysis through the prism of the family."[11] In brief, working women's central life interests are outside the workplace.

There is a strangely ambiguous quality to some of these discussions, or at least to the normative overtones in which they are clothed. The picture of women adapting to intrinsically impoverished work roles—indeed, often preferring them—is not a pretty one, and no particular effort is made to embellish it. But it also has the air of near-inevitability, for there is little recognition that the care of children and the performance of household management functions need not be exclusively "women's work." Thus, while calling for the increased public provision of household services and child-care facilities, and in some cases for reduced working time and increased maternity leaves for women, these discussions have rarely treated reduced role segregation within the family as a means of enriching work opportunities for women. The stress has typically been placed on "lightening" women's overall labor burden, less frequently on sharing household duties.[12] But some of the sociologists engaged in these discussions have gone much further than others in voicing what, under other circumstances, might be called a "feminist" position. Zdravomyslov and Iadov have been among the most forthright in this respect. Although their Leningrad study was among the first to introduce the theme of sex-linked differences in workers' interests in intrinsically rewarding work, there was no element of apologia in their discussion of this issue. Women's lesser interest in "high-content" work reflected unequal "degrees of freedom" between the sexes for personal fulfillment. It was rooted mainly in social arrangements rather than in physiological differences, i.e., in women's position in *byt*—the nonwork sphere of everyday family life. Moreover, "the unequal position of women in the conduct of household affairs under current conditions or urban life has no moral justification whatsoever."[13] The whole moral tone of these remarks seems at the furthest remove from the "managerial" orientation of those Soviet sociologists for whom women's allegedly superior adaptability to assembly-line jobs is essentially a tool for allocating labor in a manner designed to raise overall work satisfaction.[14]

Throughout the 1960s and early 1970s, Soviet discussions of sex differences in work attitudes rested on the assumption, sometimes fortified by documentation, of women's lesser claims for intrinsically challenging work. In one of its more extreme forms this was embodied in a sociologist's remark that "men and women workers attach a different meaning to the concept of 'interesting work.' "[15] For women it presumably meant "light" work; for men—"creative" work. But the late 1970s seem to have marked a turning point of sorts in the portrayal of women's orientations to work. It now appeared that the traditional picture of women's more modest claims to intrinsic work satisfaction, whatever its validity for the past, was an unreliable guide to the present. Perhaps the most unambiguous departure from the customary view appeared in Iadov's summary of his 1976 replication of the initial Leningrad study of some fourteen years earlier:

> Considerable changes have occurred during these years in women's attitudes toward wages, job content, working conditions, relations with management, etc. *Their demands are now just as high as those of men* [our emphasis]. This is a step forward demonstrating the liquidation of remnants of social inequality between the sexes.[16]

Both the scholarly stature of the author and the fact that he (jointly with Zdravomyslov) had been among the first to demonstrate women's inferior job claims in the 1960s argue against dismissing this statement as a perfunctory celebration of "social progress." It clearly was meant to signal a new situation. Moreover, Iadov made it clear that increased sex equality in demands on work content had its problematic aspect. Whatever may have happened to work satisfaction for the Leningrad sample as a whole since the 1960s, it had clearly declined in "women's branches of production." From another source which presents some results of the 1962 and 1976 studies, we can derive a more specific picture of the changes (Table 3.3). Those occupational groups in which women predominated in the 1960s (assembly-line workers and workers on semiautomatic equipment) recorded a decline in "satisfaction with occupation." Most of those in which men were a majority showed an increase or essential stability in satisfaction.

Additional evidence suggesting that the traditional view of women's job orientations is in the process of becoming outmoded has appeared in the recent (1980) work of N. M. Shishkan, one of the principal Soviet specialists on women's economic status. Shishkan note that "until recently," studies had shown that differences in work content had comparatively little impact on women's job satisfaction. The latter had depended largely on such factors as the availability of child-care facilities, convenient working hours and proximity of workplace to residence. Here we have the familiar picture of women's instrumental work orientation which dominated the sociological literature through the early 1970s, but now presented as applying "until recently" rather than in the present tense. In the new situation women's "value orientations" are such that "satisfaction with work . . . has become increasingly determined by the content of work."[17] When we recall that "work content" in the Soviet lexicon stands for opportunities for "creativity" on the job, Shishkan's remarks are seen as pointing in the same direction as Iadov's.

Table 3.3

Satisfaction with Occupation among Samples of Leningrad Workers, 1962 and 1976, and Proportion of Women in Occupational Groups, 1962

Occupational groups	% of workers satisfied with occupation		% of women in occupational group*
	1962	1976	1962
Low-skilled manual work	43.8	42.9	36.6
Assembly-line jobs	45.0	41.6	85.0
Machine operators	70.4	63.1	39.2
Jobs on semiautomatic equipment	67.1	50.5	84.9
Skilled manual work	66.5	75.8	31.7
Operators and adjusters of automatic equipment	52.7	71.0	44.0

Sources: G. Cherkasov and V. Veretennikov, "Social Factors in the Growth of Labor Productivity," *Sotsialisticheskii trud*, 1981, No. 3, p. 105; Zdravomyslov and Iadov, *Chelovek*, p. 372.

*The figures on the share of women in various occupational groups apply to workers up to the age of 30. It is not clear whether the same is true of the figures on the proportion of workers satisfied with their occupations.

It would be too much to say that Iadov's and Shishkan's comments clearly demonstrate a "leap forward" in women's work expectations. But they do suggest reduced differences between the sexes in the standards used to evaluate the adequacy of jobs. There are good reasons for this: the higher levels of general education among women workers in younger age groups, the declining impact of peasant social origins on traditional views of women's work and family roles and the continuing affirmation of an official egalitarian ethos—at least with respect to relations between the sexes. Even without a "women's movement," as the term is ordinarily understood, these factors have operated to heighten women's "claims" for both intrinsically satisfying and more highly paid work. The real problem is that at least within working-class occupations, there is no evidence of a reduction in sex-linked occupational segregation and earnings inequality in recent years.[18] Under the circumstances Iadov's finding of reduced work satisfaction in some "women's branches" is precisely what we might expect. The very language used helps explain the result.

Although women's "claims" or "demands" on work may have converged with those of men in recent years, there is one respect in which sex-linked differences in attitudes remain considerable (at least in some areas of the country). Men appear to be less inclined than women to accept the propriety and normalcy of the latter's involvement in the work force. Thus in a recent (1977) Latvian study, some 85–90% of female respondents indicated that they would continue on their jobs even if their husbands' earnings increased to a level equivalent to that currently received by husband and wife combined. But 46% of the male respondents in Riga (and 35% in the other two cities covered in the study) "voted" in favor of women leaving their jobs in such circumstances, mainly on the ground that this was necessary for improved child care. These differences in male-female attitudes seem all the more striking when we recall that the respondents were young people (up to the age of 30) and that Latvia is commonly regarded as one of the more "advanced" areas of the Soviet Union. Perhaps one indicator of the "advanced" nature of this area (or at least of its female population's work aspirations) is that the female job satisfaction rate in this study (55%) fell further below the male rate (69%) than in any of the other Soviet studies available to us.[19]

Age and work attitudes

The Soviet literature on labor problems is pervaded by a concern with the problem of adapting young workers to their jobs. This is not only a matter of reducing excessive labor turnover but of mobilizing work effort in the broader sense—i.e., developing habits of sustained work discipline, stability, precision and initiative, which Soviet writers associate with the requirements of an "industrial culture."[20] There are good reasons for the focus on young workers in this context. Perhaps the most consistent finding in Soviet studies of work attitudes is that young workers are substantially less satisfied with their jobs than older ones, with the boundary between "young" and "older" workers generally defined as the age of 29 or 30. While the precise age group exhibiting the lowest degree of work satisfaction varies in different studies (19–22-year-olds in some, 22–24-year-olds in others),[21] the greater work discontent of the below-30 age group as a whole is apparently a stable feature of these studies. Such findings have led some sociologists to regard the problem of negative work attitudes "as a specifically youth problem."[22] While this view is almost certainly an oversimplification, it reflects the common linking in the public consciousness of the unstable work commitment of individuals in younger age groups with the more general problems of work morale and poor work performance.

It should be recognized, however, that relatively high rates of job dissatisfaction among young workers are hardly an unusual or recent phenomenon. From a cross-national perspective—if the experience of the United States is a reliable guide—they are altogether "normal." At a time when ominous visions of a "youth rebellion" and a "generation gap" were still being invoked (the early 1970s), the U.S. Department of Labor summed up the historical record of generational differences in job attitudes as follows: "Younger workers have been consistently less satisfied than their elders for the last 15 years and, probably, even earlier than that."[23] Why this should normally be the case—in both the United States and the Soviet Union—has been explained in rather obvious terms by students of work attitudes in both countries. Thus the U.S. Department of Labor study cited above suggests that "older workers, especially in the case of men, are more satisfied with their jobs than younger workers simply because they have better jobs." Access to these better jobs depends on "job experience, accrued skills, and demonstrated competence," all of which are naturally less likely to be characteristic of younger than of older workers.[24] Soviet commentators point to precisely the same factors. Some have also noted that older workers are more likely to be "reconciled to the existing state of affairs." Their expectations have already been "corrected" by their actual (limited) opportunities.[25]

But these interpretations of "normal" generational differences in work satisfaction are inadequate to account for the tone of serious concern in the recent Soviet literature on young workers or for the recorded levels of their work discontent. Job satisfaction rates among young workers are not merely "lower" than among older ones. They are also "low" in absolute terms and are referred to as such. Although we cannot determine trends in these rates, it is difficult to believe that rates of job satisfaction of less than 50% (the levels reported in several studies of young workers in the 1960s and 1970s)[26] can be regarded as "normal" by Soviet authorities. Nor can the concept of "normal" generational differences in work attitudes be readily reconciled with Soviet sociologists' references to the "serious social problems" and "social tensions" associated with young people's work discontent.[27] To understand the deeper sources of this discontent and its roots in the specific circumstances of the last two decades requires that we examine the problematic impact of increased education on both the performance and perception of work. This issue has also been at the center of some lively controversies among Soviet economists and sociologists which we review below. Clearly what is new about the mass of young Soviet workers in recent years is their relatively high level of general education.

Education, work performance and job attitudes

As in other countries, the bulk of the literature on the economics of education in the Soviet Union has stressed the positive impact of increased schooling on workers' skills, labor productivity and the growth of national income. In the Soviet case this tradition has its roots mainly in empirical studies conducted during the early postrevolutionary years by the economist, S. G. Strumilin. It is not surprising that Strumilin should have had a considerable impact on later Soviet studies in the economics of education, for some of his early work has been characterized by a Western observer as "a signal contribution" to this field, "unexcelled in the West until the work of Theodore W. Schultz and Gary S. Becker in the late 1950s and early 1960s."[28] Among Strumilin's findings published in the 1920s before the start of the First Five-Year Plan were the following:[29] (a) the attainment of simple literacy after one year of schooling raised the labor productivity of lathe operators by approxmately 30%, while a year of on-the-job experience of illiterate workers increased their output by no more than 12 to 16%; (b) the addition of a year of formal schooling "gives rise to an addition to the degree of skill that is 2.6 times greater than that due to a year of training in a factory"; (c) the outlays required to introduce universal primary education (four years of schooling) among Soviet youth would be recouped in five years out of the increased national income generated by the enhanced skills of the newly educated workers. After a long absence from his studies in this field, Strumilin returned to it in a 1962 article in which he estimates that something on the order of one-fifth to one-quarter of Soviet national income could be ascribed to the increased skills from investment in secondary and higher education.[30] This was the "national economic effect" of education.

Until the late 1950s and early 1960s there was relatively little in the Soviet economic literature that added to Strumilin's findings on the "yield" of education. As late as 1965 it was not uncommon for Soviet writers, seeking to illustrate the profitability of educational outlays, to cite Strumilin's early results (particularly on the greater contribution of schooling than of work experience to worker's skills) without noting that they applied to a period when few Soviet workers had as much as five or six years of schooling and that Strumilin himself had been mainly concerned with making a case for universal primary education.[31] However, with the greater scope for economic research made possible by the post-Stalin "thaw," and with the Party's 1961 program announcing the goal of attaining "universal" secondary education among youth, a considerable body of new literature on the economics of education began to emerge in the 1960s. Much of this literature reported on the results of "micro" studies (usually based on samples of industrial workers) designed to establish the relationship between workers' educational levels and their work performance, i.e., the degree of norm fulfillment, time required to advance in skill grade, work discipline, participation in work "rationalization." The results of many of these studies seemed to accord—at least in broad terms—with Strumilin's earlier findings in the sense that they documented the favorable impact of increased formal schooling on workers' job performance, with the important qualification that workers' educational levels were now (mid-1960s) substantially higher than at the time Strumilin conducted most of his studies. At the risk of unduly oversimplifying a considerable body of research, it might be said that at least some of the newer studies conveyed the impression that as far as schooling's impact on workers' job performance was concerned, "the more the better." Here is an example of one of the more optimistic reports on the economic consequences of increased schooling which appeared in the mid-1960s. Summarizing the results of a survey of workers in two Moscow electrical equipment plants, the author noted:

How, then, does the level of education influence the output of labor? The investigation showed that for most workers, the percentage by which production norms were fulfilled rose proportionately with the level of general education. . . . Indices of norm fulfillment among workers with a complete secondary education [ten-eleven years of schooling] exceeded those of workers with an eighth-grade education by 25%. . . . As general educational levels of workers increase, the quantity of nondefective output noticeably rises, and the amount of tool breakage falls. . . . There is a direct relationship between the educational level of workers and the time they take to master new types of work. Almost all the investigations among those with a ten-year education yielded a speed of transfer to new work twice as fast as for workers with only an eight-year education. In turn, workers with an eight-year education were one and a half times superior in this respect compared with workers who had five years of education. . . . Thus the most important consequence of raising general education levels is the decrease in the time required to raise production skills. . . . The higher the education of the worker, the more usefully he employs his free time, the more sensibly he spends his leisure and as a result maintains a normal working rhythm during the course of the whole working week.[32]

The overwhelmingly positive assessment of increased schooling's impact on productive performance has remained a dominant theme in the economic literature on the "effectiveness" of education. More than fifteen years after the above lines were published, we can find essentially similar appraisals—for example, in a 1981 article which reports that "the output of workers with a complete secondary education exceeds that of workers with an incomplete secondary education [eight years of schooling] by 25%, while the output of workers with an eighth-grade education is 35% higher than that of workers with a fifth-grade education."[33] At the macroeconomic level some economists have also sought to update Strumilin's earlier estimates of the "national economic effectiveness" of outlays on education. According to one recent estimate these outlays (and the consequent increase in skills) added about 33% to national income in 1977 compared to 22% in 1960; every ruble of expenditure on education and training yielded 4.95 rubles of national income in 1977, compared to 3.72 rubles in 1960.[34] The general approach to assessing the impact of education on the economy which has guided the studies briefly summarized here has been clearly formulated by V. A. Zhamin, one of the leading figures in the revival of the economics of education since the early 1960s:

> Outlays on education are a particular form of capital investments which are ultimately recouped through an increase in output, economies of working time, an expansion in the assortment and an improvement in the quality of output and a reduction in the time required to produce it. The measure of effectiveness of any investments under socialism can only be the increase in the social productivity of labor attained as a result of these investments.[35]

It is important to recognize, however, that a quite different general approach to the significance of workers' rising educational levels and a very different set of empirical findings than those we have just reviewed have appeared in some of the sociological literature. This is not simply because sociologists have been concerned with the "social" aspects of education—the problems of adapting youngsters to labor market entry, the sources of work discontent—while economists have been concerned with the "profitability" or "returns" from increased schooling. The very manner of gauging the economic consequences of increased education and the implications for investment policy have also been in question.

Stated in its baldest terms, however, the principal issue posed in the sociological and more "popular" periodical literature concerned the alleged problem of "overeducation"—the social and economic costs associated with a more rapid rise in workers' educational levels than in the "richness" of their job content. This is the issue which generated considerable controversy out of which there emerged empirical findings and policy proposals which bear directly on the subject of our study. Among the first to invoke the concept of an "inflation" of education was the sociologist V. Shubkin in 1964–65. His own studies had shown that the great majority of youngsters completing secondary school planned to continue their schooling at a higher educational institution (*VUZ*). This had been the traditional path followed by secondary school graduates, and success in pursuing it rested partly on the relatively small proportion of youngsters completing a secondary education (no more than one-third of the age cohort in the early 1960s). But with the projected "universalization" of secondary education, most graduates' plans for *VUZ* admission would be frustrated, and they would be forced to enter the labor market and settle for jobs largely in workers' trades after ten or eleven years of general education. Moreover, according to Shubkin, skill requirements for most working-class occupations did not require this much schooling. Hence it must have seemed perfectly legitimate for Shubkin to pose the issue in the following terms:

> If the level of education is lagging, this obstructs the development of the productive forces, of scientific and technical progress. On the other hand, the premature transition to forms of education which are not generated by the actual requirements or economic, scientific and cultural development may lead to an unnecessary wastefulness (*rastochitel'stvu*), to a peculiar "inflation" of education, to a diversion of resources required for the solution of other urgent matters, to a restraint on the growth of the productivity of social labor.[36]

This was more than an appeal to explicitly consider the opportunity costs associated with an extension of secondary schooling and the delay in the labor market entry of youth. It was also a warning that increased educational levels could have certain unanticipated and problematic social consequences: the creation of "needs" for more challenging work, a level of "culture" and standards of living which, under conditions of "limited resources" and prevailing levels of labor productivity, Soviet society would not be able to satisfy.[37]

Coming on the heels of the revival of the economics of education literature reviewed above, with its unambiguously positive assessment of the "returns" from increased schooling, the notion that an "inflation" of education could be a source of new problems under Soviet circumstances obviously struck a discordant note. Indeed, given the customary fanfare with which projected or realized increases in educational levels had always been announced, it must have struck some as little short of outrageous. With an average level of schooling for members of the work force somewhere in the vicinity of seven years in the mid-1960s, and with distinctly less than one-half of Soviet youth reaching the tenth grade, could the prospect of educational "inflation" really be taken seriously?

But the legitimacy of at least posing the issue was reinforced by the results obtained by some of Shubkin's sociologist colleagues in their studies of the relationship between education and workplace behavior. Thus a study of workers in machine-building plants (by V. A. Kalmyk) found that while increased schooling up to the seventh grade promoted a rise in job skills, further increases in general education had "practically no effect on the growth of workers' qualifications." Both in this industry and in coal mining, an additional year of schooling contributed less to skill enhancement than an additional year of work experience. Clearly, the author noted, Strumilin's old conclusion that a year of schooling was equivalent to 2.6 years of job experience in workers' trades had long since become inapplicable.[38] Another sociologist (N. A. Aitov), whose research was conducted among industrial workers in the cities of Kazan and Ufa, found no clear-cut tendency for workers' "production indicators" (norm fulfillment, participation in "rationalization and innovation," ability to work on a variety of machines) to improve with their educational attainments, particularly if they had already obtained an eighth-grade education. Once again, in contrast to Strumilin's older results and those of the more recent economics of education literature, Aitov concluded: ". . . the growth of work experience by one year adds more to almost all indicators of production activity than the growth of education by one grade."[39] Essentially similar results were obtained by the authors of the prestigious Leningrad study of young workers. Zdravomyslov and Iadov reported that the correlation between workers' educational levels and their job performance was "insignificant," that for workers with more than seven or eight years of schooling, it was impossible to establish a consistent relationship between skill levels and educational levels and that in the more "monotonous" jobs (assembly-line operations) and those requiring heavy manual labor, higher educational levels were associated with a deterioration in work discipline, initiative and responsibility.[40]

It would be a mistake to assume, however, that any of the sociologists whose studies pointed to the limited "economic effectiveness" of increased general education explicitly called for restricting schooling for workers to seven to eight years or expressed open opposition to the Party's goal of a "complete" secondary education (ten or eleven years of schooling) for the young. All the principal participants in these discussions made it clear that they were not oblivious to the "social" functions of increased schooling: its positive impact on workers' participation in community affairs, the quality of family "upbringing" in the next generation, the general "cultural" level of the society.[41] What they were pointing to, rather, was that increased schooling—whatever its "social" benefits—would become a source of new problems associated with the need to absorb relatively highly educated youngsters into the large number of low-skilled ("low content") jobs that the Soviet economy would long require.

We cannot unravel the variety of factors behind the conflicting results in the economic and sociological literature. It may well be, as some of the opponents of the concept of educational "inflation" have maintained, that those who questioned the economic effectiveness of increased schooling did not properly control for differences in the work experience of the more and less educated and ignored the greater capacity of the more highly educated to adapt to anticipated changes in technology.[42] To resolve this issue and to reconcile these conflicting findings in any definitive sense hardly seems worthwhile or possible here. For our purposes the significance of Soviet discussions of the theme of educational "inflation" lies elsewhere. These discussions, beginning in the early 1960s and continuing in somewhat muted form until the end of the seventies, provided a vehicle—a forum, as it were—for airing problems of widespread job dissatisfaction, the difficulties of adapting educated workers to routine jobs and the policy alternatives available to meet such problems. These are the matters to which we now turn. What kind of evidence on job attitudes and what kinds of policy proposals emerged from these discussions?

Whatever the impact of increased schooling on job performance, it was clear that sizable proportions of young workers with more than eight years of schooling experienced their education as excessive relative to their job requirements. This perception of a "surplus" of education is apparent in the studies summarized in Table 3.4. Workers with various levels of schooling were asked to respond to questions concerning the "fit" between their educational attainments and their work assignments. Among those who had completed ten years of schooling (a "complete" secondary education), some one-fifth to more than one-third reported that "my education is more than my job requires." In what may be an extreme case—the Kazakhstan study summarized in Table 3.4—fully 42% of workers up to the age of 30 experienced their education as excessive relative to their job assignments.[43] Obviously, such perceptions alone cannot be regarded as demonstrating "overeducation." Many of the secondary school graduates in these studies were probably recent entrants into the work force, and the more long-run "payoffs" of their schooling were yet to be realized. But it does seem significant that the proportion of workers with advanced schooling whose responses voiced a sense of underutilization of education increased between the early 1960s and early 1970s (see Table 3.4). The very fact that workers' perceptions of the "mismatch" between their schooling and the jobs available to them had become a subject of "professional" (sociological) study suggests that this was not an unimportant problem. It was, in any case, a new problem.

Another type of evidence, perhaps more "qualitative" than quantitative in nature, is simply the frequency with which the notion of a "conflict" ("collision" in more apocalyptic versions) between prevailing job content and workers' advanced schooling has been invoked in the Soviet literature on labor problems. It hardly seems useful to catalogue the many instances in which this alleged "conflict" and its negative impact on work morale has been cited. But the variety of contexts in which it has been acknowledged and the extended period over which it has been reiterated merit a brief review. Even those who have explicitly re-rejected the concept of educational "inflation" (i.e., those who have argued that increased schooling almost invariably improves job performance) have recognized that job dissatisfaction among youth is connected with the recent extension of secondary schooling. In such cases, the argument goes, the problem is not workers' excessive schooling as such but the inability of managerial personnel to properly utilize it in planning work organization.[44]

Among the first to explicitly link job dissatisfaction among young workers to the "disproportion" between extended schooling and an impoverished work content were the authors of the Leningrad study on which we have drawn so frequently above. Writing in 1967,

Table 3.4

Degree of Conformity between Workers' Educational Levels and Job Requirements, Three Studies

Location of sample and educational level of workers	Workers' response to question: "Does your educational level correspond to your job?" (in %)		
	yes, the two correpsond	education is less than job requires	education is more than job requires
Kazan, 1,000 workers, 1963			
grades 1–4	81.6	17.3	1.1
5–7	88.2	10.8	1.0
8–9	87.1	8.0	4.9
10–11	75.7	3.4	20.9
Four cities in Bashkir republic, 15,000 workers, 1967–68			
grades 1–3	76.0	18.4	5.6
4	79.3	13.0	7.7
6	82.3	9.1	8.6
8	77.4	5.9	16.7
10	68.5	3.6	27.9
Semipalatinsk Meat–Packing Combine (Kazakhstan), 3,500 workers, 1972			
grades 4–6	72.3	24.9	2.8
7–8	68.5	16.5	15.0
9	65.3	11.3	23.4
10	55.4	8.2	36.4

Sources: N. A. Aitov in *Voprosy filosofii*, 1966, No. 11, p. 29; N. A. Aitov, *Tekhnicheskii progress i dvizhenie rabochikh kadrov*, Moscow, 1972, p. 66; Akademia nauk Kazakhskoi SSR, institut ekonomiki, *Upravlenie sotsial'nym razvitiem proizvodstvennykh kollektivov*, Alma-Ata, 1975, p. 80.

Zdravomyslov and Iadov noted that their observations earlier in the decade had already revealed a certain "surplus" of workers with relatively high educational levels whose expectations of challenging work could not be satisfied. They also warned that the slow pace of change in job content combined with rapidly rising levels of schooling threatened to make the problem of work morale among youth a more serious one in the deacade ahead.[45] Their warning was apparently well founded, for the same theme was to be repeatedly echoed by other sociologists in the late 1960s and early 1970s. Here is a small sampling of essentially similar findings drawn from the sociological literature of that period:

> It is no secret that with every passing year it becomes more difficult for enterprises to place yesterday's tenth-grade graduates in interesting and creative jobs where they can successfully apply their knowledge. (L. Kogan in 1968)

> One of the main reasons for job dissatisfaction among workers with high levels of education is the discrepancy between the low content of their work and their education. (N. Aitov in 1972)

> . . . a certain proportion of youth with a high level of education is forced to take unskilled jobs with no prospects of intellectual enrichment, and this creates dissatisfaction with the work itself to a greater degree than with the level of material rewards for work. (A. Tashbulatova in 1972)[46]

The *Molodoi kommunist* discussion

Perhaps the most free-wheeling discussion of the problem of young workers' job attitudes and the "disproportion" between job content and education appeared in the pages of *Molodoi kommunist*, the organ of the Komosomol, in 1972–73. Aside from providing abundant empirical evidence which supported the kinds of statements we have just cited, a significant feature of this discussion was the explicit recognition by a number of participants that technological progress alone was not the answer to the problem of increasingly educated workers in unskilled and "low content" jobs. "Her majesty, automatic equipment (*avtomatika*), is not a sorceress."[47] This was the response of a critic to the author of the article which had initiated the discussion. The latter ḧad documented widespread job dissatisfaction among young, low-skilled workers (41% dissatisfied among a sample of workers in Ufa) and had urged the conventional remedy—rapid "mechanization and automation." This remedy was based on the traditional identification of low-skilled work with "manual and heavy" jobs, jobs "unrelated to complex technology."[48] It is difficult to exaggerate the frequency with which similar appeals to technological progress as the principal solution to a variety of labor problems—including the problem of job dissatisfaction—have been voiced in the Soviet literature. At the time of this discussion (the early 1970s), in the midst of the never-ending celebration of the "scientific-technological revolution," it was hardly a common practice to question this assumption. Hence the significance of the rather casual remark that *avtomatika* was not a "sorceress" in the context of a discussion of work attitudes and job content. The critic's (V. Churbanov) point was a fairly obvious one: Work activity associated with "complex equipment" was not necessarily more intellectually demanding or challenging than purely manual work. While the former often implied a "lightening" of physically burdensome job tasks, it also could lead to their increased routinization and fragmentation and a decline in their intellectual content. The creation of "high content," challenging jobs (confronting the worker with "non-stereotyped tasks") was a more difficult problem than the simple elimination of "heavy" manual jobs. Given the spread of assembly-line work and jobs in "servicing automatic equipment," workers with a secondary education would continue to experience a "conflict" between their advanced schooling and their comparatively impoverished job content. "For an assembler on a conveyor, mental work in general is reduced to a minimum and cannot even be calculated." Indeed, success in attaining universal secondary schooling would probably intensify the sense of underutilization of education on such jobs. "The surplus of education in current production is a phenomenon that is destined to exist for a rather long time."[49]

The conflict between certain forms of technological modernization and workers' opportunities for an enriched job content was also formulated in unusually stark terms by two other participants in this discussion (the economists G. Slutskii and G. Shestakova). If assessed on purely "production-economic" grounds, the use of conveyor-line methods of production and work organization had distinct advantages: they ensured the continuity of the production process, reduced the length of the production cycle, diminished labor outlays on intraplant transportation and in general improved the utilization of productive capacity. Hence the rapid diffusion of such methods in Soviet industry. But if assessed from the standpoint of "the interests of the individual," the conveyor clearly had negative consequences. Why the "contradiction between the individual and the conveyor"?

The experience of enterprises shows that in order to train assemblers on the conveyor, to teach them its elementary operations, a few days are sufficient. The breakdown of the work process into its fractional, simplest elements inevitably leads to a reduction in the challenge of work, to an increase in its monotony, to a decline in assemblers' interests in the results of their work.[50]

As if to confirm this generalization, the authors reported on their findings at "the most advanced enterprise of native machine building," the Volga Automobile Plant. Despite its advanced technology—or perhaps more correctly, because of it—the plant, staffed mainly by young workers, was experiencing great difficulties in recruiting and retaining "stable cadres."

One of the main reasons for this situation consists in the fact that the jobs of most workers are reduced here to the performance of routine, monotonous operations in loading and unloading semiautomatic equipment, in carrying out the most simple assembly operations on numerous conveyors. In discussions with us many young workers expressed their dissatisfaction with the content of work and complained about the absence of opportunities for raising their skills.[51]

Clearly, since at least the early seventies the more serious Soviet observers of the labor process have been warning that the development of the "productive forces," understood as the replacement of manual work by "mechanization and automation," has been a new source of job discontent, especially among young workers. But not all the participants in the *Molodoi kommunist* discussion of "Education and the Labor of Youth" (the official rubric under which the discussion was conducted in 1972–73) saw the problem in precisely the same way. For some of them the problem was not primarily the rapid multiplication of routine machine-tending jobs but the negative attitude of the more educated young workers to working-class occupations generally— whether skilled or unskilled.

It is quite possible that some of the writers who pointed to the spread of assembly-line jobs as a principal source of work discontent among the more educated workers tended to overstate the diffusion of this form of production technology. Official figures on the extent of "conveyorization" are not available, and the estimates in the literature on labor problems differ substantially. Thus one of the contributors to the *Molodoi kommunist* discussion who stressed the impoverishment of job content stemming from the introduction of assembly-line technology assumed (in 1972) that "every third worker is employed on a conveyor," and that the spread of such production methods would soon absorb increasing proportions of formerly skilled metal craftsmen and lathe operators. But the sociologist O. Shkaratan cautioned that no more than 10% of workers confronted "the problems of automation and conveyorization today" (1973), and this figure would probably not increase by more than 10% by the end of the century.[52] Hence there were grounds for questioning whether the main difficulty in adapting recalcitrant young workers to their jobs lay in the rapid multiplication of low-skilled machine-assembly work. For some of the participants in the *Molodoi kommunist* discussion (as well as for others grappling with the problem of poor work morale among youth), job dissatisfaction was rooted in the attitudes which educated youngsters brought to the workplace rather than in those which they acquired as a result of their actual job experience.

In the words of one of the adherents of this view, a chief engineer of a Moscow machine-tool plant, many young people entered the work force "more afraid of workers' occupations than of a fire." Why? Because they had an exaggerated conception of the job opportunities which their secondary-school diplomas could provide, as well as of their own abilities. Too many felt that "once the graduation certificate was in hand, I am capable of creative work." The real problem, however, was the "lag" of occupational training in workers' trades behind the growing need for skilled workers. With the tone of impatience characteristic of a certain traditional style of managerial ideology, the engineer's advice to those educated youngsters who found themselves in routine, uninteresting jobs was: ". . . such work shouldn't frighten those who are capable of more. Just show that you are worth more."[53]

A more reasoned and sophisticated formulation of this position (minus the advice to show what "you are worth") appeared in the contribution of the sociologist V. Krevnevich. Without denying the negative impact on work morale stemming from secondary-school graduates being forced to accept unskilled workers' jobs, Krevnevich pointed to a more serious and "alarming" problem: the "unwillingness of some youth to seriously master workers' occupations in general," in the face of the economy's increasing need for workers in "challenging, highly skilled jobs."[54] Numerous sociological studies over the preceding decade had demonstrated that 80% or more of secondary-school graduates planned to continue their schooling either at a higher educational institution *(VUZ)* or a specialized school (*tekhnikum*), leading to semiprofessional occupational status. Very few such graduates aspired to become skilled workers. When forced to enter working-class occupations as a result of failure to gain admission to advanced schooling, they frequently regarded these jobs as "temporary" and for an extended period resisted the prospect of making a "career" in workers' occupations. For Krevnevich the responsibility for this situation rested largely on the content of education in the upper grades of the general secondary school, with its "theoretical" orientation fostering expectations of "mental work" among those who remained to graduate.[55]

The view that widespread job dissatisfaction among the more educated young workers often reflected a certain "social orientation" acquired prior to labor market entry was frequently voiced in the sociological literature of this period. "Social orientation" in this context meant essentially a striving for "social position," more specifically, for intelligentsia social and occupational status. Whether this orientation was directly fostered by the content of education in the upper grades of secondary school (as suggested by Krevnevich), or whether advanced schooling was seen by some youngsters as mainly an instrument for realizing their aspirations for a higher-level "social position" (as suggested by the sociologist I. M. Popova), the point was essentially the same. For youngsters entering the labor force in workers' jobs after ten years of schooling, the orientation to college admission and eventual attainment of intelligentsia social position which they brought to the workplace could be a more important source of job dissatisfaction than the actual content of their work tasks.[56] The problem was not so much that they were forced into routine, unskilled workers' jobs, but that they found themselves in any kind of workers' jobs. In Popova's words, "The orientation to college admission determines to a considerable degree the attitude of tenth-graders to the enterprise" (i.e., to their jobs in working-class occupations).[57] In her own study of ship-repair workers, Popova had found that the higher the level of workers' schooling, the less satisfied they were with both their schooling and their jobs. The greater degree of satisfaction among the less educated—both with their schooling and their jobs—signified their adjustment to and acceptance of working-class status. In Popova's somewhat elusive language, the dissatisfaction of the more educated workers was associated with "claims" of a "nonproduction" character—their frustrated aspirations for intelligentsia (professional) social position.[58]

Enough has been said here to demonstrate the absorption of the sociological and "popular" literature in the early 1970s with problems of poor work morale and job dissatisfaction among young workers. The variety of attempts to identify the sources of these problems stressed two factors—one "objective" in nature, the other "subjective." The former referred to the rapid multiplication of low-skilled machine-tending and assembly-line jobs increasingly staffed by secondary-school graduates. While precise figures on the relative share of such jobs in total industrial employment are unavailable ("official" figures showing close to three-quarters of industrial workers in "skilled" jobs are hardly credible), none of the participants in the *Molodoi kommunist* discussion challenged the view of one writer who noted that more than 50% of workers' jobs were still in "low content and unskilled types of work," or the views of another who remarked that "the future belongs to serial production," which requires mainly low-skilled workers.[59] The "subjective" factor referred to the negative attitudes toward working-class occupations as a whole which many graduates of second-ary school brought to their jobs. These attitudes were rooted in the inability of increasing proportions of these youngsters to follow the traditional career paths open to the relatively small number of such graduates in the past—access to higher education and intelligentsia status. Fewer than one-fourth of these graduates were being admitted to full-time college study at this time, compared to more than one-half a decade earlier. It would clearly be an error to regard the greater stress on "objective" factors by some writers and on "subjective" factors by others as representing alternative interpretations of the problem of job discontent among youth. These were two sides of the same coin—the growing "contradiction" between job content and rising educational attainments.

Although we have focused thus far largely on the late 1960s and early 1970s, there is no reason to assume that this "contradiction" and its negative consequences for job attitudes and work discipline have lessened significantly in more recent years. The available evidence points to the continuity rather than the easing of these problems. Thus in reporting on his study of Leningrad machine-building workers in 1976–77, O. I. Shkaratan summarized his findings in terms that were remarkably similar to those used a decade earlier by Zdravomyslov and Iadov: "Leningrad . . . is training the most highly educated and voca-tionally schooled workers, but the content and character of work at the city's enterprises are changing much more slowly. . . ."[60] The conse-quences included "relatively high rates of dissatisfaction with their jobs" by graduates of secondary schools providing vocational training (only 48% reported satisfaction with their current jobs). The work performance of these graduates, as judged by norm fulfillment and the quality of their output, was inferior to that of workers in the same age groups but without a secondary-school diploma.

It is hardly remarkable, of course, that workers in low-skilled jobs but with relatively high levels of schooling should express dissatisfaction with their workplace roles. But it does seem significant that in Shkaratan's sample as a whole (which presumably included representatives of occupations of varying degrees of skill), higher levels of job dissatisfaction appeared to be positively associated with higher levels of schooling. Here are Shkaratan's figures (in number of years of school completed) for various job satisfaction (dissatisfaction) groupings among Leningrad machine-building workers in 1976–77:

more satisfied than dissatisfied with job	8.9
more dissatisfied than satisfied with job	9.6
fully satisfied with independence on job	8.8
completely dissatisfied with independence on job	9.2[61]

Whatever its long-run positive consequences, therefore, the steady rise in workers' educational levels in the late 1970s continued to be regarded as a source of "additional problems" (in Shkaratan's phrase) for those entrusted with managing the work process. Nor were Shkaratan's findings the only indicator that this was the case. Essentially the same point was made in studies conducted in Moscow and Taganrog during this period.[62] But it seems most appropriate to conclude this review with the rather casual though highly significant remark made in 1979 by one of the first sociologists to warn of the problematic consequences of the increased schooling of young workers. Reporting on his recent study of changes in the work attitudes and behavior of young Leningrad workers since the early 1960s, V. Iadov noted: "In the period that has elapsed there has been some increase in the indiscipline of workers."[63]

The evidence is persuasive that job dissatisfaction among the younger members of the work force remained a widely recognized problem throughout the decade of the seventies and later, and that it was related to the much discussed "disproportion" between increased schooling and the largely routine, low-skilled nature of most youngsters' work tasks. What have been some of the principal responses to the evidence of work discontent?

4
Responses to Work Discontent

A few words of qualification are in order as we turn to an examination of Soviet efforts to improve work morale and to elicit a more disciplined and committed work effort from the laboring population. Although we have focused in the immediately preceding pages on Soviet concerns with the attitudes and performance of young workers, there is no reason to assume that job dissatisfaction and poor work performance are exclusively confined to the younger age groups. But since the public discussion of labor problems has so often concentrated on the job attitudes of young workers, we should not be surprised to find that some of the principal policy responses and proposals for work reform have been directed at this group. It should also be clear that only certain types of proposals to counter the dissatisfaction and indifference of workers are likely to surface in the public discourse on labor problems. Thus we can hardly expect suggestions for increasing workers' real wages, or for improving the availability of food supplies and other consumer goods, or for introducing radical changes in opportunities for the airing of workers' grievances to appear in these discussions. The right to raise such issues—indeed, if they are viewed as legitimate issues at all—is obviously reserved for those at the highest levels of authority. Within these limits, however, we shall see that a rather wide range of measures has been proposed. If the actual policy measures implemented to confront the problem of work discontent seem few and far between, the variety of ideas which have begun to surface in the literature are part of the intellectual environment in which a modest Soviet version of work reform has begun to emerge. Hence in the material which follows we are interested in the ideas and concepts that have appeared in these discussions no less than in the limited range of policy measures thus far adopted.

Finally the various measures and proposals to be reviewed here have not always been presented as responses to explicit manifestations of job discontent. More often they have been defended as necessary to improve workers' "productive potential," to reduce excessive labor turnover, to heighten work discipline. These formulations should not obscure their obvious connection to the problem of job dissatisfaction. It seems convenient to divide the various responses into two broad categories: (a) those directed at changing the content of schooling, and (b) those designed to improve the work environment.

Changes in schooling

Cautiously worded warnings against excessive investment in workers' schooling have occasionally appeared in Soviet discussions of the proper "fit" between education and work.[1] But they have been subordinate to the stress on changing the content of schooling in the upper grades of secondary education. We have seen that the completion of the tenth grade of a general-education school was long regarded as essentially a stepping-stone to college admission and thus escape from working-class status. Beginning in the late 1960s, a serious effort was made to change the career expectations of the vast majority of youngsters who continued their schooling beyond the eighth grade. The process was one we might loosely call "consciousness-lowering." The principal instrument was to be a substantial increase in enrollment of youngsters in vocational-technical schools (*professional'nye tekhnicheskie uchilishche*) providing training for semiskilled and skilled workers' occupations. These schools had long been widely regarded as "second-rate" educational institutions to which "difficult" youngsters who performed poorly in general education schools were channeled.[2] The workers' vocational schools had also been "dead-end" institutions in the sense that graduation did not make a youngster eligible for postsecondary schooling. Beginning in 1969, in an effort to enhance the attractiveness of this form of education, an increasing number of these schools were shifted to a three-year course of study (compared to 12–18 months in earlier years) which would simultaneously provide a "complete" secondary education and vocational training in workers' trades. The purpose was not merely to promote early acquisition of workers' skills but to "implant in youth an interest in workers' occupations,"[3] i.e., to avoid the development of the kinds of unrealistic career expectations fostered by the general education schools. Graduates would be considered eligible for college admission (this feature was obviously intended to raise the prestige of these schools), but the principal objective was clearly the early socialization of youngsters to future employment in working-class occupations.

High hopes were placed on the ability of these schools to divert students from the more academically oriented general education schools. With the customary enthusiasm acompanying new policy initiatives, some commentators saw the secondary vocational-technical schools as harbingers of "universal vocational-technical education of youth." They were to become "the principal source of recruitment of the working class."[4] But perhaps the most significant feature of this form of schooling has been its relatively modest expansion thus far. By 1978 only 15% of youngsters completing the eighth grade of daytime general education schools continued their schooling in secondary vocational-technical institutions (see Table 1.2). Over the whole period of the Tenth Five-Year Plan (1976–80), approximately four-fifths of all youngsters completing a secondary education (10–11 years of schooling) graduated from general education schools. These are the very institutions so often criticized for orienting their students to "mental labor" rather than working-class occupations. Moreover, in the words of the deputy minister of education in 1981, the general education schools "will remain . . . the principal path for receiving a secondary education."[5]

How can we explain these "mixed signals," in particular, the failure to more rapidly expand a form of schooling explicitly designed to adapt youngsters to working-class jobs, and the continued dominance of a type of upper-level secondary education traditionally associated with preparation for college entry under conditions in which such entry is impossible for most graduates? Part of the answer lies in what might be called—to borrow a strange phrase from a Soviet commentator—"sociological resistance" to the expansion of the new vocational schools.[6] The resistance has come from a variety of sources. First, the more ambitious youngsters and their parents can hardly be expected to view with enthusiasm a type of secondary schooling offering the least likely prospect of access to higher education. Graduates of the new vocational schools, although eligible for admission to a *VUZ*, are clearly at a disadvantage in the competition for college entry compared to the more "academically" trained graduates of general education schools. Moreover, the importance of early "professionalization" of youngsters (through attendance at workers' vocational schools immediately upon completion of the eighth grade) must seem less urgent as families' living standards gradually increase. But resistance to making the workers' vocational schools the principal form of secondary education has also come from sections of the educational establishment. Their concern has been that the excessive diversion of youngsters from the general education schools, under conditions in which the demographic base for recruitment of college students has already begun to narrow (reflecting the low birth rates of the 1960s), may cut into both the number and quality of *VUZ* applicants.[7] (The number of applicants per *VUZ* vacancy had already begun to decline in the 1970s.) In effect the effort at early adaptation of school-age youngsters to working-class occupations might prove too "successful." Finally, studies of the work performance and job attitudes of graduates of secondary vocational-technical schools in areas where this type of education has become widespread—Leningrad, for example—have not always been encouraging (see our summary of Shkaratan's findings on pp. 72–73). Thus the relatively slow change in an educational system widely regarded as contributing to the problem of negative attitudes toward workers' jobs among the more educated youth.

It would be a mistake, however, to assume that efforts to moderate youngsters' career expectations have had no impact. The extension of a more prestigious form (i.e., one offering a "complete" secondary education) of vocational schooling in workers' skills, the increased stress on "vocational guidance" in the schools (essentially "guidance" into workers' trades) and the sheer passage of time since the days when secondary-school graduation meant a high probability of college admission have all operated as part of a "cooling-off" process gradually adapting educated youth to the prospect of a lifetime in workers' jobs. The point is that by its very nature, such a process of adaptation cannot be expected to produce a marked and rapid improvement in the job attitudes of young people entering working-class occupations. There is no shortage of evidence that in the early 1980s, the low prestige of working-class occupations remained an obstacle to adapting many youngsters to their occupational fates.[8]

Proposed changes at the workplace

Some of the policy measures proposed or actually adopted at the workplace in recent years have been "external" to the labor process itself in the sense that they have not sought to alter job content or work organization. While such proposals seem less important than those bearing directly on the labor process, they deserve at least brief mention as indicators of the range of work reform measures under consideration in the effort to reduce job dissatisfaction.

One illustration, voiced in the *Molodoi kommunist* discussion of the early 1970s reviewed in Chapter 3, was the proposal for introducing measures of "social compensation" for workers employed in "low content" jobs. "Social compensation" encompassed the elimination ("wherever possible") of night shifts, the reduction of the normal length of the working day, increased vacation periods and preferential access to enterprise housing facilities.[9] The context of the discussion made it clear that the proposals were aimed mainly at reducing work discontent among educated youth in "unattractive" jobs. The term "social compensation" was certainly appropriate—rewards off the job (mainly increased nonwork time or more convenient work schedules) would partially offset an unchanged and unrewarding job content. The proposal was not favorably received by most of the other participants in the *Molodoi kommunist* discussion, nor is this the route which political authorities have recently pursued in confronting the problem of poor work morale (although there is scattered evidence that as a matter of local rather than national policy, managers occasionally grant above-normal or seasonally preferred vacation periods to workers in unpleasant jobs).[10] The high costs of such an approach, both in terms of output sacrificed and in its incentive effect on skill acquisition and occupational mobility, have apparently been effective arguments against its widespread implementation. But it seems unlikely that such proposals would have emerged in public discussion unless they represented one of the options under active consideration. Suggestions in Soviet publications to reduce the working day and extend vacations for a large body of workers cannot be regarded as simply expressions of "one man's opinion."

Although such proposals have little prospect of implementation under the conditions of labor scarcity of the 1980s, they are important as one expression of a more general response to the problem of work discontent: the search for "compensating factors" (off the job) to offset or reduce negative attitudes to unrewarding work. The same approach is reflected in the appeal to managers to recognize the urgency of improving the "social infrastructure" of the enterprise—its housing and recreational facilities, its medical and child-care services—where there is little prospect of making work itself more satisfying.[11] But quite apart from the limited prospects for large-scale decentralized investments in "social infrastructure," a more significant and promising Soviet response to job dissatisfaction and poor work performance lies elsewhere. We refer to attempts to "enrich" job content by altering the organization of the work process and to create a sense of mobility opportunities as well as a consciousness of worker "participation" in plant-level decision-making. Thus we now turn to the Soviet version of "work reform." This is a large theme which merits extended examination. Hence we introduce the theme here and continue our discussion of it in the following chapters.

The assimilation of "work humanization"

One manifestation of the search for new forms of work organization may be seen in the process of assimilating into Soviet public discourse the concepts associated with the "humanization of work" and "quality of work life" movements in Western countries. Thus the Soviet management literature has begun to report in relatively positive terms on the variety of work reorganization experiments undertaken in both Western Europe and the United States. This literature includes straightforward accounts of such practices as job rotation, job enlargement, work "enrichment," the modification and elimination of conventional assembly-line work (especially in Volvo plants in Sweden), and the organization of autonomous work teams (with the authority to "independently plan and organize their own work activity" and in some cases to elect their own team leaders). The sheer volume of such literature (more than half a dozen substantial articles in the leading Soviet management and economics periodicals in the late 1970s and early 1980s) suggests a serious effort—bordering on a "campaign"— to popularize the more "progressive" forms of work reorganization being implemented in Western plants.[12] Not much reading between the lines is required to see that this Soviet literature is part of the search for solutions to domestic problems of managing work. When a Soviet writer describes the traditional "methods of organizing capitalist production" which the adherents of work humanization seek to change ("the subdivision of work processes into the simplest and briefest operations . . . the detailed planning of work 'from above' and the elimination of any possibilities for decision-making . . . the extremely rapid, forced pace of work determined by the speed of the conveyor"), the Soviet reader does not have to be explicitly told that similar conditions prevail in Soviet plants.[13]

Any such discussions must, of course, contain a necessary minimum quota of critical commentary. The introduction of work reform measures in the West does not alter the "class essence" and "exploitative character" of labor under capitalism.[14] But these critical remarks seem

almost perfunctory compared to the predominantly positive characterizations of the enriched "group methods" of work organization which,
in the Soviet view, have begun to replace "Taylorism" and "Fordism"
in the more advanced capitalist enterprises. A tone of unabashed admi-
ration is particularly apparent in Soviet portrayals of the consequences
of Volvo's "pioneering" efforts to replace the conventional conveyor
by team assembly and job rotation. These consequences have included:

> . . . the elimination of one-sided physical overloading, the reduction
> of monotony, increased opportunities for the manifestation of
> workers' abilities and independence, the growth of skills. . . . Yes,
> the new form of work organization in industry has led to some
> lightening of workers' labor, has made it richer in content, has in-
> creased the sense of involvement of working people. Industrial safety
> measures have been raised to a new level, and the quality of the
> surrounding work environment has been improved.[15]

While this description of the Volvo experiments may be somewhat
more enthusiastic than most Soviet accounts, even the more restrained
discussions make it clear that Soviet industrial practice can benefit
from a study of Western humanization of work policies. If anything
signals this recognition, it is the explicit invocation by some Soviet
commentators of Lenin's often cited characterization of Taylor's "scientific management" (". . . it combines within itself the most subtle
brutality of bourgeois exploitation and some of the richest scientific
achievements . . .") as now being "no less applicable" to the new
stress in capitalist work organization on job autonomy and reduced
fragmentation of work.[16]

It would be a mistake to assume, however, that the Soviet popularization of Western work reform experiments represents simply an
"importation" or "borrowing" of previously unfamiliar and alien
concepts. It is precisely the familiarity and ideological compatibility of
these concepts that has facilitated the popularization of Western "work
humanization" experience. The idea of job rotation has strong roots in
the Marxian ideological heritage, and proposals to implement it have
long been made in the Soviet lilterature. The same is true of the idea of
organizing work on the basis of "group" ("team" or "brigade")
rather than individual work assignments and of "enlarging" and
"consolidating" fragmented and specialized job tasks, especially on
assembly-line operations.[17] But such concepts had long been subordinate to the faith in "mechanization and automation" as inherently
work-enriching processes. This is no longer the case. The possibility

that technological advance without regard to the "human factor" may impoverish work tasks and increase job monotony has recently become a common theme in the Soviet management literature.[18] Hence the readiness to assimilate, or at least to seriously consider, the experience of Western efforts to improve both workers' job attitudes and productive performance through changing the organization of work and—within limits—the distribution of authority within the work process. The fact that the "progressive" methods of work organization have been introduced in some Western enterprises in response to problems of excessive labor turnover, absenteeism and poor work discipline—a point stressed in Soviet accounts—clearly contributes to Soviet interest in them.

But the comparatively favorable portrayal in Soviet publications of the concepts and practices associated with work humanization in the West obviously does not constitute evidence of their implementation in the Soviet Union. To what extent is it appropriate to speak of a Soviet version of "work reform"? What is the evidence, if any, that Soviet responses to job discontent have been translated into measures to redesign and "enrich" job content, to change the way in which work is organized and managed? The problem here is to distinguish between advocacy of and appeals for such changes, on the one hand, and hard evidence that they are being introduced, on the other.

Leaving aside for the moment the issue of whether anything resembling "work reform" has been introduced into Soviet industrial practice (the phrase "work reform" does not ordinarily, or ever, appear in Soviet discussions), it should be recognized that appeals for organizational and technical innovations in the work process have been widespread in recent years. We are not referring here to the perfunctory calls for mechanization of "heavy" manual labor that have long been routine in the Soviet labor literature but to the need for the kind of restructuring of work that would address the problems arising out of technological advance. As might be expected, the conveyor and assembly-line jobs are probably the most common context in which the appeal for work reorganization has been expressed. Why this should be the case is apparent from the almost routinely negative terms used to characterize such jobs: monotony, specialization carried to absurdity, one day or less required to master the work.[19] Discussions of this issue have often been more concerned with stressing the urgency of redesigning work rather than providing ready-made answers:

> Ford's invention must be abolished, eliminated, replaced, destroyed. But how to do this? What is the most appropriate and promising al-

ternative? Many participants in the production process [*proiz-vodstvenniki*] are waiting impatiently for an answer to this question from scholars.[20]

Some sociologists have even urged that the time has come for the question of rejecting the conveyor as a form of work organization to be raised "at the state level,"[21] and the few instances in which conveyor assembly-line methods have been abandoned have received a fair amount of publicity.[22] However, the more typical form which the advocacy of work reorganization has taken involves not the elimination of assembly-line technology (especially where large-sized components are concerned) but its redesign to permit team assembly and job rotation:

> We must assume that the conveyor will be the basic method of assembling autos and other types of large-scale production for a long time to come. In the future the place of man at the conveyor apparently must be taken by robots. But until their use becomes a mass phenomenon, we cannot ignore any opportunities for struggle with the negative consequences of conveyorization. The experience of team assembly at Volvo can be of definite assistance in this respect.[23]

The "conflict between man and the conveyor,"[24] however, is not the only context in which appeals for work reorganization have appeared. A reformist spirit, if not a specific reform program, is apparent in the criticism recently directed at some of the more extreme aspects of the "scientific organization of labor"—essentially a Soviet version of Taylorism. One critic (V. Markov) has directed his fire at the tendency of this movement to stress the importance of specifying in advance and in excessive detail precisely how each workplace is to be organized, how the job is to be performed, the knowledge and skills required. He warns against the danger of "strict regulation" (the context suggests "overregulation") of the details of the work process "which cannot help but inhibit initiative and creativity and sometimes lead to the justification of antiquated methods." The kind of *reglamentatsiia* associated with this managerial ideology often conflicts with the personal qualities required of workers under conditions of rapidly changing job content, qualities like "a capacity for creativity . . , an ability to take decisions in nonstandardized situations . . , a positive and receptive attitude toward technical and organizational innovations."[25] Although couched in general terms, this is—at the very least—a plea for a less authoritarian, more open and "participatory" style of management. These sentiments may also be found in some of the literature concerned with the problem of the low prestige of working-class occupations in the thinking of youth. The way to overcome this problem is not through "sloganeering appeals" but through the enrichment of work content: "The worker must make independent decisions . . , must not be tied to a single job operation or monotonous type of activity, must see prospects for advancements."[26]

What we have called the advocacy of work reform has also appeared in the appeals to machine-design organizations not to be guided by exclusively "technical-economic criteria" but to consider "social criteria" as well. However abstract and imprecise such formulations may seem, their essential meaning is clear: to apply "social criteria" to machinery design means to reject the kinds of technological options that reduce workers' skills and/or worsen conditions of work. The appeal to apply such criteria is obviously a call to abandon traditional practices which must have frequently ignored these "noneconomic" considerations. It seems hardly surprising that the same Soviet writer who has urged the use of "social criteria" in machinery design should also stress that the development of communist work attitudes "presupposes the elevation, enrichment and humanization of all types of work activity."[27]

Enough has been said here to indicate that quite apart from the comparatively favorable portrayal of Western experience, the vocabulary—some might say the rhetoric—of work reform has begun to permeate Soviet public discourse on labor problems. We now return to the question asked earlier. Has the increasingly familiar language associated with the idea of "humanizing" work ("adapting work to man . . . not man to work"[28]) had its counterpart in the actual organization and management of work? Is there a "real" process of work reform underway in the Soviet Union?

Work humanization in practice

Students of Soviet society are familiar with the common Soviet practice of singling out certain "leading enterprises" as models of economic and social organization which others are constantly urged to emulate. In the area of managing and organizing work activity, the most celebrated of these "leading enterprises" has undoubtedly been the Volga Auto Plant at Togliatti. Others serving a similar function, although obviously ranking a few notches below the Volga plant in the frequency with which their experience has been popularized, include the Kaluga Turbine Plant, the Perm Telephone Plant, the Minsk Tractor Plant. One way of establishing the meaning and dimensions of work reform under Soviet circumstances is to examine the portrayal of a few salient features of the labor process at some of these model enterprises. What emerges here obviously cannot be regarded as "typical" but as representing the acceptable boundaries of work reform under current circumstances and as specifying prevailing Soviet conceptions of the humanization of work.

It is well to recognize at this point that there is no need to regard the various policies to be discussed below as sudden manifestations of a more "humane" attitude toward labor. These policies are essentially "management tools," responses to the worker discontent and indifference documented in earlier chapters. With this in mind, some of the main elements in recent Soviet work reform efforts may be considered under three headings: (a) improvements in working conditions, (b) the regularization of promotion procedures, and (c) the institutionalization of work teams (or brigades) as the basic units of work organization.

a) If serious work reform efforts are underway in the Soviet Union, it would be perfectly natural for them to encompass measures to improve the complex of job factors associated with industrial health and safety, "sanitary-hygienic conditions," the pace of work and general "comfort" on the job—the variety of job elements normally falling under the rubric of "conditions of work" (*uslovii truda*). Iadov noted at the end of the 1970s that the relative importance of these job characteristics as determinants of work attitudes (job satisfaction/dissatisfaction) had increased since the early 1960s.[29] A similar conclusion is suggested by a study of Siberian industrial plants which found that unsatisfactory "conditions of work" accounted for an increasing proportion of job turnover over the period 1964–70.[30] A 1976–77 study of workers in Leningrad machine-building enterprises reported that more than half of those questioned voiced "dissatisfaction with conditions of work," a finding not unusual in studies of work attitudes in the 1970s.[31] Why the apparently heightened importance of these elements of the work situation? We have already encountered the answer suggested by Iadov—recent changes in the nonwork sphere of Soviet life: "Having become accustomed to comfort in everyday life, people want comfort on the job. If a plant director today wants to retain young workers . . . and attract new ones, he must be concerned not only with material incentives and the richness of work content but also with conditions of work."[32]

The traditional meaning of improvements in conditions of work has centered largely on the idea of eliminating (or at least reducing) "heavy

manual labor'' by introducing ''all-sided mechanization and automation of work.'' More recently the emphasis has increasingly shifted to
the problems of ''heightened monotony and nervous-emotional stress''
associated with the extension of conveyor-belt technology.[33] It is in this
context that a set of ''psychophysiological measures'' in effect at the
Volga Auto Plant are worth examining. These measures represent the
Soviet conception of the humanization of conditions of work in a
''leading enterprise.'' Such measures include:[34] regular changes in the
speed of the conveyor over the course of the working day (beginning at
less than the ''optimal level'' at the start of the day, rising to this level
after 40 minutes, slowing down somewhat before the lunch break,
speeding up after lunch, and slowing down at the end of the day); two
regular work breaks of ten minutes each per shift, with a separate rest
area for each work team equipped with such amenities as ''tables,
benches . . . dominoes and newspapers''; the piping in of ''functional
music'' to workers employed on conveyor lines for two hours per shift.
In somewhat less specific terms the claim is also made that the Volga
Auto Plant has created ''optimal sanitary-hygienic conditions,'' and
that special care has been taken to enhance the ''esthetic'' qualities of
work areas (by installing such furnishings as ''decorative greenery,
fountains . . . exhibition stands, fish tanks, decorative rocks, etc.'').

Whether all these measures are in fact regularly implemented or not
seems less significant than the general conception they convey of what
constitutes exemplary ''conditions of work.'' The avowed objective of
these measures is to ''lessen fatigue'' and ''reduce the influence of
monotony.'' The choice of words is not accidental. As a Soviet writer
puts it, these measures are designed to ''remove some of the symptoms
of monotony, some of its consequences, but not to eliminate monotony
itself.''[35] They are thus essentially mechanisms for better adapting
workers to what is widely recognized as a work-impoverishing technology. This was implicitly acknowledged by the chief of the Volga plant's
Department of Working Conditions in 1979 when he described a new
aspect of his organization's work: ''. . . to reduce to a minimum the
assignment to the conveyor of workers who, because of their psychological makeup, cannot tolerate monotonous and routine work.''[36]

The relatively modest nature of some of these measures (regular
work breaks, variation in assembly-line speeds) should not obscure the
possibility that they are part of a serious effort to improve working
conditions. The fact that such measures are described as prevailing at a
''leading enterprise'' suggests that there must be considerable scope
for improvement at the more numerous ''lagging enterprises.''

b) It comes as something of a surprise, at least initially, to learn that the systematizing of job promotion procedures and of rules governing the filling of vacancies is regarded by Soviet writers as one element in current efforts at work humanization (or work reform in non-Soviet vocabulary).[37] The surprise stems from the expectation that such obvious, if not trivial, matters as clear-cut criteria for job promotion and occupational advancement would have been settled long ago. But closer study reveals that this clearly has not been the case. The absence of consistently enforced formal rules governing the movement of workers within the enterprise has long been accompanied by complaints against arbitrary promotion and hiring policies and appeals for a "system of promotion that would be equal and clear for all." More specifically, the complaints (as reflected, for example, in workers' testimony recorded in a job turnover study of the early 1970s)[38] have been directed at such managerial practices as withholding job advancement opportunities until workers submit notice of job quitting, filling newly created skilled positions by hiring from the "outside" rather than by promotion from within. In a study published in 1979, two of the principal Soviet investigators of labor turnover found that "at the present time almost all enterprises are characterized by the absence of a well thought-out and systematically implemented policy of job advancement for workers."[39] But the need to create a sense of "career" opportunities within working-class occupations in recent years must seem all the more urgent given the increased inflow of secondary school graduates— many of them frustrated *VUZ* applicants—into relatively low-skilled workers' jobs. For such workers the concept of a "career" is undoubtedly normally associated with intelligentsia occupational status. Having failed to attain it, how can they be persuaded that "career" prospects are worth aspiring to and planning for in working-class occupations? It is against this background that we can understand the importance attached to popularizing and institutionalizing the job allocation and promotion procedures said to be in effect at the Volga Auto Plant and similar model enterprises.

In some of their essential features these procedures are analogous to those associated with the concept of "internal labor markets" in the United States:

> . . . new workers are hired only to fill jobs in the mass occupations of low-skilled labor. The filling of vacancies in skilled jobs is implemented by drawing only on workers with the required length of service at the factory and those who have completed special training.[40]

Thus "port of entry" jobs through which workers enter the organization's employment are concentrated at the bottom of the job ladder, while the more skilled positions are filled by promotion from within. Eligibility for promotion is governed by "fixed and predetermined requirements" based on a combination of seniority at the plant, formal schooling and attendance at the plant's job-training courses. The plant periodically issues an Information Bulletin (as a section of the factory newspaper) which announces the vacancies available in the more skilled job classifications and the currently operating training courses which workers in less skilled jobs must pass through on their way "upward." While some accounts of this job allocation process also note that workers' promotion prospects are affected by such civic virtues as "attitude toward work, conscientiousness, . . . attitude toward one's comrades, participation in the public life of the collective," principal stress seems to be placed on the more objectively defined "fixed and predetermined" criteria cited above.[41]

Once again the important point is not whether these practices are in fact strictly observed, even at enterprises heralded as models for other economic units to follow, but one of the meanings commonly attached to work reform measures under current Soviet circumstances. In this case such measures involve an extension of rules designed to reduce arbitrary decisions by supervisors in the area of job allocation. The objective is to encourage job stability and work commitment by instilling in workers—particularly the younger, more educated groups—the sense that disciplined work promises upward movement along predetermined job ladders. It can hardly be accidental that the rules in question (limited ports of entry, promotion from within to fill the more skilled positions, reliance on "objective" criteria for job advancement, the specification of promotion ladders) appear to be, at least on the surface, not unlike those in effect in "primary" labor markets in the United States, where the promotion of on-the-job training and employment stability have also been principal objectives.

c) "The brigade method of work, extensively applied at the Volga Auto Plant, is an effective means of humanizing conveyor production."[42] Whether such a description is appropriate or not, it is certainly true that serious efforts have been undertaken in recent years to extend the use of brigades or work teams and to make them the basic structural units of work organization throughout Soviet industry. There are good reasons to regard this as a principal component of Soviet work reform policy. Work teams (we shall use "team" and "brigade" interchangeably for the Russian *brigada* henceforth), of course, are not a recent phenomenon in the Soviet Union. But the large scale on which they have been implemented of late, as well as some of their newer organizational features, suggest more than a simple continuation of earlier policies. We are also interested in the manner in which the discussions surrounding their implementation disclose both the pressures for and resistance to change in the Soviet labor process.

The public justification for extending reliance on any organizational form must necessarily rest, at least in part, on "productionist" or "technological" grounds. Thus a principal argument for increased reliance on work teams as the primary units to be assigned job tasks is that the most advanced types of industrial equipment require "collective forms of work organization." Here is one way in which this idea has been expressed:

> In industry there is a gradual transition underway from the creation of individual machines to the elaboration and introduction of systems of machines geared to one or another technological process as a whole— not only to basic but to auxiliary operàtions as well . . . All or almost all powerful, highly productive machines and aggregates constitute essentially a technology of collective utilization, the full productive potential of which can only be realized if operators and adjusters servicing it work in coordination, helping one another—in other words, if they are associated in a single collective united by common interests. The high cost of modern equipment and its rapid obsolescence require a rise in the intensity of its utilization and an elimination of stoppages [*prostoi*] connected with deficiencies in the organization of production and work. The brigade form of work organization facilitates the solution of these tasks.[43]

A somewhat different version of the "productionist" justification for work teams invokes the pressure which teams allegedly exert on the "loafers, drunkards and shirkers" in their midst. The slack job performance of these types may reduce the earnings of the more conscientious workers under conditions of the brigade form of work organization (since earnings are geared to the output of the brigade as a whole). Thus the more conscientious make life difficult for the slackers and presumably reduce the number of the latter—or so the argument goes.[44] The claim that the team form is an effective means of raising the intensity of work effort has also been made in that genre of Soviet labor literature which makes no secret of the "constant conflict between workers and the norm setter. . . ."[45] The argument here is that the normal resistance to the norm-fixer's effort to "improve the labor process" (i.e., to raise work norms) is weakened under conditions of team organization. Once again the group pressure of the team (or as a Soviet writer puts it, citing Lenin, "the discipline of comradely ties") makes it difficult for individual workers to resist changes in production norms intended to raise the productivity of the team as a unit. The very possibility of conducting time-and-motion studies as the basis for norm setting is apparently facilitated by the team form of organization:

> Before [the introduction of work teams—M. Y.] the norm-fixer would arrive to conduct a time study on a worker and might not even find him present: the worker simply did not want to be studied. Today the team leader [*brigadir*] designates the worker who will be subject to the time study. If, out of old habits, someone wants to conceal himself or "spoil the comedy" [*polomat' komediiu pered normirovshchikom*], all he has to do is observe how his comrades in the brigade are working, and he will continue to work normally.[46]

All these alleged advantages of work brigades obviously do not suggest a process resembling work humanization. If anything, they point in the opposite direction. Thus far the work team appears to be essentially an instrument for speeding up and intensifying the work process. But it would be a mistake to see this as its only function. The extension of work teams in recent years (more than half of industrial workers were organized in the brigade form in the early 1980s compared to 20–40% in "most branches" in the late 1970s)[47] has also embodied reformist objectives which should not be dismissed as a mere "cover" for a work speed-up. That work teams should encompass reformist functions (in the Soviet vocabulary—"social" functions) should come as no surprise when we recall that poor work morale—especially among comparatively well-educated youth in low-skilled jobs—is widely acknowledged to be a serious problem for those who manage the labor process. The extension of the brigade form is a response to job discontent and the difficulty management confronts in retaining workers no less than to poor work performance. Whatever else it may be, it must also be understood as an attempt to improve work attitudes.

The hallmark of the reformist justification for work teams is a concern for "enriching" the work experience under conditions in which modern technology often seems to impoverish it. It is curious that in this respect the reformist justification runs almost directly counter to one version of the "productionist" or "technological" argument. Work teams become instruments designed to offset the extreme specialization and fragmentation often imposed by modern machinery rather than organizational forms required for its efficient utilization. The idea that the kind of division of labor normally associated with technological advance may have negative consequences for work attitudes which must be "compensated for" by means of work reorganization is an essential part of the reformist justification for work teams. Thus the authors of an article on work design at the Likhachev Auto Plant:

> In designing technological and labor processes, it is desirable that . . . every assembler perform a technologically complete cycle of operations . . . that the content of work be enriched, that workers' fatigue be reduced. But under the existing practice of division of labor, it is difficult to observe these requirements. This is precisely why we turn to the team form of work organization.[48]

As we noted earlier, the general phenomenon of work teams is not a recent innovation. But the claim of Soviet writers is that since the late 1970s the preferred types of teams (the most "progressive" ones) have incorporated organizational features designed to increase opportunities for job enlargement, job rotation and "self-management" (within the team).[49] Thus preference has been given to organizing "complex" teams consisting of workers in a range of occupations (rather than "specialized" brigades of workers in a single occupation), thereby facilitating opportunities for the kind of job rotation that could promote genuine diversity in work. The more general principle frequently stressed and apparently applicable to "specialized" teams as well is that of not "locking" workers into a single job task for extended periods. Another aspect of the new direction concerns the manner in which workers receive individual work assignments. In contrast to earlier years such assignments are not "handed down" by managerial personnel. At least theoretically, the team as a unit receives a "single assignment" (*edinyi nariad*), which is then allocated among individuals as a team-level decision. Money rewards are supposedly based mainly on collective effort—the team's output—rather than on individual piece rates. (The view that the latter system left an unhealthy individualistic imprint on worker psychology and that it had a divisive rather than unifying impact on work collectives has been openly expressed by now.) Although the brigade leader is normally appointed by management, isolated experiments in "elections" and appeals to regularize this method of choosing such leaders have been reported.

Clearly, the actual functioning of most work teams departs from the somewhat idyllic picture which emerges here. But our discussion of some of the new elements in work team organization should indicate the sense in which the extension of the team principle may legitimately be regarded as one component of recent work reform (humanization) policies. Even if Soviet claims are accepted at face value, however, these reform measures seem rather modest when compared with some recent Western work humanization experiments, including those popularized in the Soviet literature reviewed earlier.

Those who doubt the Soviet system's capacity for reforming work (or anything else) will probably be most skeptical of the claim that the new work brigades can become genuine instruments of worker self-management. Is this not so much empty rhetoric not taken seriously by either Soviet workers or managers? We suggest some caution is in order before responding to this question. Whatever the ultimate fate of these work teams, it is important to recognize that public discourse on this issue has revealed conflicting conceptions of the ''optimum'' degree of team indpendence and of the desirability of redistributing managerial authority. Some observers (the industrial sociologist O. I. Shkaratan, for example) have described the new work teams in highly positive terms as essentially ''small, self-managing work collectives which take on many of the functions normally belonging to line managers. . . .''[50] A similarly enthusiastic response appears in those writings which ascribe the highly successful economic performance of a ''leading enterprise'' (in this case the Kaluga Turbine Plant) mainly to the opportunity for worker participation in management provided by the brigade form of organization.[51] On the other hand some have warned against the danger of excessive autonomy for the new work units, the possibility that ''the transfer of brigades to self-management . . . the granting to them of the right to independently decide all production questions'' will impede managerial efforts to intensify work and expand output.[52] A similar meaning can be attached to warnings against the ''narrow group interests'' and ''group egoism'' allegedly exhibited by some work brigades.[53] That such warnings should be necessary suggests that there are social groups which take seriously the dangerous idea of self-management through autonomous work teams.

The importance of recent Soviet discussions of the brigade form of organization is that they have provided a vehicle for airing the principal issue in the work reform literature, that of worker participation in management, to which we now turn. It is in this larger context that we shall return to the subject of work teams.

5
The Participatory Current: The Management Literature and Empirical Studies

In 1974 the Komsomol journal, *Molodoi kommunist*, carried an article which reported on the results of some psychological experiments involving "intrinsically motivated" behavior. The experiments had been conducted by an American researcher at the University of Rochester who published his results in an issue of *Psychology Today* in 1972. The bulk of the Soviet article was essentially an accurate summary of the findings reported in *Psychology Today*.[1] What interests us, of course, is the use which the Soviet writer (V. Kokashinskii) made of these findings in the context of Soviet concerns with the problems of work morale and work effectiveness.

The American researcher was interested in the question of the impact of "extrinsic reinforcements" on "intrinsically motivated" behavior. He asked a group of college students to work on "an intrinsically interesting task"—a puzzle consisting of seven three-dimensional pieces. The students were requested "to use the pieces to reproduce several configurations that were outlined on paper." The subjects of the experiment were divided into two groups, one of which was paid for successful solutions of the tasks, while the other was not. When the assigned period for solving the puzzles was over, the two groups were placed in circumstances where they were "free to do what [they] wished: read magazines, solve more puzzles, or whatever." The researcher's reasoning was that the students were intrinsically motivated if they continued to work on the puzzles when the assigned period for solving them had ended. The additional time spent on the puzzles was the measure of intrinsic motivation. Here is the American researcher's summary of this stage of the experiment (accurately paraphrased in the Soviet article):

> Money made a difference. Those students whom we had paid spent significantly less time with the puzzles when they were alone later than did those who had done the puzzles for free. Once they got money for doing a fun game, their intrinsic motivation decreased; to an extent they had become dependent on the external reward.

Other phases of the experiment involved determining the impact on "intrinsically motivated activities" (puzzle-solving) of such "extrinsic" factors as threats of punishment (which seemed to reduce intrinsic motivation) and "verbal rewards"—praise—(which, of course, increased it). There is no need here to examine additional details of the reported experiments, but it is worth noting those comments of the American researcher which seemed of particular interest to the Soviet writer. Noting that educators were not alone in wanting to maintain intrinsic motivation, the *Psychology Today* piece pointed to the concern of managers of business firms with those factors in the work situation which promoted workers' intrinsic interest and ego-involvement with their jobs. Such managers stressed the kinds of work that promoted creativity and involved participation in the decision-making processes of the firm. The American writer also noted that one of the implications of his research was that reward systems which link money to work performance, such as piece rates and sales commissions, probably decrease the intrinsic motivation promoted by interesting work and sharing of decision-making. The general conclusion, which seemed to follow naturally, was: "We must create more activities that are inherently interesting and gratifying, and we must not use extrinsic rewards in a way that will lower the interest level of those activities that are intrinsically motivated."

The Soviet author, following his straightforward summary of the American researcher's principal points (including extensive verbatim quotations from the *Psychology Today* piece), made it clear that he "could not help but agree" with the American psychologist that interesting work and participation in management decisions raised intrinsic work motivation. Moreover, in a socialist society where worker participation in management is "assumed" by the very nature of the production process, this is "presumably" (*pozhalui*) the "decisive channel" for increasing intrinsic work motivation. Worker participation was particularly important as a means of enriching work content: ". . . the more uninteresting, routine and fatiguing the work itself, the more attention must be devoted to the active, informal participation of working people in management for the purpose of increasing the intrinsic interest in work.''

Clearly it was the support which the article in *Psychology Today* lent to the argument for worker participation which explained why Kokashinskii was calling it to the attention of *Molodoi kommunist* readers. Even the former's critical remarks on piece rates and other payment systems which linked income with work performance—systems long officially approved in the Soviet Union—were treated with understanding. After all, the activity in question (whether solving puzzles or doing ''creative'' work) was inherently interesting. ''Payment by results'' would probably reduce intrinsic motivation in such cases. This was not to deny the special importance of ''material stimuli'' in those many cases in which the potential for intrinsic rewards was severely limited by the very nature of the work tasks.

Although the general tone of the Soviet article's comments on the American study was distinctly appreciative in nature, there was one idea in this study that the Soviet author could not explicitly accept—at least for the present. The American researcher had used his findings to argue for the removal or reduction of ''external controls'' in a variety of spheres—curfews imposed by academic institutions, ''threats'' of employers, grades awarded by teachers. The initial response may well be some chaos, the American argued, but ''internal controls'' will be reestablished. ''Controlling others seems to insure that others will not control themselves.''

Following extensive quotations from the American article spelling out this point, the Soviet author commented:

> These concluding observations . . . seem to me highly interesting. From an ideal point of view they can hardly be faulted. But in practical terms it is impossible to fully implement these ideal recommendations today even in a socialist society, not to speak of a bourgeois society.

Our justification for reviewing at some length this Soviet reaction to an American magazine article is that it provides an illustration of what we shall henceforth designate as the ''participatory current'' in Soviet discussions of domestic labor problems, i.e., a serious effort to pose the issue of enlarging opportunities for workers' involvement in enterprise decisions. Although the *Molodoi kommunist* article is a comparatively minor illustration, it embodies some features which are typical of this current—the readiness to draw on Western ideas and experiences,

the affirmation that a socialist economy is (should be?) "participatory" by its very nature but that this principle requires substantial
extension in practice, the implied reassurance to those who exercise
"external controls" that their powers need not be threatened (at least in
the immediate future). Perhaps most important is the treatment of
worker participation not primarily as an achievement to be celebrated
but as a problem in need of solution.

Pressures for more participatory forms of organization at the
workplace are not a new phenomenon in Soviet life. In an earlier study
we examined some of their manifestations during the late 1960s and
early 1970s.[2] Hence in the material which follows we shall focus
mainly on more recent years. The variety of forms taken by the
participatory current may be conveniently subdivided as follows: (a)
discussions in the management literature, (b) empirical sociological
studies of the extent and effectiveness of worker participation, (c)
recurring proposals to introduce "elections" of lower-level managerial
personnel, (d) efforts to implement reliance on semiautonomous work
teams as the basic units of work organization. Our review of these
discussions and experiments should demonstrate that they have provided a kind of "platform," as it were, from which appeals for a Soviet
version of "production democracy" have been aired. It should also be
clear that pressures for worker participation are—no less than the "job
enrichment" policies reviewed in Chapter 4—responses to work discontent and ineffective work performance.

One problem that we must confront here is why some of the recent
principal manifestations of the participatory current appear to be largely echoes of earlier discussions and experiments, variations on a familiar theme. Obviously we are not referring to the unending din which
accompanies various, mainly fictitious forms of "participation" (socialist emulation campaigns, attendance at production conferences,
membership in the plant's "social organizations"—essentially the
trade union and Party units) but to measures intended to go well beyond
them. What factors seem to constantly block the introduction of institutional changes which promise improved work morale and work commitment and thus require "starting all over again"?

Discussions in the management literature

The case for enlarging the scope of workers' involvement in enterprise
decisions is sometimes made in the familiar language of the Leninist
principles of management. Discussions in the management literature

framed in the traditional litany of democratic centralism, one-man management, collegiality, etc., do not lead one to expect that serious proposals are being made to alter existing management practices and increase opportunities for worker participation. But arguments framed in these familiar terms have one distinct advantage. The very familiarity of the terminology tends to allay suspicions and reduce the risk of attack from guardians of existing workplace procedures. Thus we should not be surprised if manifestations of a genuine participatory current sometimes appear in the ritualistic and stodgy language of official managerial ideology.

The meanings normally attached to concepts like one-man management (*edinonachalie*) and collegiality have been sufficiently elaborated in the Western literature,[3] and only the briefest exposition should suffice at this point. One-man management is essentially a way of specifying the necessary "relations of subordination" that must prevail in any economic organization. It assigns to incumbents of particular positions in the economic unit's organizational structure the authority to issue instructions which must be obeyed "without question" and holds such individuals personally responsible for the unit's economic performance. It is a way of affirming that a unitary structure of authority prevails in the enterprise. The principle of collegiality, on the other hand, involves the general notion that reaching the "best" decision on any managerial problem requires reliance on "collective opinion," i.e., that the views of the work collective must be elicited by the one-man manager in the process of decision-making. Collegiality is thus the "democratic" component of democratic centralism as applied to the management of a work collective. The "organic unity" of the principles of one-man management and collegiality may be implemented in one of two forms: "(1) the collective [group] thinks, the one-man manager decides and acts; (2) the collective [group] thinks and decides, the one-man manager acts."[4] The responsibility for implementing the decision, whether the latter was reached by the manager alone or by the "group," is the manager's (he "acts").

The hallmark of the participatory current in this kind of management literature is that while affirming the continued relevance of these principles, it recognizes their historically contingent nature and stresses the increasing relative importance of collegiality and the desirability of extending its application. A recent volume by Kaidalov and Suimenko provides a case in point.

> In certain situations either one of these principles [one-man management or collegiality—M. Y.] may play the leading role in the organi-

zation of management, temporarily limiting the significance of the other. They may lose this role when new circumstances require fundamental changes in management organization. If for some reason this does not occur, then either one-man management or collegiality becomes hypertrophied, generating either excessive centralism or departmental separation [*razobshchennost'*], excessive priority to local interests [*mestnichestvo*].[5]

Nor is there any mystery about where the danger of ''hypertrophy'' comes from under present circumstances for these writers. With appropriate quotations from Lenin, they argue that under conditions of the ''historical immaturity'' of the masses, preference must be given to ''dictatorial'' one-man management; but when the stage of ''developed socialism'' is attained (currently), ''collegiality not only can but must become the most important—and with time—the *decisive element* [our emphasis—M. Y.] in the management of the socialist production collective.''[6] The very terminology used by Kaidalov and Suimenko to characterize these principles constitutes an implicit argument for increased reliance on collegiality. While one-man management, with all its ''historical necessity,'' contains the potential for ''bureaucratism and subjectivism,'' collegiality tends to eliminate such dangers by allowing for a ''struggle of opinions'' and serves a desirable educational function by creating conditions in which the prestige of a single individual (''the leader'') is replaced by the heightened prestige of the work collective.[7]

The desirability of implementing a ''democratic style of management'' (i.e., extending the principle of collegiality) in organizing work activity is defended by Kaidalov and Suimenko on very pragmatic grounds by invoking the familiar theme of the ''scientific-technological revolution.'' The very nature of the production process under these conditions increases the importance of the flow of accurate information ''from below''; it requires a ''democratic atmosphere'' which encourages ''the free discussion of problems, the confrontation of differing views, controversies. . . .''[8]

It would be a mistake to dismiss these hymns of praise to collegiality as mere elaborations of a participatory tone or style in the management literature, although they clearly do perform this function. But they do more than this. They also serve as a ''safe'' point of departure for urging the introduction of specific reform proposals like election to managerial positions, the downgrading of individual piece rates and increased reliance on self-managing work teams. We examine some of these issues in a wider context below and will not dwell on them here.

Let us turn briefly instead to the way in which, beginning with the familiar (the theme of collegiality), Kaidalov and Suimenko develop some barely charted concepts in the Soviet management literature. Consider the concept of "production conflicts" in work collectives. Such conflicts, whatever the images they evoke to a Western reader, obviously do not embrace organized work stoppages, but they do account for some 15% of total working time. The conflicts referred to here are characterized as stemming from "a clash [*stolknovenie*] of interests, opinions, orientations and aspirations" within a producing unit.[9] This is a subject which must be treated with considerable caution in the Soviet literature, and the more serious discussions readily acknowledge that only the first steps have been taken in the systematic study of production conflicts. For a long time the subject was either ignored, or such conflicts were regarded as an "exclusively negative phenomenon."[10] While the more recent discussions (as illustrated in the writings of Kaidalov and Suimenko, as well as some others) will hardly strike the reader as a great leap forward in the social analysis of workplace conflicts, it is well to remember the distance which had to be transversed before this stage could be reached.

For Kaidalov and Suimenko conflicts are an inherent feature of the life of a work collective. ". . . the interaction between the leader and the collective [management and labor?—M. Y.], as well as among members of the collective, inevitably involves various types of collisions and frictions which frequently turn into conflicts, the kinds of situations which in social psychology are customarily called conflict situations." The reference to social psychology should not deceive us, for the kinds of conflicts the authors have in mind are not merely the consequences of psychological quirks of individuals or social groups; they are embedded in the organizational structure and authority relations of the enterprise. The typology of conflict situations presented here distinguishes between (a) "vertical" and "horizontal" conflicts (those whose participants occupy differing slots in the unit's hierarchy of positions, as distinct from those involving identical positions), (b) conflicts on matters of substance (*delovye konflikty*—literally, "businesslike conflicts") and interpersonal conflicts, (c) constructive and destructive conflicts. The affirmation of the "constructive" or "positive" nature of certain workplace conflicts is no small matter, although they are defined in the most general terms (they "stimulate the development of the production collective" and involve "issues of principle" rather than "squabbles and petty unpleasantries"). But it is clear that the category of constructive conflicts largely overlaps with "businesslike" or functional conflicts. The important point here is that the latter are associated with a "democratic, collegial style of management" and are a sign of the "vitality" of the work collective. With an "authoritarian style of management" there is no opportunity for businesslike conflicts to emerge; or if they do, they are likely to be transformed into interpersonal conflicts.

What is the subject matter of businesslike (and hence constructive) conflicts? Here the discussion becomes more specific. Such conflicts may be rooted in "material-technical" factors—antiquated equipment, unpleasant premises, dangerous working conditions (excessive fumes, noise, vibrations). "Conflict situations in such circumstances arise most often between the collective and the leader." They may also arise from the mistaken economic policies of enterprise managers, when the latter "misinterpret" the state's interest as requiring neglect of "individual and group interests," i.e., when managers ignore workers' needs. Such cases include the establishment of "*excessively high* [our emphasis—M. Y.] or unduly low work norms, the unjustified revision of work norms. . . ." Since work norms are typically revised upward rather than downward, the latter point is clearly a criticism of unjustified increases in norms. Readers with even a cursory acquaintance with the Soviet labor literature will recognize the unusual nature of such references to excessive work norms in Soviet public discussion. Perhaps this is why Kaidalov and Suimenko do not fail to note that justified "collisions" over work norms need not arise only in a labor versus management context. They may also stem from "protests" by the more "conscious" workers of the enterprise ("and especially from the communists" among them) directed at those workers who enjoy unduly low work norms or "obstruct the realization of available reserves" (i.e., those who consciously restrict their work effort). But the more important source of conflict (and "businesslike" or "functional" conflict at that) for Kaidalov and Suimenko is clearly the kind of situation in which enterprise management is guided by the slogan "the plan at any price," for in this case "dissatisfaction may embrace a wide range of workers."[11]

How do these views, some of which seem to merely recognize the obvious, bear on what we have called the participatory current in Soviet discussions of workplace relations? There is surely nothing striking or new, even in the Soviet context, in admitting that individual workers may have justified grievances. What is significant here is the notion that a particular kind of collective conflict, serving as a signal alerting management to workplace problems, can play a legitimate role in improving the functioning of an economic enterprise. The conflicting parties may be "advanced" workers and slackers, but they can just as easily be workers and their managers (under the pseudonyms of the "collective" and its "leaders"), with the former resisting the imposition of an excessive work pace ("the plan at any price") or hazardous working conditions. Such conflicts must be "principled" and "responsible," of course, stopping short of interruptions of work. But they should be brought out into the open through a collegial, "democratic style of management." None of this, however, requires abandoning the principles of one-man management, for as another writer (very much in the spirit of Kaidalov and Suimenko) puts it, after the "yeas" and "nays" have been weighed, and workers and their organizations have had their say, somebody after all "must strike a balance"—i.e., the plant director or shop chief must make the binding decision.[12] The attempt to adapt the familiar, apparently rigid Leninist principles of management to the task of legitimating the concept of "constructive" group conflicts may be seen as a cautious effort to promote a more participatory ethos at the workplace without upsetting too many applecarts. Thus the image of participation which emerges here is a process in which openly expressed collective grievances may influence the binding decision ultimately made by officially designated authorities. Rarely, if ever, is it a process in which the decision is made directly by the "collective" itself.

When Soviet writers on management problems largely ignore the traditional Leninist formulations and attempt to strike out in new theoretical (and terminological) directions, they run the risk of a hostile reception. But in at least some cases such discussions have made a significant contribution to the participatory current. We refer, in particular, to some of the Soviet literature on "organization theory" or "the sociology of organizations." A critical idea in this literature is that there is no single measure of the organizational effectiveness of a socialist production collective. Its direct contribution to production (its *produktivnost'*) is only one criterion of the organization's successful functioning, which together with other criteria such as the satisfaction of its members with their work, their "participation in the management of production and the social life of the collective" and the "dynamism" of the collective (its capacity for change) must all be viewed jointly as constituting a single, "integral system."[13] What interests us in this set of multiple criteria of organizational effectiveness is how the concept of "participation" in managing the affairs of the collective—its members' "social activity"—is defined and elaborated. Sometimes, perhaps in most of this literature, this is done in a way that is difficult to take seriously. We refer to those cases in which the principal indicators of workers' participation include their membership in the plant's "social organizations" (Party, Komsomol, union), their participation in "socialist emulation" campaigns, their involvement in "innovating and rationalizing" work processes and their participation in various (unspecified) forms of "self-management" in production. Having elevated workers' participation in management to the status of a criterion of organizational effectiveness, most Soviet writers on management problems seem unable or unwilling to treat it in any but the most perfunctory and vacuous manner.

It should be recognized, however, that this is not always the case. An important exception to this trivialization of the concept of worker participation appears in the work of A. I. Prigozhin, one of the leading figures in Soviet organization theory. Perhaps one measure of the importance and controversial nature of Prigozhin's writings is that the principal Soviet sociological journal found it necessary to publish two opposing reviews of his book on the sociology of organizations in a single issue, a most unusual occurrence.[14] There can be no doubt that Prigozhin breaks new ground in his attempt to make worker participation in management a meaningful and operational concept under Soviet circumstances.

Unlike the writings of Kaidalov and Suimenko reviewed earlier, Prigozhin's starting point is not the Leninist principles of management (although these are given their due) but certain universal structural principles of any organizational system—whether biological, technical or social. One such principle is hierarchy. With respect to social and economic systems, "this principle may be observed at all levels, from the small group to society as a whole. Apparently mankind knows no mode of association other than pyramids."[15] Although Prigozhin presents this characterization as corresponding to the way in which hierarchy is generally "defined today," there is nothing in what follows to suggest that he rejects it.

But the necessity of hierarchy also involves the appearance of certain problems generated by hierarchical social relationships—"relationships of subordination, dependence and inequality." The blunt and direct nature of these formulations is somewhat unusual in the Soviet social science literature:

> . . . hierarchy appears as . . . a human relationship, in particular as the one-sided personal dependence of one individual on another. This

means that some persons [in an organization—M. Y.] may exert influence on the position and behavior of others without the latter being able to act similarly in relation to the former. Obviously, in the relationships between people there exist many variants of one-sided dependence, but in a hierarchy this dependence is locked in by [differing—M. Y.] statuses and functions as a factor in social inequality.[16]

The relations of subordination characteristic of hierarchical organizations means that the individuals composing them are differentiated into two basic social groups—"the managers and the managed." Hierarchy may also be conceived as a system of power.

The specific features of this aspect of hierarchical relations consist in control over the will of the worker by impersonal requirements of the organization, in the adaptation of his individuality to organizational functions. Marx understood power as "the appropriation of an alien will." This is attained by limiting the freedom of behavior of the individual in organizations and requiring certain necessary behavior. Thus power presumes compulsion, since such requirements may . . . be in opposition to the worker's own inclinations and interests. . . .[17]

It should be stressed that there is nothing in these characterizations of hierarchical organization that suggests Prigozhin meant them to apply only to presocialist societies. The same is certainly true of his remarks on the "organizational pathology" rooted in certain forms of hierarchy as manifested in "bureaucratism, careerism, the isolation of leadership from execution, conflicts, etc." Little wonder, then, that Prigozhin's work has found its hostile reviewers. One such critic seemed particularly distressed by Prigozhin's apparent failure to distinguish between the nature of organizational structures in presocialist societies (based on relations of "domination-subordination") and under socialism (where the principle of "equal rights" prevails along with "conscious discipline"), and by the distinction he draws between the two basic social groups of managers and managed.[18] But if there is some validity to the critic's charge that Prigozhin focuses on certain "universal" features of organizational structures (why this merits criticism is not clarified), it is no less true that Prigozhin stresses the variability and flexibility of hierarchical structures. The pyramid is subject to a "changing geometry"; it may be inverted, flattened, placed on its side. Some forms of hierarchy may be "historically transitional."[19] The justification for studying organizational hierarchies is to improve the organizational mechanism of the existing socialist society. How is this to be achieved? This brings us to Prigozhin's contribution to what we have called the participatory current in the Soviet literature on management.

One of the most urgent organizational problems of economic enterprises is that of changing the "social relations" that prevail in them. More specifically this requires a convergence (*sblizhenie*) in the position of managers and managed, the "overcoming of the boundaries" between these two distinct social groups. "The principal direction of this convergence is the development of a system of participation of all working people . . . in the management of organizations."[20] That these general formulations by Prigozhin (along with references to the need for "socialist self-management" and "the democratization of management relations") are meant to be more than empty phrasemaking is clear from the way in which participation is defined, its necessary preconditions specified and various operational indicators of its presence elaborated.

The essence of management is decision-making. Thus "democratic participation" in management must be gauged by the extent to which workers contribute to the making of management decisions at the enterprise, in addition to their normal job functions.[21] For such participation to be a reality, certain preconditions are required. One of them is an adequate flow of information to workers bearing on the production and organizational issues on which decisions must be made. To assure competence in decision-making, such information must come systematically from "official channels" and must also be attainable "independently, through inquiries, from colleagues, etc." A less tangible requirement is an appropriate psychological climate at the enterprise, one in which both the work collective as a whole and its management react positively to *vnesluzhebnoi aktivnosti*, i.e., to activities by workers outside of their normal job functions, so that worker participation comes to be accepted and encouraged as a "collective norm."

Finally, "what is the system of operational indicators that may be used to describe this phenomenon" (of collective participation in management)? The distinctions which Prigozhin draws here, the specificity of his criteria of participation, go well beyond any Soviet discussions known to us. Categories or levels of participation may be distinguished according to the "form of contribution of the worker to the adopted decision." That is, does the "contribution" involve a "positive proposal," and if so, was it adopted or not? It may take the form of an objection. Once again, was it considered or not? Or does the "contribution'' take the form of ''simple agreement'' with an already adopted decision? Distinctions may also be made according to the ''source of development of the decision'':

> Did the collective adopt the prepared version of the decision without changes, or was the initial version itself prepared collectively? Did the discussion introduce any significant corrections? This aspect of the participation of the collective in management characterizes the degree of activity (or passivity) of workers at the initial—frequently the decisive—stage of decision-making, as well as the managerial initiative of those who are to execute the decision.

Another important indicator concerns the ''outcome'' (*rezul'tativnost'*) of collectively adopted decisions. Here the critical distinctions concern the relative shares of such decisions which are fully implemented, implemented with changes (and who was responsible for the changes) and not implemented at all. In one of those incidental statements packed with meaning, Prigozhin notes: ''It would be interesting . . . to compare the extent to which similar decisions adopted with the collective's participation and by managers on their own are implemented.'' A further distinction is drawn between various ''subjects of participation'' in management—''social organizations,'' individual workers and groups of workers. The significance of distinguishing these ''subjects'' is apparent from another pointed aside by Prigozhin: excessive reliance on ''organized'' forms of participation (*zaorganizovannost'*) through ''official representatives'' (the example given is trade union leaders) may ''inhibit the activity of the remaining workers.'' The final summary measure—the ''integral indicator''—of worker participation in management suggested by Prigozhin is simply the proportion of all management decisions over a given period which were ''adopted with the participation of the collective.'' The system of indicators reviewed here, a ''fully operational and measurable'' set of parameters, in Prigozhin's words, may be used to compare the degree to which ''democratic management'' prevails at different enterprises.

There is no need here to elaborate the full range of Prigozhin's implicit arguments for worker participation: his relatively favorable portrayal of non-Soviet experience in this area, his rejection of a rigid technological determinism, the linking of participation with increased work satisfaction. The various specific indicators of democratic management reviewed above and the unfolding of the argument from its roots in organization theory seem to mark what is most distinctive about Prigozhin's work. But for all the boldness of some of his formulations, there is one obvious gap. The criteria of participation—the apparent attempt to make participation an "operational" concept—are all confined to what might loosely be called decision-making procedures, not to the specific content of managerial decision-making. What are the concrete issues, the matters of substance, to which collective decision-making (worker participation) can be legitimately applied under Soviet circumstances? Perhaps Soviet writers seeking to say something both new and useful on the general theme of the democratization of management must be guided by the principle: one (or a few) step(s) at a time.

Another set of ideas deserves at least brief examination in our review of the various forms taken by appeals for more participatory modes of management. We refer, in particular, to some of the writings of industrial sociologists like A. K. Nazimova and O. Shkaratan. Nazimova has sought to develop the concept of the "social potential" of the work collective (for Shkaratan the equivalent is the "human potential"). In this view effective work performance and work satisfaction depend not only on the presence of advanced technology and high levels of occupational skills but on the extent to which existing modes of work organization provide increased scope for "self-organization, self-discipline, self-supervision" (Nazimova). The needed improvements in the social organization of the workplace, invoked by Prigozhin in rather broad terms (narrowing the gap between the managers and managed), are defined here more specifically as measures which would "extend the functions of the worker in managing his own work process, increase his on-the-job independence (*proizvodstvennaia samostoiatel'nost'*) in planning and organizing his own work and increase his control over its results. . . ."[22] The principal instruments for implementing increased workers' discretion over their own job activities must be brigades or teams of workers delegated functions traditionally reserved for management. Such functions are to include the distribution of work assignments among team members and at least partial authority over the distribution of team earnings. Output assignments (norms) are to be specified from above for the team as a unit rather than for individual workers. This seems to be the essential meaning of the "increased degree of freedom in work" (Nazimova) associated with "collective" (as distinct from "individual") forms of work organization.

The identification of the activities of relatively small, semiautonomous work groups with concepts like self-management and "production democracy" (Shkaratan)[23] may initially appear to be a rather restricted application—if not a trivialization—of these ambitious-sounding concepts. We reserve for later a more detailed discussion of the problems confronting attempts to introduce such work groups and the redistribution of managerial authority which they imply. For the moment, what is most significant about this variant of the participatory current is not so much the specific organizational mechanisms being proposed as the more general arguments offered by Nazimova and Shkaratan to justify the idea that reforms are urgently needed in the organization of work and management. These justifications draw on a theme we have already noted in passing—the gradual disappearance of the illusion that technological advance and the alleged decline in unskilled manual work that accompanies it can be relied on to significantly reduce work discontent, raise work morale and inspire improved job performance. The illusory nature of this view is exposed here in the most unambiguous terms and with considerable empirical support.

Shkaratan describes in rather lyrical terms the view which prevailed until "quite recently" and its demise:

> . . . another step, another half-step of scientific progress, of a technically intoxicating leap to beautiful workshops and clever machines—and everything would be fine. Happy, joyous faces of young romantics enthusiastically employed in creative quests. Everyone is interested and working intelligently. . . . But alas. Technical progress does not fly at supersonic speeds, and its fruits are not always sweet. In our own day they sometimes generate a bitter taste, not only in the form of ecological tragedy but also in monotonous work and nervous exhaustion. . . .[24]

The fact is, Shkaratan notes, that the much celebrated scientific-technological revolution has intensified the "polarization" of work into creative and routine jobs (although he is quick to add that the relative share of the former will increase "with time"). Moreover, complaints have multiplied "throughout the whole industrial world" (the context makes clear that the Soviet Union is included here) against the extreme standardization and excessive division of labor which inhibits workers' initiative and flexibility. Instead of relying on technological "leaps," what is needed is a "qualitative leap in organization and management." For Shkaratan this appears to mean the organization of "minibrigades" with "extensive, genuinely managerial rights." One is tempted to remark that this author's formulation of the problem is more persuasive than the solution offered. But the important point is surely the logic of the argument for some kind of work reform.

In a similar vein Nazimova (in an article jointly written with L. A. Gordon) poses the question: Why is it that in contrast to the present, some 20–25 years earlier (i.e., in the late fifties and early sixties) there was no "acute" (*ostryi*) problem of worker dissatisfaction among those employed in relatively simple, unskilled jobs, although such jobs absorbed a considerably larger proportion of the work force than is now the case. The answer lies essentially in a marked disjuncture between the (low) rates of decline in the number of relatively low-skilled jobs and the (high) rates of increase in average educational attainment levels. The authors do not pretend to precision in their estimates (particularly in their figures on the relative share of low-skilled jobs), but the general order of magnitude of the figures cited seem to confirm their reading of the problem. At the end of the 1950s the share of the work force with an elementary-school level of education or less and the share in jobs that could reasonably be classified as low-skilled were both in the range of 50–60%. By the late 1970s the relative share of the poorly educated (by the above criterion) had declined to less than one-fifth, but the proportion of industrial workers employed in the "simplest" jobs (those requiring no prior "occupational training") was still close to one-third. Moreover, the rate of decline in the latter category of jobs had slowed considerably in the decade of the seventies. The result was an unprecedented situation: "For the first time society has a considerably larger number of low-skilled jobs to fill than the number of workers of that cultural type which in the past readily filled them."[25] Dissatisfaction with low-skilled jobs becomes a "social problem," in Nazimova's words, not when such jobs predominate but when their gradual decline lags behind the increase in educational levels. "Such a situation has emerged at the present time. . . ." Although Nazimova's discussion here refers explicitly to workers in low-skilled "manual" jobs, the more general concept of a significant "underutilized educational potential" among Soviet workers (particularly among the young) has become a common theme in the sociological literature,[26] and it is clear that the problem referred to is not confined to "manual" workers alone.

The lesson to be learned from recent trends in occupational and educational structure for Nazimova is essentially the same as that implied by Shkaratan. Improvements in "socialist relations of production" are just as vital as "the maximum possible reduction" in low-skilled jobs which can be expected from technological advance.[27] If the traditional Marxian language ("relations of production") seems to require some clarification, its meaning is more explicitly spelled out in her appeal (in another article) for "the democratization of management at all levels, beginning with the higher organs of power down to the primary work collective."[28]

Once again, the distinguishing features of these discussions by Nazimova and Shkaratan are the development of a rationale for increased worker participation, the search for social rather than exclusively technological solutions to problems of work, and the stress on widening workers' discretion ("self-organization") in the organization and distribution of their own job tasks. In the midst of the variety of approaches expressed in these and the other illustrations of the participatory current reviewed earlier, there is one essentially similar quality that unites them all. Putting it in negative terms first, and quite simply, none of these appeals for participatory management is made in the name of workers themselves. They are all formulated from a management perspective, under such rubrics as improving the "social-psychological atmosphere" of the collective, raising its "organizational effectiveness," liberating its "social potential." The managerial ideology expressed here may be a comparatively enlightened one, and it may be responsive to pressures from below, but its principal concerns are clearly not workers' well-being and the quality of their work experience. It is surely no revelation that Soviet workers lack the institutions and publications through which they could speak freely and in their own "voice" on the issues posed in this management literature. This raises some interesting questions. How much do we know about Soviet workers' attitudes toward meaningful participation in managerial decisions? How urgent an issue is it for them? How are workplace behavior and job satisfaction affected by increased opportunities for worker participation? How extensive is such participation? Although the evidence is hardly abundant, we are not completely in the dark on these matters.

Empirical evidence on worker participation

The initial picture which emerges from a review of Soviet empirical materials on worker participation is highly confusing and often contradictory. Some studies claim that such participation is extremely widespread ("Investigations show that at the present time an absolute majority of Soviet workers, in one form or another, participate in the managemenat of production"),[29] while others point in precisely the opposite direction. The problem here is compounded when, as occasionally occurs, the same study seems to provide evidence to support

Table 5.1

Illustration of "Fictitious" Workers' Participation in Management: Workers at Four Auto Plants, 1974*

Types of activities: "Methods by which workers influenced decisions of enterprise managers"	Proportion of workers indicating involvement in specified activities (in %)
1. Participated in production conferences and meetings of union, Party and Komsomol organizations	98.4
2. Participated in work of union, Party and Komsomol committees and commissions	56.5
3. Stated their views to direct supervisors or representatives of administration	89.1
4. Stated their views to representatives of union, Party and Komsomol organizations	70.3
5. Communicated with representatives of union, Party and Komsomol organizations outside the enterprise	19.0
6. Communicated with state agencies (ministries, soviets, government departments)	7.1
7. Engaged in collective pressure on enterprise management (refusal of overtime, "working to rules," strikes)	0

Source: Akademiia nauk SSSR, Institut mezhdunarodnogo rabochego dvizheniia, *Rabochii klass v usloviiakh nauchno-teknicheskoi revoliutsii*, Moscow, 1979, p. 235.

*Although the study was conducted in 1974, the questions which elicited these figures applied to workers' activities "over a two-year period," presumably 1973–74.

claims of both extensive and negligible worker participation. Our natural inclination, of course, is to dismiss the former type of evidence as simply unbelievable and to accept the latter as the truth. But the empirical material invoked in Soviet studies to justify the view that workers have a substantial input into management decisions is not simply the product of "free invention" of supporting statistics. The main problem in such studies is not that the statistics are unbelievable but that they do not constitute evidence of genuine worker involvement in management decisions. What they do reveal is a kind of "fictitious" or pseudo-participation that tells us nothing about the presence or absence of workers' impact on workplace conditions. Although our point here may be an obvious one, a brief illustration of such "fictitious" participation may help clarify the nature of the genuine participatory current expressed in the management literature we have just reviewed. Whatever else it may be, the participatory current is, after all, a reaction against "fictitious" participation.

Table 5.1 provides an illustration of the latter. In the words of the Soviet authors of a study of labor conditions and work attitudes in four automobile plants, it shows the "methods by which workers influenced the decisions of enterprise managers" over a two-year period (1973–74). There is no particular reason to question the approximate accuracy of the figures in this table. That is, it seems quite believable that more than 90% of a sample of auto workers attended production conferences and meetings of union, Party or Komsomol organizations, and that approximately half or more were members of "committees and commissions" set up by these organizations. These are the "institutionalized forms" of worker participation in the management of production (in the view of the authors of this study), in contrast to points 3–7 of the table, which refer to forms of worker "influence . . . other than permanent forms of participation."[30] Nor is there any reason to question the rough accuracy of the figures shown for these latter points. It does not strain credulity that substantial proportions of workers "communicated" in some form with officials of "social organizations" and state agencies (about what, and what were the consequences?). Certainly the claim that no workers were engaged in "collective pressures" in the form of strikes (point 7 of the table) seems to accord with most of what we know about Soviet labor relations.

But there is no good reason to accept the authors' claim that this table demonstrates that Soviet workers "make very extensive use of varied forms of participation in the management of production for effectively influencing the decisions adopted."[31] This is pseudo-participation with a vengeance, for what we don't know is precisely what we need to know. What transpired at the heavily attended production conferences and meetings of the plants' "social organizations" and their committees? How much scope was there for workers' initiative at these meetings? Did workers' experience their attendance at meetings and membership on plant committees as having a significant influence on managerial decisions? We shall see below that at least some of the available evidence on these questions does not reinforce the conclusion just cited by the authors of the auto industry study. It is even possible that to apply the concept of "pseudo-participation" to this situation might exaggerate the degree of actual participation that prevailed—if the "pseudo" form is used in Carole Pateman's sense of "techniques used to persuade employees to accept decisions that have *already* been made by the management" (emphasis in the original).[32] We simply lack the information to ascertain the "mix" of persuasion, mobilization, command, decision-making or merely functionless consumption of time that characterized the activities of the meetings and committees referred to in points 1 and 2 of Table 5.1.

When writers linked with the participatory current warn against excessive reliance on "organized" forms of participation (Prigozhin) or call for "noninstitutionalized forms" or "new forms" of worker involvement in the enterprise's "social activity" (Nazimova),[33] they are clearly appealing for something more than the kind of participation portrayed in Table 5.1. Moreover, in recent years there has been at least as much evidence published to counter (or at least to question) the claim of extensive worker participation as to support it. Table 5.2, which brings together some of this evidence, provides some indicators of workers' own perceptions of their involvement in or impact on management decisions. The implications here are very different than those suggested by the authors of the auto industry study. Thus most workers (at the Cheliabinsk Tractor Combine) claimed that their suggestions were insufficiently considered, or not considered at all, by managerial personnel. In a study of Murmansk enterprises in 1977, only a small minority of workers (12%) claimed that they "personally" participated in management. In yet another study (in Gorky in 1980) less than a fifth of a sample of workers responded that they could "affect decisions" in their collective. It is impossible to disagree with the author of one of these studies who declared, in what must be regarded as a masterpiece of understatement, "Not all of them [the workers questioned—M. Y.] perceive themselves, in full measure, as masters of social production. . . ."[34]

The participatory current appears here not only in the readiness to publicize the sense of exclusion from decision-making so common among Soviet workers but in the very nature of the questions asked. In the auto plants' study, which we have taken as symbolic of "fictitious" participation, most workers answered in the affirmative when asked whether they or "their representatives" could participate in decisions bearing on "the management of enterprises."[35] The operational phrase here is "their representatives," i.e., officials of Party, Komsomol and union organizations who obviously have some influence on workplace decisions. But the questions included in the studies summarized in Table 5.2 (our indicators of "real" participation) are of a different nature. They are framed so as to elicit workers' assessments of their *own* opportunities to influence managerial decisions, without reference to "their representatives" (for example, does the respondent feel that he "personally participates" in managing the affairs of the enterprise?).

Clearly there is no incompatibility between what we have termed the

Table 5.2 **Selected Indicators of "Real" Workers' Participation in Management: Workers' Responses to Questions on Participation**

Location and year of study, questions	Workers' responses (in %)	
Cheliabinsk Tractor Combine, 1974		
"To what extent do managers of the shop consider workers' suggestions?"	They do consider them	45.0
	They do not consider them sufficiently	43.7
	They do not consider them at all	11.3
"To what extent do managers of the plant consider workers' suggestions?"	They do consider them	28.2
	They do not consider them sufficiently	48.7
	They do not consider them at all	23.1
Five enterprises, Murmansk, 1977		
"Do you personally participate in managing the affairs of the enterprise?"	Yes	12.2
	No	65.7
	Difficult to answer	22.1
Do workers have a significant influence on deciding questions of your collective?"	No	20–25
	I don't know	20–25
Gorky enterprises, 1980*		
"Do you feel that you can affect decisions on matters concerning the development of your collective?"	Yes	16.4
	Not always	19.7
	In reality no	16.5
	Difficult to answer	47.4

Sources: A. K. Orlov, *Sovetskii rabochii i upravlenie proizvodstvom,* Moscow, 1978, pp. 181–82; V. A. Smirnov, *Sotsial'naia aktivnost' sovetskikh rabochikh,* Moscow, 1979, pp. 168, 170; "Problems of Social Planning and Educaitonal Work," *Kommunist,* 1982, No. 2, p. 52.

*Our source here does not mention the precise location or number of enterprises; but since the study was conducted by the Gorky Regional Committee of the Party and the Gorky Higher Party School, it seems safe to assume that the enterprises studied were located in the Gorky region.

"fictitious" and "real" indicators of participation shown in Tables 5.1 and 5.2 respectively. They are essentially different sides of the same coin. The fragmentary evidence in the sociological literature on the nature of workers' meetings and production conferences helps explain why this should be the case. Thus a study of workers' meetings at the Svetlana Combine in Leningrad published in 1978 revealed that while most workers attended "regularly," more than 90% either never joined in the discussion or did so only "rarely." Little wonder that the majority characterized their "involvement" (*aktivnost'*) in these meetings as "low." The same study makes it clear that while the issues discussed at these meetings were not unimportant (improvements in working conditions, extent of fulfillment of production plans, problems of work discipline, material and moral incentives), the typically low sense of worker involvement reflected the fact that such meetings did not function mainly as mechanisms of decision-making.[36] An essentially similar picture emerges from a description of the production conferences attended mainly by workers (and allegedly representing a principal form of "worker participation") at the Cheliabinsk Tractor Plant in the mid-1970s. Those who "introduce proposals and recommendations, pose questions, participate in the discussion and verification (*kontrol'*) of adopted decisions," i.e., those who dominate the activities of production conferences, are explicitly identified as "representatives of the administration and social organizations."

This may help explain why only a minority (42%) of the Cheliabinsk workers "regarded the activity of this form of social management as effective," and a similar proportion declined to answer the investigator's question concerning the effectiveness of production conferences.[37] These attempts to document the limited role of workers in "official" channels of worker participation are particularly clear illustrations of a genuine participatory current. They are, in effect, exposés of "fictitious" participation.

All this would be less of a problem if it was clear that Soviet workers were generally uninterested in an increased role in enterprise decision-making. But if there is anything on which all the studies reviewed here—whether based on "fictitious" or "real" indicators—agree, it is the generally high level of interest among workers in the extension of participatory opportunities. Estimates of the proportion of sampled workers expressing such interest range from 60 to 90%.[38] It is conceivable, of course, that workers answering sociologists' questions in this manner are simply giving what they know to be socially approved responses, i.e., telling "official" investigators what they want to hear rather than conveying their real sentiments. But this seems to us an implausible explanation. Why would workers conceal their genuine sentiments in responding to questions bearing on their desire to participate in managerial decisions and then (at least in the more serious studies summarized in Table 5.2) often reveal that their actual opportunities to influence such decisions were highly limited? It is surely significant that in most of the studies of work attitudes examined in Chapter 2, a distinct majority of workers expressed general satisfaction with their work; but in the only studies known to us in which workers were directly asked whether they were satisfied with their opportunities to influence management decisions, only a minority (some 30–40% at most) answered in the affirmative.[39] The issue is formulated persuasively in a recent Soviet work in the following terms: ''Thus the problem now is not that of inculcating in workers' consciousness the idea of the need to participate in management but of creating the conditions for realizing the already quite highly developed interest in participation in the management of production.''[40] Considerable support for this view is provided by Table 5.3, which illustrates (for a 1979 sample of workers in the Gorky Region) the marked divergence between workers' relatively modest assessments of their actual opportunities to participate in workplace decisions, on the one hand, and their more ambitious views concerning the ''necessity'' of creating such opportunities on the other. For most of the decision-making areas shown here, the proportion of respondents affirming the ''necessity'' of worker participation is some two to three times the proportion agreeing that such opportunities actually exist.

Soviet writers who have sought to make the creation of a more participatory work environment a serious public issue have drawn on a variety of empirical materials other than those we have just reviewed. We refer, in particular, to studies which have demonstrated the positive impact of worker involvement in managerial decisions on job satisfaction and work performance. N. Alekseev's investigation of work attitudes in a sector of the Soviet fishing fleet in the early 1970s provides one illustration.[41] Although this is a comparatively minor sector of the economy (the study applied to ''collective fisheries,'' apparently organized on the same principles as collective farms), the issues raised are obviously applicable elsewhere. Alekseev showed that workers who had opportunities to participate in decisions bearing on the organization of the work process, the distribution of premiums and the maintenance of work discipline were more likely to find their work interesting and to express higher levels of job satisfaction than the rest of the work force. Some of his claims are presented in rather extreme terms and are not supported by the evidence he adduces—for example, the claim of a "sharp polarization" of job attitudes and behavior depending on "inclusion or exclusion" in management decisions. But the principal objective of the article was obviously to call attention to certain policy implications. Prevailing opportunities for worker participation were inadequate; their extension would bring into play "a main reserve for increasing labor productivity" and would foster "optimally positive" attitudes toward work.[42]

Table 5.3

Workers' Assessments of "Actual" and "Necessary" Participatory Opportunities, Gorky Region, 1979

Areas of decision-making	Proportions of workers indicating opportunities to participate exist (in %)	Proportions of workers indicating "necessity" of providing opportunities to participate (in %)
Improvements in working conditions	32.8	79.2
Improvements in work organization	28.7	70.9
Distribution of travel passes and allowances	28.2	70.7
Establishing procedures for socialist emulation	38.3	67.4
Planning the construction and distribution of housing	22.5	70.3
Awarding prizes in socialist emulation	33.2	64.9
Introduction of new machinery and equipment	27.5	59.9
Determining premiums	21.5	61.5
Examining grievances and labor disputes	24.1	60.5
Increasing wage grades and deciding on promotions	23.3	55.7
Setting wages and work norms	18.6	53.6
Working out production plans	27.5	52.3

Source: Akademiia nauk SSSR, Institut sotsiologicheskikh issledovaniia, *Sovetskaia sotsiologiia*, Vol. 2, Moscow, 1982, p. 20. The sample was approximately 1,500 workers.

Probably the most influential and widely popularized Soviet study in this area is A. V. Tikhonov's investigation of the relationship between workers' job performance and their participatory opportunities. The significance of this study lies not only in its empirical findings but in its introduction of a new conceptual apparatus into Soviet public discourse on work organization. Tikhonov developed the concept of the "production independence of the worker'' (*proizvodstvennaia samo-stoiatel'nosti rabochego*).[43] As earlier, we shall refer to this as on-the-job independence or work autonomy. Its presence in a particular situation, as we noted in Chapter 2, depends on the degree to which ordinary workers are delegated the authority to plan, manage and supervise their own work process. It is not equivalent to the familiar Soviet category of ''high content'' work, which depends mainly on the extent to which machinery has replaced physically burdensome and unpleasant tasks. It is largely a function of ''social relations'' at the enterprise, the opportunity accorded ''direct producers'' to combine within their own work activity the functions of execution of work along with its management and supervision. Thus on-the-job independence is embedded in the very organization of work—in its ''self-organization''—and is distinct from activities in the official channels of worker paticipation via the enterprise's ''social organizations.'' While necessarily paying his respects to this form of participation (obviously the type illustrated in our Table 5.1), Tikhonov notes that such activity is ''merely a compensation for the social costs of strictly regulated labor of execution of tasks.''[44] The striking contrast drawn here between workers' on-the-job independence and the functions of official channels of participative activity serves to clarify the nature of both. Here is how Tikhonov justifies posing the issue of work autonomy and his attempt to derive some empirical indicators of its importance.

> What level of independence of workers in the planning, organization and control of their own labor should be regarded as optimal from the social and economic points of view? How should the system of long-run and operational decision-making at various levels of management be restructured? At present it is difficult to get fully substantiated answers to these questions.[45]

Two of Tikhonov's findings seem particularly significant for our purpose. First, a clear majority (about two-thirds) of the oil-extraction workers he investigated exhibited ''low'' or ''medium'' opportunities for on-the-job independence. Most work tasks were planned, assigned and supervised by managerial personnel. Second, and more important, the differing degrees of work autonomy inherent in the various occupational roles were found to be closely associated with the quality of workers' job performance (the ''results of their work''). More specifically, Tikhonov claimed to have derived a correlation coefficient of 0.84 between on-the-job independence on the one hand and workers' labor productivity and quality of output on the other.[46]

Taken together, the formulation of the concept of on-the-job independence, the attempt to demonstrate its positive impact on work performance and the almost casual dismissal of official channels of worker participation constitute an appeal for the extension of what Western writers have variously called "high discretion work" or "self-directed work."[47] While important in its own right, Tikhonov's study has been repeatedly invoked since the late 1970s by other representatives of the participatory current (at least by Nazimova, Shkaratan and Iadov) in their efforts to popularize the idea of democratization of enterprise decision-making. The need for "self-organization" in the performance of work, for recombining "the functions of management and execution of work" and for encouraging workers' "initiative, responsibility and ability to make independent decisions" have now become part of the common vocabulary of Soviet public discourse on work reform.[48] The hallmark of all these discussions is a shift of focus from technological advance to the need for restructuring "social relations" at the workplace. We need hardly add that there is a world of difference between the introduction and popularization of a new vocabulary (perhaps a new rhetoric would be more appropriate) on the one hand and its translation into new workplace practices on the other. But if repeated often enough, the new rhetoric gradually becomes part of the work environment.

The material we have reviewed makes it clear that the combined effect of a considerable body of management literature and empirical studies by industrial sociologists has been to popularize and lend "scientific" credibility to the themes of increased discretion, work autonomy and participation in decision-making for Soviet workers. The general arguments and concepts reviewed here have also had their counterpart in more specific policy proposals, to which we now turn.

6

The Participatory Current: Elections and Work Teams

How should we regard repeated proposals in the Soviet literature to introduce "elections" for selected managerial positions and occasional reports of "experiments" in applying the electoral process to such positions? Can they be taken seriously? Given the nature of Soviet elections, it may strike some readers as the height of naïveté to even pose such questions. We shall seek to demonstrate that it is not. It will become clear, in any case, that the view of some Western specialists that "the issue [of elections—M. Y.] was never taken up after the initial elan of the economic reform (1965), which continued until about 1970,"[1] is surely mistaken. We regard the continuing Soviet discussions of this issue as one expression of the participatory current. To ignore these discussions and experiments is to miss what they reveal: the markedly differing reactions of different social groups to proposals for elections, the publicly expressed grounds for approval and disapproval of the idea, the recurring—indeed, in some respects, the escalating—nature of these proposals. It is quite probable that nothing worthy of being designated as "elections" will appear in Soviet economic enterprises in the near (or distant) future; or if it does appear, it will make no essential difference in the quality of the work experience and the distribution of managerial authority. But then, anticipating somewhat one of the findings which will emerge below, we are still confronted with the question of why the great majority of workers sampled in Soviet studies approve of the idea while a substantial proportion of managers clearly oppose it.

The issue of elections

Although we shall focus our attention here largely on the late 1970s and early 1980s, some of the Soviet discussions of the election issue in this period invoke and build on the experiments and public opinion surveys of earlier years. The most important of them was undoubtedly the one authored by Ia. S. Kapeliush in 1969 under the imprimatur of the Institute of Concrete Social Research and the Institute of Public Opinion of the newspaper *Komsomolskaia pravda*.[2] Thus a brief review of the circumstances surrounding this early study and some of its principal findings should serve as a useful introduction to our consideration of this issue as it has emerged in more recent years.

The explicit justifications offered by Kapeliush for surveying public opinion on the issue of elections were rooted in the particular historical circumstances of the late 1960s. In 1966–67 Soviet newspapers reported that experiments in the election of lower-level managerial personnel had been conducted at construction projects in Krasnoiarsk and Baku, and that consideration was being given to extending the experiments to industrial enterprises. (We shall see below that the designation "election" was something of a misnomer, as Kapeliush himself admitted.) Judging by the volume of mail received from readers, these reports had generated "widespread interest" among Soviet citizens.[3] Such interest was perfectly "natural," Kapeliush noted, in the light of the expectations created by the economic reforms announced in 1965. The reforms appeared to hold out the promise of a substantial increase in "the economic independence of enterprises" by reducing the flow of directives from "above" and giving enterprise managers increased decision-making powers on questions of choice of technology, number of workers to be hired and levels and systems of wage payment. But the implementation of such reforms could also become a source of workplace social tensions unless the extension of managerial authority was to be somehow matched by increased opportunities for workers' involvement in enterprise-level decisions. Although the decrees announcing the reforms referred to the "further extension of democratic principles of management . . . and the broader participation of the masses in management" which could now be expected, they provided no new institutional mechanisms to assure such participation. The point was explicitly recognized by Kapeliush:

> . . . changes in rights and authority in deciding basic questions are less significant for ordinary workers [*u riadovykh*] than for managers. . . . While the extension of the economic independence of enter-

prises automatically assumes an increase in the rights of its managers, ordinary working people will not be able to immediately occupy a position which would permit them to feel themselves to be masters of the enterprise on a par with managers. There arises a disproportion which bears within itself a certain danger. If it develops, it could have a negative impact on moral (and possibly on material) incentives. . . . The perception by workers of this disproportion will hardly promote a growth in production, an increase in labor productivity, etc.[4]

The "disproportion" which Kapeliush warned against is obviously that between the expected increase in managerial discretion and the continued subordinate status of workers. In this context provisions for the election of some categories of managerial personnel could serve as a kind of balancing mechanism averting the intensification of such "disproportions." "Participating in elections . . . every worker and engineer thereby receives an additional opportunity to exercise, through the person of the elected, a real influence on the life of his enterprise." Thus Kapeliush's justification for a survey of public opinion on what seemed to him a vital issue was simultaneously an argument in favor of extending the experiments in elections already undertaken. It will be well to recall the nature of these justificaations when we find, later, that appeals for elections (and descriptions of ongoing experiments) continued to be heard even when the initial momentum of the 1965 reforms seemed to have largely dissipated.

Although he was obviously an adherent of the idea of elections, the study conducted by Kapeliush seemed carefully designed, with the respondents drawn from a broad spectrum of occupational groups ranging from ordinary workers to plant directors and covering a fair diversity of geographic locales. The principal question asked of respondents in this study of the late 1960s was: "Is it advisable at present to fill certain managerial positions through elections?" We have brought together some of the study's main findings in Table 6.1. The most striking, although hardly surprising, result was that while a clear majority of respondents favored the idea of elections, the degree of support was generally inversely related to the height of the social group's ranking in the occupational hierarachy, or as Kapeliush put it, "the higher the step on the ladder of official position, the greater the opposition to elections."[5] Thus, while almost 90% of the workers, technicians and engineers questioned supported the proposal, opposition to the idea was particularly strong among upper-level managerial personnel, with fully one-half of plant directors and more than one-third of shop chiefs voting "no." Party and trade union officials were also distinctly less enthusiastic about elections than workers, with one-quarter to one-third expressing their opposition. There were solid grounds for Kapeliush's conclusion that "the attitude of people to elections is connected above all with their socio-occupational position, with the degree of their involvement in management."[6] These results were in general agreement with other surveys on this question conducted in 1969–70,[7] but the "all-union" nature of this study and the rather prestigious "scientific" auspices under which it was conducted must have reinforced the impression of deep social divisions on the issue of elections.

We have no way of reading the minds of the "voters" in these

Table 6.1

Institute of Social Research Survey of Attitudes toward Election of Managerial Personnel[*] 1969: "Is It Advisable at Present to Fill Certain Managerial Positions through Elections?"

Groups of respondents	N	Categories of answers, in %				
		no	yes	difficult to answer	no answer	total
1. Workers	363	4.7	89.0	6.3	—	100.0
2. Workers, deputies of soviets	105	6.6	82.9	8.6	1.9	100.0
3. Engineers and technicians	51	5.9	88.2	3.9	2.0	100.0
4. Lower-level managerial personnel	86	26.7	66.3	5.8	1.2	100.0
5. Upper-level managerial personnel	84	42.8	52.4	3.6	1.2	100.0
directors of enterprises	38	50.0				
shop superintendents	46	34.2				
6. Executives of Party, trade union and Komsomol organizations	114	19.3	77.2	1.7	1.8	100.0
union officials	31	32.4				
Party secretaries at enterprises	30	26.7				
7. Scholars (uchenye) and journalists	97	16.5	81.4	—	2.1	100.0

Source: Ia. S. Kapeliush, *Obshchestvennoe mnenie o vybornosti na proizvodstve*, Information Bulletin No. 39 (54) of the Institute of Concrete Social Research of the Academy of Sciences of the USSR, Moscow, 1969, pp. 9, 10, 13, 14.

[*]The precise period in which the survey was conducted is not clear, although it was probably some time in 1967–68. The results were published in 1969. Respondents in the categories of workers, engineers and technicians, and lower-level managerial personnel were drawn from eight cities. The other categories were more widely dispersed.

surveys, and it would be foolish to speculate excessively on the meaning of the findings. But one thing is clear. All of the respondents must have been thoroughly familiar with the nature of elections in the Soviet Union; yet—as we have just seen—various social groups responded quite differently to the proposal for elections of managers. At the very least this suggests the perfectly obvious point that representatives of various social groups must have differed in their assessment of the impact which elections would have on their position in the enterprise. For the overwhelming majority of workers, the symbolic meaning of elections, the semblance of worker involvement in enterprise decisions which they seemed to promise, perhaps even the anticipation that they might be a forerunner of other changes in a participatory direction all apparently combined to make even Soviet-style elections a welcome prospect. For many of those in managerial positions, already harassed by constant pressures and instructions from "above," the principle of "accountability" of managers to the managed—whatever the strictly formal manifestation it might take under Soviet conditions—must have seemed an additional and unnecessary burden. Besides, could elections be readily reconciled with the still sacred principle of one-man management? More than 40% of upper-level managers in the Kapeliush study agreed that elections would weaken the principle of one-man management, and another 16% "partially agreed" with this proposition. Thus the proportion of these managers opposing elections and the proportion agreeing (fully or partially) that elections would weaken one-man management were essentially of the same order of magnitude. Parenthetically, it is worth noting that among workers this relationship was quite different: the proportion holding that elections would weaken one-man management was some three to four times the proportion opposed to elections.[8] It can hardly be a surprise that the prospects of a dilution of one-man management should have seemed a less powerful argument against elections among worker-respondents than among managers.

We have already noted that Kapeliush was not only the principal investigator of the 1969 study but clearly an advocate of the idea of elections. The significance of this study lay not only in its disclosure of worker-manager differences in responses to the prospect of elections but in the author's readiness to pose questions which would take the issue beyond the limited stage it had already reached. Thus Kapeliush noted that what had recently been described in Soviet newspapers as elections of foremen at construction projects in Krasnoiarsk and elsewhere were not really "direct elections by workers" but a process of "competitive selection" (*konkurs*) to fill vacancies in foremen's posts.[9] Why? Apparently when the vacancies appeared, a "special commission" was set up comprising "representatives of management, social organizations [one of which was obviously the Party—M. Y.] and workers." This commission examined the aspirants (candidates) for the vacancies, selected those it considered "worthy of consideration" (*dostoinykh*) and presented them to a general workers' meeting. Following an extensive "discussion" of the candidates, those in attendance expressed their sentiments through "voting"—in some unspecified form.[10] But the key point was surely this: in Kapeliush's words, "*the final decision remained with the commission*" (our emphasis—M. Y.). Thus the latter was to be guided, but apparently not bound, by the sentiments of the work collective in the choice of foremen. The very manner in which Kapeliush described the Krasnoiarsk proceedings ("In this case the opinion of the meeting and the opinion of the commission coincided, but this need not occur") seemed an implicit appeal for going beyond current half-measures to a process in which the formal selection of the winning candidate would be made "from 'below' directly by subordinates,"[11] i.e., a situation in which the "final decision" would be in the hands of the work collective rather than the "special commission."

In one additional respect, as well, the Kapeliush survey raised the possibility of taking the electoral process (or the process of "competitive selection") further than current experiments permitted, indeed, further than most of the survey's respondents seemed prepared to go. Most of those expressing approval of the general principle of elections had in mind elections to lower-level managerial positions—brigade leaders, foremen, section chiefs (*nachal'nik uchastka*)—the kinds of positions involved in the ongoing experiments. In none of the socio-occupational groups into which Kapeliush divided his respondents did support for electing upper-level managers (plant directors, shop chiefs) reach as much as one-fifth of those polled. The reason seemed fairly obvious. In the case of lower-level managers, workers were likely to be directly familiar with the candidates and the nature of the work involved, and hence a case could be made for trusting their assessment of the candidates' performance. The same argument could not readily be made to support the idea of workers directly electing upper-level managers. But here Kapeliush cited, with apparent approval, or at least in a manner which indicated that the idea was worthy of serious consideration, the proposal of one of the survey's respondents: Why not consider the possibility of "multistage" (*mnogostupenchatyi*) elections or indirect elections of higher-level managers? That is, workers could elect foremen, foremen could elect shop or department chiefs and the latter could elect the director. After all, noted Kapeliush, the essential element distinguishing the "election" of a leader from his "appointment" is the source of authority. Does he receive it from "subordinates" or those standing above him? "When a director receives his authority from his subordinates, this means an election [*vybornost'*], even if large masses of workers do not participate in the selection of his candidacy and in the voting."[12]

Clearly the subject of possible elections of selected categories of enterprise managers—in some not yet specified form—was a relatively "open" one in the late 1960s, and for some participants in these discussions the prospects for extending and modifying prevailing experiments must have seemed promising. But if such heady expectations did exist, they were to be disappointed in the years immediately following. Little was heard on the subject in Soviet public discourse in the early 1970s, and what was said had been heard before. The fact that a leading writer on "scientific management," V. G. Afanas'ev, could do no more in the 1973 edition of his textbook than repeat—word for word—his proposal of five years earlier that it would be appropriate to test the principle of elections "experimentally at some enterprises" suggests that the issue was essentially at a standstill.[13] This impression is reinforced by the rather perfunctory comments of another prominent Soviet management specialist in 1974 that in the "not too distant past," experiments in elections of lower-level managers in some "primary production collectives" had yielded "hopeful results."[14] In neither of these cases, nor in any others that we are aware of in this period, was there any reference to new experiments, public opinion surveys or elaborations of arguments for or against the idea of elections. The obvious "cooling down" of this issue in the early 1970s was undoubtedly connected with the failure of the reforms of the mid-'60s to generate the kind of "economic independence" of enterprises that some had anticipated. But the very boldness and partisanship of studies like that by Kapeliush, and their documentation of substantial management resistance to proposals for elections, may have played a no less important role in inhibiting further discussion at this time. The evidence that Party officials at economic enterprises were much less inclined to perform a "vanguard" role on this issue than ordinary workers might have hoped for (compare the "no" votes of ordinary workers and Party secretaries in Table 6.1) was another good reason for caution.

All the more important, therefore, that public discussion of the election of managers reemerged in the late 1970s and continued into the early 1980s, apparently quite independently of any sign of the kind of economic reforms that had triggered the earlier experiments and discussions. We cannot unravel all of the pressures associated with this revival, but one obvious fact should be noted. The resurgence of the issue of elections occurred in the same period in which we observed the participatory current in the management and sociological literature reviewed in Chapter 5 and the increased interest in policies of "work enrichment" examined in Chapter 4. All of these concerns were rooted in a set of interrelated problems which, although not new, showed no signs of disappearing: declining rates of labor productivity growth, intensification of "disproportions" between workers' relatively high educational levels and their limited job content and the poor—perhaps the worsening—state of work discipline. Clearly there were pressing reasons for continuing the search for mechanisms (including participatory mechanisms) that offered some prospects of enhancing the state of work morale and job performance—even in the absence of a more general "economic reform."

Perhaps the first signal that elections of managers could again become a legitimate subject for public discussion was the appearance, in 1976–77, of reports describing the somewhat unusual procedures used at a Riga communication equipment plant of the "Kommutator" Combine to fill vacancies in foremen's and section chiefs' positions. Like the Krasnoiarsk experiment of a decade earlier, the Riga model has had its imitators (the number of them is not clear, but it is certainly not large) and has become the focus of recent discussions of this issue.

The first detailed report on the Riga plant's procedures (appearing in *Literaturnaia gazeta* late in 1976) was entitled, significantly, "Workers Choose the Foreman." The pertinent details of what Soviet published sources refer to as the election process are essentially these.[15] The public announcement of the forthcoming election is made two weeks before it is scheduled to take place. Following the announcement, nominations for the vacancy are submitted to the particular shop's "social department of personnel" (*obshchestvennyi otdel kadrov*). This agency includes representatives of plant management and functions "under the leadership of Party and trade union organizations." Just who can submit nominations is not clear, although one source assures us that the "masses" of workers can do so.[16] In its considerations of candidates, the shop's personnel department has at its disposal the plant's "cybernetic system," which yields information ("ratings") on the various candidates' "personal qualities," including their "professional competence, creative activity, independence in making decisions. . . ." The personnel department's deliberations are also guided by the views of the "unorganized masses" (the phrase and the quotation marks are *Literaturnaia gazeta's*): ". . . anyone who wishes may speak in favor of a candidate or present his weighty objections." At the conclusion of these deliberations "there remains one aspirant, the most worthy one in the view of those who have submitted their recommendations. His candidacy is then presented for voting." For the proposed candidate to be elected, at least 80% of the workers employed in the affected shop must be present at the election meeting, and he must receive at least 75% of the votes (in a "secret" ballot) of those present. Thus unlike the earlier Krasnoiarsk experiment (in which the voting was "open," possibly for a multiplicity of candidates but not binding on the "selection commission"), workers at the Riga plant formally have at least the theoretical right to veto the personnel department's (i.e., management's) choice of foremen and section chiefs. In fact, the 1976 *Literaturnaia gazeta* report indicated that at least one such veto had been exercised since the project was initiated early in the decade.

It is impossible, of course, to assess the degree to which actual practice at the Riga plant corresponded to the published accounts of the formal election procedures. These procedures, whether applied in practice or not, are in any case less important for our purposes than the interpretive commentary which accompanied the initial accounts and the varied reactions to the experiment which followed. As might be expected, the organizers of the experiment justified it in the familiar language that would normally accompany any such undertaking: it would promote "the democratization of management and foster the feeling of being a master of one's enterprise." In the somewhat less familiar language of social psychology—and perhaps to stress the limited nature of the electoral experiment—they also invoked "the theory of small social groups" and the desirability of combining within one individual the "functions of both formal and informal leader." In somewhat more pragmatic terms the expectation was that elections would raise the prestige of lower-level managers and (together with a recently promulgated wage increase) attract more competent people to these positions.

But the most striking and unusual aspect of the initial *Literaturnaia gazeta* report on the Riga experiment was that it posed a question rarely raised in public discussions of Soviet election procedures:

Perhaps it would be appropriate to present several candidates for final judgment by the comrades at the meeting where the election is held. At the "Kommutator" plant it was decided that it would not be appropriate.[17]

Why not? The response of the Riga experiment's organizers (speaking through the *Literaturnaia gazeta* correspondent) can hardly be considered persuasive, but it does reveal something about the initial difficulties that would confront any serious effort to introduce multicandidate elections in the Soviet context. The decisions not to "present several candidates for final judgment by the comrades" was allegedly based, in part, on "humane considerations," i.e., "to avoid pushing people away pointblank, to avoid a moral trauma for those whose candidacy would be rejected." The rare experience of being a defeated candidate in a Soviet election could certainly be personally devastating, although it seems unlikely that this was the principal concern of the experiment's organizers. The latter also claimed to be guided by "managerial" (*delovye*) considerations, i.e., they were concerned to avoid complicating the situation of future foremen and section chiefs who would have to work alongside those who had almost "seized the reins of government in their own hands." Neither of these justifications hinted at what must have been the principal obstacle to presenting voters with a choice of candidates: the incongruity of a single plant implementing such procedures, and the problem of containing them, in a society in which elections are typically designed to display the maximum possible unanimity of the electorate.

That the question of "several candidates" should have been raised at all seems more significant than the rather pathetic answers which were provided. It is highly doubtful that the question posed reflected merely the naïve curiosity of a *Literaturnaia gazeta* correspondent. We suggest that the issue of workers choosing from a multiplicity of candidates for lower-level managers' positions was very much alive—at least for representatives of the participatory current—and that the correspondent (if not his readers) was probably aware that in its initial stages in the early 1970s, the Riga experiment had, in fact, presented two or three candidates per vacancy to its worker-voters.[18]

The existence of an undercurrent of support for extending the electoral process beyond the limits permitted by prevailing experiments, which we noted in the case of Kapeliush's public opinion survey of the late 1960s, had its counterpart a decade later. One illustration is provided by a 1977 article in *EKO* (an economics journal of the Siberian branch of the Academy of Sciences) by O. I. Kosenko, a researcher attached to the All-Union Central Council of Trade Unions. Following a detailed description of the Riga plant's official procedures for choosing foremen, Kosenko noted that "a number of questions remain for those conducting the experiment."[19] The questions concerned precisely those features which showed that workers' discretion in the selection of lower-level managers was clearly limited by the prior decisions of upper-level managers. "For example, in the great majority of departments only one candidate figured in the election campaign, so that 'competition' was essentially absent." Furthermore, in the whole period of the experiment there had only been "a single case" in which a candidate had been "voted down." Another reason for concern was that while the "broad masses" could propose candidates, the "final list" of those who came up for discussion at workers' meetings was "determined by the administration." Without proposing specific alternative procedures, Kosenko appealed for "following through" on the experiment (*eksperiment trebuetsia dovodit'*) by involving the work collective in "all stages" of the consideration of candidates so that "elections could embody a content corresponding to their purpose." Perhaps most challenging was Kosenko's summary appraisal of the restricted nature of the Riga experiment:

> . . . either the administration of the Riga plant acts with sufficient insight in appointing lower-level managers, and elections merely confirm this indisputable fact, or elections are only the outward appearance [*vidimost'*] of the actual participation of the collective in the promotion of cadres.[20]

The decision to permit the revival of public discussion of elections of managers in connection with the Riga experiment provided an opportunity for Kapeliush to reenter the fray in 1977 ("I will say it at the outset. I am a supporter of the idea of elections of organizers of production").[21] His perception that the idea was "in the air" at this time may seem surprising in the light of the almost complete absence of discussion in the first half of the decade; but if this perception was at all widely shared, it helps explain the rather blunt comments of Kosenko cited above. Kapeliush welcomed the news of the Riga experiment but was critical of its reliance on the "theory of small social groups." The "narrowness" of such an approach had "impoverished" the Riga undertaking and did not offer good prospects for "developing a system of elections in production." His main objective, however, was not to criticize the Riga "sprout" but to appeal for "an extensive experimental verification of the idea of elections." He also reviewed, apparently for the first time in a "popular" publication (*Literaturnaia gazeta*), the principal findings of his 1969 public opinion survey—including the evidence that support for elections, while overwhelming among workers, declined steadily as one moved up the managerial ladder. Although avoiding the delicate issue of how many candidates might be presented for workers' consideration, he renewed his proposal for indirect elections to higher-level managerial posts (workers elect foremen, foremen elect shop chiefs, etc.). All this review of earlier findings and proposals seemed to be a way of saying that the issue of involving workers in the selection of managers had a history and was once again on the order of the day. Kapeliush acknowledged that opposition to elections was still considerable, "especially among directors," but the "social circumstance" for elections had improved. That is, the number of trained specialists had vastly increased so that there were more than enough "from whom to choose," and the increased educational level and "consciousness" of workers meant that there were enough of them to do the choosing. "In a word, there has been a change in the objective circumstances and subjective characteristics of both potential electors and candidates for position in the system of plant management."

The serious quality of some of the arguments adduced in support of elections of managers in the late 1970s emerges most clearly when adherents of the idea have sought to rebut the principal objections of opponents, or at least those objections which have been openly stated. It is this quality which makes it difficult to dismiss these discussions as merely idle chatter about a process which participants must have known would be essentially farcical—Soviet-style elections. Whether supporters of the idea really believed that genuine elections were possible, or simply used the opportunity to argue for elections as a means to focus attention on the need for whatever participatory mechanisms political authorities might find acceptable, makes little difference for our purpose. It is the logic of the argument for worker participation and its potential for improving work performance that deserves our attention.

The response of Kaidalov and Suimenko in their 1979 volume to an opponent of extending the principle of election to middle- and upper-level managers provides a case in point. The opponent had invoked an argument by analogy that may be as familiar in some Western management circles as in the Soviet:

Just as the passengers of an airliner are not in a position to pass
judgment in detail on the professional training of the air crew, and can
only speak of their own sensations of the flight, so it is true that a
work collective can not comprehensively assess the merits of a candidate for a leadership post. Even on the basis of its experience of joint
activity, the collective will draw more superficial conclusions than
higher-echelon managers.[22]

For Kaidalov and Suimenko the airline analogy was a false one. The
members of a work collective could not be regarded as "passive
passengers" who had entrusted their fate to the crew; they were "interested and active participants" in the "aggregated activity" of the
enterprise. Moreover, it was not legitimate to equate the managerial
aspirant's "professional training" with his "merits," i.e., with his
capacity to properly perform management functions. This also
depended on his personal and "workmanlike" (*delovye*) qualities, his
method and style of leadership, which could be adequately assessed by
"the majority of conscientious, politically literate and qualified members of the collective."

Nor did these writers accept the view that a certain level of "social
and cultural maturity" of work collectives—presumably not yet attained—was a necessary condition for selecting managers through an
electoral process. In effect Kaidalov and Suimenko turned the issue
around and argued that workers' "maturity" was, in part, a function of
their participatory opportunities. The danger was that "antiquated
organizational structures" (the nature of which the authors did not
identify) could "condemn ordinary workers to permanent
'immaturity.' " The way out of this "enclosed circle" required

the creation of the kind of organization-managerial conditions in
which the masses would be included in management and would learn
to manage through actual practice. The creation of a system of elections of managers is a necessary condition through which workers
could really raise their cultural level and have the necessary stimulus
to do so.[23]

Perhaps the most "militant" expressions of support for the general
idea of elections of managers, and for transcending the limitations of
the Riga experiment in particular, have been voiced in the writings of
the journalist A. Levykov. His articles on management and work organization in *Literaturnaia gazeta* and a volume of essays published in
1980 (*Kaluzhskii variant*) are clear expressions of the participatory
current and have probably attracted more public attention to the issue of

elections and worker participation than any of the more "scientific" literature. The journalistic technique of speaking in the voices of the (real or fictitious) workers and managers he interviews (or from whom readers' letters have been received) may also help explain a certain boldness of formulation in discussing sensitive issues not often found in the "professional" literature. Much of what he has had to say on the issue of elections need not detain us since it is essentially a report to Soviet readers on the various electoral experiments, public opinion surveys and arguments of supporters and opponents which we have already reviewed. But a tone of unrestrained partisanship, almost of engagement in a kind of battle, pervades his writings. Here is Levykov's retrospective perception—perhaps not altogether credible— of how eagerly the revival of discussion of the election issue was awaited in the period immediately preceding public accounts of the Riga experiment:

> Public opinion, adequately prepared to grasp the idea, was in a state of agonizing expectations, ready for a new round of discussion concerning something more substantial than the extinguished Siberian flame [this appears to be a reference to the Krasnoiarsk experiment, which apparently had lapsed—M. Y.]. At any moment it appeared that a new one would arise. Who would be bold enough to take the next step? The idea was in the air. Readers sending their letters to the paper referred to it more and more often; they were looking for an occasion to continue the discussion. . . . And the occasion arose![24]

The "occasion" obviously refers to published reports of the Riga plant's election procedures which began to appear in 1976. Readers' responses, according to Levykov, reflected the varying views of opponents of the experiment, of "hesitant supporters" and of "energetic supporters," including those who were dissatisfied with its half-way measures and were "burning with feelings of militant maximalism."[25] We cannot help but wonder how many "militant maximilists" there were on the issue of elections among *Literaturnaia gazeta* readers and precisely how far they were willing to go. What we do get from Levykov, however, is perhaps almost as illuminating. Using the device of lengthy extracts from letters presumably received from an "advanced" worker, Levykov presents what must be regarded as his own views on the elections of managerial personnel (in the context of the Riga experiment) and related matters. These views do seem to deserve the label "militant"—if not obviously "maximalist"—under Soviet circumstances.

The main elements of the "message" conveyed by Levykov's worker-correspondent were essentially the following:[26] Of course the Riga experiment is to be welcomed. But why did its organizers abandon the initial practice of presenting several candidates for every foreman's vacancy? If the principal concern was to avoid a traumatic blow to losing candidates—and this is a legitimate concern—there is a simple solution. Instead of "following the path of least resistance," why not let workers "name," through a secret ballot, any candidates they wish. The individual receiving the largest number of votes in this process would then be presented as the single candidate at the final election meeting. Nothing needs to be said which would identify the losing candidates. The prevailing procedure, in which the personnel department—largely "under the influence of the administration"—chooses the final candidate shows that "workers at this Riga plant are not fully trusted, that some people are afraid to lose control and initiative." What a pity that those who conceived and implemented the "splendid idea" of electing foremen have not taken the next step, as if suddenly "someone activated a stop-valve."

What is significant in the remarks of Levykov's worker-correspondent is not simply the appeal for a genuine workers' voice and discretion in the selection of superiors but the clarity with which they reflect what Alan Fox has called the "low-trust syndrome" in relations between managers and managed: managers' insistence on the need for close supervision (in this case of the electoral process), the existence of an appropriate "social distance" between the two groups, the recognition of divergent group interests, the perception by the managed of their status as one of subordination (perhaps even of "class" subordination). Nor are these sentiments merely implicit. In the words of Levykov's "advanced" worker: "Workers and management [*administratsiia*] generally assess the merits of a foreman differently." In what sense? What management looks for is essentially someone who will be "an executor of its will." But the kind of foreman the worker "needs" (especially a worker on piece rates) is someone capable of organizing the work process efficiently, ensuring that the worker's wages are adequate and "representing his interests before the bosses" (*nachal'stvo*). In defending the proposal for elections of managerial personnel, Levykov's worker relies, in part, on the conventional language that is almost obligatory in such cases (elections would "promote the democratization of management . . . and develop the feeling of being a master of one's enterprise"). But what is surely the larger point is stated with unaccustomed bluntness: "People are tired of the identical model of being pressed into a cast-iron mold (excuse the comparison), where they are taken from above by the hand, pinned down and then moved here and there.'' One reason for the failure of the Riga experiment's organizers to carry the electoral process further, to fully trust the plant's workers, is the normal human fear of the unfamiliar: "For many of the even highly sensible directors the workers' environment is a kind of 'darkness.' Their contacts with it are few, not frank, official.''

We cannot assess how common are the perceptions voiced here by a Soviet journalist or his worker-spokesman, how numerous the strata of workers or "enlightened" managers who share them. But in an intellectual environment in which published writers do not speak only for themselves, it must be assumed that these ideas have a sizable number of adherents, including some in positions of political authority. Once again we can observe how public discussion of a particular policy proposal, however slight its chances of meaningful implementation, serves as a vehicle for posing the broader issue of institutionalizing participatory opportunities for workers and for revealing dimensions of the work experience barely touched on in sociologists' studies of work attitudes and job satisfaction examined earlier.

As for the specific issue of elections of managers, published references to it became quite common in the early 1980s and almost invariably in the context of support for the idea.[27] When open opposition was expressed, it took the form of what might fairly be called "sympathetic criticism.'' Thus for G. Kulagin (a retired plant director and prominent writer on management problems) reliance on an electoral process in managerial selection was simply not a feasible form of worker participation given the underlying organizational principles of the Soviet economy.[28] State industrial enterprises are not producer cooperatives whose managers deal with property belonging only to members of the work collective and who manage its affairs mainly in their members' interests. In such cases elections of managers and their accountability to the work collective would be "absolutely necessary.'' The typical industrial enterprise and its assets, however, are public property, "property belonging to society as a whole" (*obshchenarodnaia sobstvennost'*), and its "interests" must be represented by "higher-level state agencies" with the right to appoint and dismiss managers. The fact is that the public interest (equated here with "state interests") may diverge from the interests of a particular enterprise, just as the interests of the enterprise as a whole may diverge from those of a particular group of workers. "Should we always, in such a situation, rely on the unselfishness of one or another group of workers, or even on their competence?'' The answer seemed all too obvious to Kulagin. This did not mean that the need for worker participation was a false issue. On the contrary, Kulagin affirmed that work satisfaction depended largely on workers' participation in ''decisions bearing on the common objectives of the organization.'' But he was concerned that pressure for elections would only serve to ''compromise'' more realistic opportunities for participation. It would be wiser to concentrate on strengthening existing participatory ''structures''—and here Kulagin cited trade unions and semiautonomous work brigades—than to ''elevate oneself prematurely to the clouds.''[29] The nonpolemical tone and substance of these comments by an opponent of elections[30] was itself an expression of respect for the larger set of ideas we have subsumed under the label of the ''participatory current.''

One thing is certain, however. Public discussion of the issue of elections has progressed very much further than the actual implementation of the electoral process. There seems to have been no significant increase in reliance on this process for managerial selection since the late 1970s. This is suggested in a 1983 review (in *Pravda*) of the Riga plant's version of elections, which could do no more than claim that the Riga model had been duplicated at a Lvov industrial combine (Mikropribor) ''and others.''[31] The range of elected positions had been extended to shop chiefs, along with foremen and section chiefs. But the selection procedures had apparently remained essentially unchanged, i.e., a single final candidate for the managerial vacancy,[32] with workers having the theoretical right to veto the proposed candidate (whenever the latter received fewer than 75% of the ballots cast at the election meeting). The only hint that alternative procedures were still under consideration was the *Pravda* writer's suggestion that ''a more careful and comprehensive accounting of the views of the work collective'' would be desirable along with greater reliance on the ''methods, forms and possibilities of trade union work.'' Also of some significance is the fact that the *Pravda* article generally avoided characterizing the Riga plant's managerial selection process as an ''election,'' preferring instead the more modest term ''competitive procedure.'' It seems clear that if the idea of elections of managers was ''in the air'' in the late 1970s (as some election enthusiasts had suggested), it had not moved very far from this somewhat nebulous location by the early 1980s.

We shall suggest some of the more obvious obstacles to the implementation of this idea, as well as the broader meaning of the discussion it has generated, in the concluding observations which follow our

examination of an additional manifestation of the participatory current—the brigade (or team) form of work organization.

Work brigades (teams)

Since the late 1970s a serious effort to redesign and restructure work
arrangements and wage-payment systems has been underway in Soviet
industrial enterprises. The principal instrument of this work reform has
been the extension of the brigade form of work organization. We have
already noted (in Chapter 4) that work brigades, in the general sense of
groups working jointly on a set of interrelated tasks, are not a recent
innovation in Soviet industry. But until the late 1970s the brigade form
was largely confined to those sectors and production processes in which
prevailing technology seemed to require reliance on the coordinated
efforts of work teams. Perhaps the clearest examples would be steel-
industry work groups employed on blast furnace and open-hearth furnace operations or lumber-industry work teams in logging operations.
While a "technological" explanation is never entirely absent in Soviet
justifications for any economic policy, what distinguishes recent efforts to introduce work brigades is the stress on the alleged "social
advantages" to be expected from this form of work organization. It is
now recognized that a given technology is compatible with diverse
ways of organizing work activity. Thus the brigade or team form is
being extended even where prevailing technology does not seem to
dictate it—for example, in machine building, light industry, the chemi-
cal industry, all of which are sectors in which this form of work
organization encompassed one-quarter or less of employed workers in
the late 1970s. A 1979 decree of the Party and Council of Ministers
called on all ministries and enterprises to implement the "extensive
development" of work brigades and to make this form of work organization "basic" in the Eleventh Five-Year Plan (1981–85). By 1983 the
decree was well on the way to being carried out—at least in strictly
quantitative terms: about 59% of industrial workers were organized in
work brigades by the beginning of that year, compared to 43% in mid-
1981. The previous peak, in the late 1970s, probably did not exceed
one-third.[33]

We are well aware that official explanations for particular economic
policies and organizational changes must be treated with caution, but
the meaning of the potential "social advantages" invoked to justify the
brigade type of work arrangement seems fairly clear. They refer to the
opportunities for "work enrichment" which this form of organization

appears to provide, i.e., opportunities for job rotation, job enlargement and an increased role for workers in shop-floor decisions. Whether such opportunities are, in fact, being widely utilized is not the point here. Our concern for the moment is with the public justifications commonly offered for increased reliance on work-team arrangements. Why the recent stress on "enriching" work? The answer will seem familiar. The increased "cultural" and educational level of the Soviet work force creates—in the words of a Soviet writer—a new "structure of interests" among workers, a need for "interesting, high-content work,"[34] a work environment in which they can satisfy their "strivings not only to perform specific tasks but to participate in the organization of the production process. . . ."[35] Technological advance, however, while it reduces the proportion of "heavy" manual jobs, also continues to "intensify the division of labor, to fragment jobs into the simplest of operations," and requires "the performance of monotonous work, sometimes even intensifying this monotony."[36] Hence the urgency of adapting the structure of work arrangements to the "structure of interests" of Soviet workers. In this situation the work-team form of organization holds out the promise of simultaneously improving both job satisfaction and worker performance.

To this argument is joined another based on the obviously unsatisfactory nature of the individual piece-rate system that has long been associated with traditional ways of organizing work. (We shall see below that the brigade form, at least in some of its versions, largely eliminates individual piece rates.) Whatever its justification in the years of early industrialization, with their focus on strictly quantitative output indicators, the piece-rate system is now seen as having certain inherent flaws which may have become aggravated with the passage of time. It fostered an unhealthy "everyone-for-himself" kind of psychology, with no particular incentive for the more "advanced" to aid the "lagging." Under conditions in which frequent changes in technology and product characteristics are common, it is difficult to set equally "tight" output norms (the basis for individual piece rates) for all workers. The result often turned out to be a division of jobs into "profitable" ("loose" norms) and "unprofitable" ("tight" norms), with all workers scrambling for the former. In this competition older, more experienced workers—particularly those standing "closer to the foreman"—were at an obvious advantage compared to newcomers. In all these respects work arrangements based on relatively fixed individual task assignments and individual piece rates fostered divisions among workers, a sense of "separation" rather than group solidarity.[37]

At least in theory the team form of work organization, by basing output norms and wage payments largely on the joint output of the work group as a whole, fosters a cooperative rather than divisive and competitive orientation and simultaneously creates an "internal" group pressure on "laggards" so that workers can discipline each other rather than relying on "external" supervision to do so.

Finally, Soviet justifications for the brigade system have invoked favorable Western experience with autonomous work groups,[38] as well as the alleged campatibility of brigade organization with some general principles of "management science." Kulagin's defense of brigades provides an illustration of what might be termed the brigade-as-management-tool type of argument. Enlightened managers recognize that effective management cannot be conducted only from "above." Under conditions of excessive centralization, the flow and processing of information and its application in decision-making are unavoidably delayed. Hence under present circumstances the "best" system of management "is one in which decision-making is entrusted to the maximum number of individuals at the lower range of the managerial hierarchy. . . ." This tends to minimize information flows and thus makes it possible to adopt and implement decisions more rapidly. "All this is ensured by the brigade organization of work."[39]

Our review of some of the more common Soviet justifications for brigade work arrangements is not intended to set the stage for a comprehensive examination of Soviet experience with this form of organization. Our interest is somewhat narrower and more closely related to the general theme of this and the preceding chapter. That is, we shall try to demonstrate how public discourse on work brigades, as well as their actual operation, has become an arena of conflict between those who seek to implement the ideas associated with the participatory current and those who seek to contain them. For some groups at the Soviet workplace (and those who speak for them) the officially sanctioned brigades are seen as an opportunity to translate the principles of "self-supervision, self-management, self-regulation" into shop-floor practice.[40] For others a principal concern has been to limit brigade autonomy and to adapt the formal application of brigade arrangements to the prevailing mode of work organization and the traditional distribution of managerial authority. We cannot always identify the precise social composition of these two broad groupings, but it will become clear that it is not a simple matter of all workers on one side and all managers on the other. The nature of these conflicting responses should become clear following a brief review of some of the formal or "official" principles of Soviet work-brigade organization and accompanying wage-payment systems.

Perhaps the core principle is the simple idea that a group of workers on a set of interrelated tasks (the brigade) is given a "single assignment" or single work order (*edinyi nariad*) by management. The latter does not set individual workers' output norms, only the "collective" norm for the work group as a whole. The distribution of job tasks within the work group is the responsibility of the brigade itself, acting under the leadership of a brigade leader. This leader is a worker—not part of the management staff (like a foreman)—and is appointed by management "with the agreement of the brigade."[41] In work teams with ten or more members, a "brigade council" may be selected by members in "open voting" to assist the brigade leader in the distribution of work assignments.

The total wage of a brigade takes the form of a price paid for its "final results," i.e., for "the job as a whole." Thus the brigade's wage pool depends on the degree of its fulfillment of the work group's "collective" norm. This is usually expressed in relatively "whole" units—a final product, some discrete component of that product or a specified set of "complete operations." The distribution of the collective wage pool among brigade members is a brigade-level decision:

> . . . issues of material rewards for brigade members are now basically decided by the brigade council or the brigade as a whole.
>
> The distribution of wages and premiums among brigade members is not subject to ratification [by management?—M. Y.].[42]

The individual's share of the team's wage pool normally depends on some combination of three factors: the basic wage grade (*tarifnyi razriad*) established for his occupational classification, the number of hours he worked on a team assignment and a "coefficient of work participation." The latter is essentially a point rating assigned to individual team members and reflecting the team's assessment (i.e., the brigade council's and/or leader's assessment) of the individual's work effort: the degree to which he performed a variety of team tasks, assisted other team members in their work, attained higher than average levels of productivity, abided by rules of work discipline. The team may also formally recommend to management that special premiums and supplements be awarded to particularly worthy individuals or that their basic wage grades be increased.

If we were to end our brief review of the formal principles of brigade work organization at this point, there would appear to be considerable substance to the Soviet characterization of the brigade as "an autonomous collective of workers"[43] with substantial discretion in the assignment of job tasks and distribution of brigade earnings. Indeed, at least on the surface there are undeniable similarities here with Western experiments with "autonomous work groups"—where "members regulate their behavior around relatively whole tasks" and "task control is located within the work group rather than external to it."[44] But a closer examination reveals a number of ambiguities and inconsistencies in the "official" portrait of brigade organization which raise serious questions about the possible scope of worker self-management and brigade autonomy. One issue is related to the size of work teams. As might be expected, there is considerable variation in average size of brigades depending on industry and the nature of technology. Although about 70% of brigades had ten persons or fewer in the early 1980s, workers at the Volga Auto Plant—frequently publicized as a model for other plants to follow—were typically organized in brigades of 50–70 workers, with the largest containing 100 or more workers. In such cases a brigade is directly led by a foreman ("a representative of management"), not by a worker-brigade leader.[45] Additional doubts about the scope for genuine worker participation in shop-floor decisions are raised by the discovery that brigade councils are expected to work "under the leadership of the administration and the trade union committee," and that the recommended composition of brigade councils (allegedly selected, it will be recalled, by "open voting") includes a "party organizer [*partorg*], trade union organizer [*proforg*], Komsomol organizer [*komsorg*]," in addition to brigade leader, foreman and "advanced workers [*peredoviki*]."[46] Are worker "self-management" and "brigade autonomy" compatible with a structure dominated by representatives of those "control" institutions whose traditional function in the Soviet plant has been to "mobilize" work effort and supervise the work process?

We raise this question not as a rhetorical device designed to demonstrate that worker participation in management through the work-brigade mechanism is necessarily pure sham but to suggest that the variety of elements included in the formal guidelines governing brigade organization provide legitimation—a procedural "cover" or legal shield, as it were—for two opposing camps: those who see improved economic performance and worker morale as dependent on the introduction of at least the semblance of genuine participatory mechanisms on the one hand and those "conservative forces" (in the words of two Soviet sociologists)[47] who either fear the potenial for democratization of workplace relationships embodied in semiautonomous work teams or are simply indifferent to the issue on the other. What follows are some illustrations of the "voices" coming from these two directions and the workplace traditions they draw on.

The brigade as artel

In Soviet discussions of work organization since the late 1970s, the Kaluga Turbine Plant has emerged as a symbol of the opportunities which the brigade system can provide for worker participation in shop-floor decisions. There is no claim that the "Kaluga variant" is at all typical, but it has become something of a rallying cry for those journalists, sociologists and management specialists whose writings give voice to the participatory current. Once again (as on the issue of "elections") the writings of the journalist A. Levykov have done much to publicize the Kaluga model, although there is also a fair amount of "professional" management literature on its operation. The significance of Levykov's reports from Kaluga lie not only in the details which they provide on the plant's work arrangements (to which we turn shortly) but in the reformist spirit and the larger theme which infuses them: "The main problem consists of improving social relations. . . ."[48] The "social relations" in question are, of course, the relations between managers and the managed, and the "improvement" required refers to the democratization of work through worker involvement in shop-floor decisions. This larger theme is formulated in a manner which suggests that the author is concerned with more than the usual empty sloganeering:

> The requirement to involve workers in management is interpreted by some managers and even social organizations in a formal manner, as a "correct slogan," and that's all! The more insightful among them recognize its benefit for the economy, for production, and react favorably to initiative from below, giving it some scope. But only very few suspect that the issue is not one of economic benefits. Human beings have a need to manage—every person, whether chauffeur, lathe operator, steel worker or assembler.
>
> But every need, whether recognized or not, requires some satisfaction. Every director recognizes workers' needs for rest, recreation, spiritual nourishment, not to speak of wages and good working conditions. . . . If not, the factory committee will take him by the throat. But the need to manage? A fog, mysticism, chimera. . . . No, it is not a chimera! We need convincing forms of satisfy-

ing this specific demand [*spros*], including new forms in addition to the traditional ones . . . the kind that would permit every worker to choose, to take risks, to think, to decide, to affect in one way or another the whole process of conducting affairs. The Kaluga variant is one of the striking examples of this.[49]

The explicitly reformist context in which Levykov envelops his reports on work teams at Kaluga and the nature of the "production relations" which he regards as worthy of emulation (or at least of attention) are also revealed in his favorable accounts—in the midst of his Kaluga volume—of earlier attempts to apply the principle of workers' self-management. Of particular significance here is his readiness to recount some of the principal features of a state farm experiment in norm-free, autonomous work teams which received considerable publicity in the late 1960s and early 1970s before it was "prematurely concluded." The significance of Levykov's evocation of the Akhchi experiment[50] in 1980 can only be appreciated if we realize that his report on it was probably the first since the experiment was aborted in the early 1970s on the grounds that it was "an attempt to 'drag' into being a communal form [*artel'naia forma*] of work collective—clearly in conflict with the collective and state farm forms—known in Russia since prerevolutionary times and representing a rudimentary form of organization of work collectives on democratic principles. . . ."[51] Some of the key features of the experimental farm's organization which appear in Levykov's account help explain why the subject should be a sensitive one and also suggest the symbolic meaning of his decision to review it in the midst of his discussion of work brigades in an industrial plant. The farm's skeletal administrative staff included only two members (a director and economist-bookkeeper). Thus it lacked the usual "cumbersome managerial apparatus" which so often "limited the independence" of direct producers and generated a "sense of dependence, the feeling that 'the bosses know best' [*nachal'stvu vidnee*]." The basic units of organization were autonomous work teams "managed independently" from within and led by a team leader who was himself a farm worker. No output norms were established either for teams or individual workers; the team's pay depended on its "final output" (the crop available for delivery to the state). One of the objectives (never attained) was to apply the principle of "managing in turn," so that all would have an opportunity to become team leaders; the principle of job rotation would also apply to the position of director, which would be filled at regular intervals by drawing on the most "worthy" team leaders. Levykov acknowledged the utopian element in this experiment: "Perhaps they tried to look somewhat ahead of their time. But is this reprehensible?"[52]

Thus the principle of autonomous work groups has distinguished forebears, Levykov seems to be saying, and their history should be known. But what about the current embodiment of this principle in the form of the "Kaluga variant" of brigade work organization? The picture which emerges may well be a somewhat idealized one, but even in this form the limited conception of worker participation which it projects and the divergence of this conception from traditional Soviet workplace arrangements seems fairly clear. In most respects work organization at Kaluga (as it appears in the writings of Levykov and others) follows the "official" guidelines for brigade arrangements outlined above. Unlike the large work brigades at the Volga Auto Plant, which obviously cannot be managed from "within," work teams at Kaluga range from 5 to 25 members, with the "optimum" size considered to be 12–15.[53] Brigade leaders are management appointees, but their selection is guided by the work group's consensus determined by issuing questionnaires to brigade members. The final choice, however, is clearly a management decision.[54] (Levykov expresses his regret here that brigade leaders are not directly elected but regards the use of questionnaires as a step forward.) The plant's aggregate production targets are distributed among its shops and then among more than 300 brigades and become the basis for team output assignments expressed in units of "final product" or some distinct "set of components." The magnitude of these planned team assignments is apparently not subject to team discretion—at least officially—although some bargaining is possible over the resources required to meet them. In response to Levykov's question as to whether brigades have any say over their output targets, the answer of the turbine plant's director is unambiguous:

> The shop and brigade have no right to reduce their plan. Here all democracy stops. The plant receives a plan—it's law [*zakon*]. It's allocated to shops—that's law. The shop [shop chief—M. Y.] then distributes its plan to brigades—that's law. But as to what they need, on this matter they can speak out and they do—a particular implement, an additional couple of machine tools, the need to resolve certain technological, organizational and other problems. All requirements of this type are strictly verified and met. . . . If a brigade . . . accepts a plan and asks for nothing, says nothing, that is suicide. . . .[55]

Thus the "ends" of the brigade's activity are established for it by management, with the work group having some influence on the technical "means." But if "democracy stops" where the decision at hand concerns the work team's assigned production target, where does it begin? If we are prepared to have as much confidence in the deputy director's testimony on this issue as in the director's statement cited above, a general answer is provided by the following rough-and-ready formulation:

> In ideal terms it is necessary that the brigade have incoming and outgoing channels. You, brigade leader, turn over so many and so many complete units, render an accounting of them and you will receive so much and so much money for your "artel." *All other questions are decided within the brigade* [our emphasis—M. Y.]. This is, in practical terms, the way things are with us.[56]

The "all other questions" obviously refer to the assignment of individuals' job tasks and the sharing of the work group's earnings pool among brigade members—decisions made by the appointed brigade leader and the team's "elected" brigade council. "In each of more than 300 brigades . . . brigade councils, independently, without the administration, decide the fate of workers' wages—who to pay, how much and for what."[57] Individual piece rates have been "dethroned," and the individual's wage share depends on his basic wage grade (which can be "adjusted" by the brigade council) and the "coefficient of work contribution" set by the council for each brigade member. The total wage pool for the brigade, of course, is not a brigade decision but depends on the degree of its fulfillment of the work group's production assignment established by management. It is on this basis—the work group's control over intrateam task assignments and wage distribution—that the claim is made that "the brigade decides up to 70% of the questions formerly in the competence of the foreman."[58] These are also the apparent grounds for Levykov's repeated invocation of the term "artel" to characterize the Kaluga plant's work brigades. Although the picture of management-selected work teams (albeit with the power to "expel" loafers), subject to externally imposed production norms and headed by management-appointed brigade leaders clearly falls somewhat short of an artel-like, fully independent, self-managing workers' cooperative, there is at least a core of validity to the "artel" characterization—providing, of course, that the Kaluga brigades actually function as we have just described.

Two additional elements of the Kaluga brigade system should be noted. Brigade leaders within the various shops are organized into brigade leaders' councils which meet at certain intervals with shop management (shop chiefs—*nachal'niki tsekha*). The management-appointed chairmen of these councils in turn constitute a plantwide brigade leaders' council which meets with the plant director. Although these councils seem to be mainly concerned with ironing out production problems, they also serve as vehicles for bringing workers' grievances that cannot be settled within brigades to the attention of top-level management.[59] For example, if a foreman unjustly interferes with a brigade's decision on wage distribution to its members, the issue can be taken to the appropriate shop-level brigade leaders' council.[60] If the latter recommends that the brigade's decision be upheld and the shop chief gives his approval—affixes his "stamp" (*viza*) to the recommendation—the foreman is overruled. If brigades are not receiving the resources (materials and equipment) they require to meet their production targets, a similar procedure is followed. If the particular grievance is not settled at the shop level (in negotiations between shop-level management and the brigade leaders' council), it goes to the plantwide council, which has access to the director. In the words of the latter, the brigade leaders' councils "can quickly pose any problem before the administration." Although the councils' recommendations are repeatedly referred to as "decisions" or "instructions," they can only be implemented if countersigned by the appropriate shop chief or the plant director. Thus they are essentially consultative or grievance-handling rather than decision-making bodies. If Levykov's testimony (speaking, as usual, in the words of the workers and managers interviewed at the Kaluga plant) is taken at face value, however, the "decisions" of the brigade leaders' councils are invariably considered seriously by plant management. But as advocate, active propagandist and friendly critic of the "Kaluga variant," he also cannot help but note how much more "logical" it would be if chairmen of brigade leaders' councils—who, after all, might find themselves "in conflict" with management—were elected rather than appointed.

Finally, a feature which is important by virtue of the comparatively minor role it plays in public reports of the Kaluga model of work organization. While the usual "social organizations" (mainly the Party and Komsomol) are obviously present at the Kaluga plant, as they are everywhere, there is nothing to indicate that their representatives must be incorporated into the formal structure of brigade organization. There is no indication, for example, that all brigade councils as a matter of principle must include Party, Komsomol and trade union representatives (as suggested by some of the literature on brigade organization). Indeed, it is the relatively unobtrusive role of these "mobilizing" and "policing" agencies at Kaluga that is a striking feature of Levykov's account. Our impression is that this is no mere oversight of the author's. After all, the essential "message" he seems to be conveying is: "trust the people"[61] (i.e., the workers)—under conditions in which they have genuine opportunities for participation in managerial decisions. Or in a somewhat different formulation which embodies the same "message": The director of the Kaluga plant may not agree with the Riga plant's practice of electing foremen, and the Riga people may not find some things at Kaluga "to their taste"; but the important thing is that "we must search in the direction of further democratization."[62] To stress the importance of including representatives of the usual "control" organizations in brigade councils (chosen by "open voting") would then surely sound a ludicrous note.

Whether its work arrangements in fact correspond to the rather benign picture drawn by its publicists is less important than the fact that the "Kaluga variant" has become a symbol of a move toward workplace democratization and the reformist potential inherent in the system of partially autonomous work brigades. This explains why those whose writings give voice to the participatory current often invoke (explicitly or implicitly) Kaluga-like work arrangements in defense of their arguments for a more participatory work environment. These arguments have undoubtedly enriched Soviet discussions of labor problems by enlarging the range of issues normally posed and questioning some conventional explanations of poor work performance and motivation. A few illustrations will suffice to demonstrate this point.

For example, some economists and sociologists have begun to challenge the simplistic appeals for anti-egalitarian wage policies so often presented as necessary to promote more conscientious work effort. How would such increased wage differentials be implemented, ask the economists Pavlov and Gavrilenko?[63] Surely not by reducing prevailing levels of minimum wages. Thus a policy of increased wage differentiation would require differential increases in the wages of various work groups. But the planned wage bill is already often overexpended, and increases in average earnings frequently press on increases in labor productivity. Moreover, is it really likely that increased wage differentials would generate a "leap" in work intensity? "If a person works listlessly for 8 rubles a day, he would hardly put himself out for 10 rubles." As for proposals to ease or lift state-imposed limits on the wage bill, they would threaten to create a worse evil than prevailing egalitarianism, namely, "unjustified increases in money incomes through the kind of differentiation that could generate social tensions." The authors' point is simply that the traditional framework within which problems of the relationship between wage structure and work motivation are discussed is misguided. The key question to ask is what is the source of the constant "pressure on wages," the striving "to receive more at any price," and how to reduce this pressure?

For Pavlov and Gavrilenko the problem is rooted in "social relations" at the enterprise, in the worker's sense of being a "hired hand": "He is taken on the job by a 'hiring department' [*otdel naima*], the administration pays out his wages, in many cases he observes that all functions of management are performed by the administration." It is perfectly natural that in such cases workers will not feel themselves to be "masters" or "bosses" of production and will not be concerned with the methods used by their colleagues (or themselves) to increase earnings (including various illegal supplements). The resulting feeling will be "it doesn't come out of my pocket." The solution to this problem lies in the direction of the brigade form of work organization, particularly as exemplified by the "Kaluga variant" which has implemented "more fully than others" the principle of worker participation in management. Thus the logic of the authors' argument is that genuine opportunities for worker involvement in managerial decisions, by fostering a sense of being in command of one's own enterprise, will reduce wage pressures. Establishing proper wage differentials remains a genuine issue, of course, but such differentials should be determined by the work group (brigade) itself, which alone can assess the contributions of individual members to the team's final product.

The closest thing to an explicit justification for certain egalitarian wage-distribution practices—in the name of the higher principle of work-group autonomy and solidarity—has appeared in the literature on work brigades. Readers with even a cursory acquaintance with the Soviet labor literature will be aware that "egalitarianism" (*uravnilovka*) has been little less than an epithet for some 50 years in Soviet public discourse (even during periods when official policy was to reduce wage inequality), so that expressions of contrary sentiments assume special significance. One such example (there are others) appears in an article by the sociologists Kaidalov and Suimenko in defense of brigade autonomy.[64] While the "Kaluga variant" is not explicitly invoked, the basic argument is certainly in the spirit of this model of work organization. Why, these writers ask, do some brigades ignore the income-differentiating "coefficients of work participation," preferring to share brigade income in a relatively equal manner. The answers given by some workers to inquiring sociologists reflect a tradition of working-class egalitarianism rarely revealed in Soviet publications. In one case: "Today a young, inexperienced worker contributes less to production than I do. Tomorrow I will be older, and he will work better than me. Then we'll be even." Or in another case ("without a formal arrangement and without publicizing it"): ". . . to help a comrade with a sick wife and two children." The reaction of Kaidalov and Suimenko is interesting. They do not directly endorse even this "benevolent" form of egalitarianism, although it arouses their "profound respect." The larger issue, in any case, is not egalitarianism but brigade autonomy: ". . . let them [the workers—M. Y.] decide themselves, without external interference," how to distribute brigade earnings. Clearly, for these representatives of the participatory current, the importance of establishing the credibility of the idea that workers can have decision-making powers through the brigade system transcends whatever urgency there may be to combating traditional egalitarian sentiments.

A particularly prestigious source of support among social scientists for the idea of workplace democratization through the brigade system, and the "Kaluga varaiant" in particular, has come from the sociologist V. Iadov and his colleagues. In a sense we return here to our starting point. Iadov, it will be recalled, was a coauthor of the initial study of work attitudes of young Leningrad workers in the early 1960s and headed the replication of that study in 1976. Thus he is among the principal figures in Soviet research on job attitudes and workplace behavior. Only those of his recent findings which bear directly on the argument for worker participation need concern us here (a fuller account appears in Chapter 2). Insofar as job attitudes are concerned, we have seen that Iadov's evidence pointed to the emergence of an increasingly "instrumental" orientation to work among young Leningrad workers. That is, the "motivational significance" of monetary rewards and "conditions of work" (i.e., safety measures, sanitation, general "comfort" on the job) had increased in relative importance as determinants of work attitudes compared to the role of those factors subsumed under the heading of "work content" (i.e., creativity, variety, intellectual challenge). Thus instead of becoming more intrinsically rewarding, a "self-valued" end, the work experience was increasingly perceived as a means to other ends—increased consumption, material comfort and "enriched" leisure. The basic values of work activity had been increasingly "displaced" to the nonwork sphere. This, of course, was precisely the opposite of the expectations that had prevailed at the time of the initial studies of work attitudes, expectations fostered by the Marxian vision of the approach of a communist society. Part of the explanation offered by Iadov for the enhanced role of "instrumental" work values was, quite simply, the emergence of increased consumption opportunities and the "spillover effects" of increased household amenities. But there was another element in the explanation that was more disturbing and had a direct bearing on the need for workplace reform. Young workers were entering the work force with much higher levels of education and "cultural" development, precisely the characteristics that might be expected to increase the importance of "work content" (rather than material rewards) as a source of job satisfaction. Such workers, at least at the start of their work careers, brought rather ambitious "needs" or "demands" to the workplace—for creativity on the job, for variety in work, for "participation in public life and the general affairs of the plant. . . ."[65] But here was the rub. The antiquated social organization of the workplace frustrated the realization of these "demands" and "blocked" the expected impact of workers' increased education and "culture" on their attitudes toward work. Hence the increasing importance of workers' "instrumental" orientations and their widespread indifference to workplace production problems. Instead of promoting "a feeling of involvement," managers confined themselves to "tiresome exhortations" and "appeals to conscience."

The consequence of all this for workers' behavior—another of Iadov's principal findings—was a deterioration of work discipline (increased lateness, absences from work, "refusal to carry out assignments"),[66] more frequent labor turnover and a "rational" pacing of work effort designed to avoid either excessive overfulfillment or underfulfillment of work norms. The striking feature of Iadov's characterization of these elements of workers' behavior is that he does not regard them in exclusively negative terms. They reveal a kind of "self-regulation" of worker behavior, a sign of "self-reliance, independence and rationality," all of which traits could be mobilized for more productive purposes if opportunities were created for worker participation in management. Thus Iadov's findings on the job attitudes and behavior of young Leningrad workers provide logical and empirical support for an appeal to democratize workplace relationships:

> Either the managers . . . assign a task to the managed . . . and strictly control the sequence and mode of implementing the process,

in which case the managers are themselves wholly responsible for the result. Or an objective is assigned, and the mode of attaining it is chosen by the managed themselves, who then become responsible for the result which now depends on them. . . . One of the most urgent requirements of the present day is to extend the application of the second approach. . . . The main issue is the objective necessity of increasing the participation—moreover the direct participation—of the masses in management. It is difficult not to see the connection between all the basic problems of the economy and [the need for— M. Y.] the democratization of production.[67]

More specifically, Iadov cites the brigade system (and the "Kaluga variant"), with work teams having the right to decide how to fulfill their work assignments and distribute team earnings, as pointing in the right direction. But the limited nature of workplace democratization through the brigade mechanism is also explicitly recognized. Thus one of Iadov's colleagues, A. N. Alekseev, notes that since the enterprise's wage bill and average earnings are "given" to it from above, the workers can "democratically decide only how to slice up a predetermined . . . slice of the social pie." But suppose a given enterprise (or, for that matter, a whole branch or sector) merits a larger or smaller "slice"?[68] This theme is not pursued further, but the implicit question posed by Alekseev is why should democratization begin only *after* (our emphasis—M. Y.) central planning authorities have determined enterprises' wage allocations? Thus, like those representatives of the participatory current who have raised the issue of going beyond officially sanctioned "electoral" experiments, others have pointed to the possibility of extending democratization of economic decision-making well beyond the limits permitted by the brigade system—even in its "artel" (Kaluga) version.

But what about the actual implementation of the brigade form of work organization? In the struggle on this issue between the two camps we identified earlier, there is little doubt that the "conservative forces"—the opponents of worker participation—have thus far prevailed. The section which follows presents some of the evidence and suggests some of the reasons.

The brigade as façade

Any attempt to implement reforms in the Soviet economy, whether in the underlying planning mechanism or in traditional modes of work organization, is obviously bound to confront the resistance of those groups whose authority and material well-being seem threatened by the proposed change. All the more so when the appeal for reform is made under the banner of worker participation in management and democratization of work. To characterize all such resistance as "bureaucratic inertia" does not seem very useful or illuminating. In what follows we attempt to identify some of the ideological mechanisms, attitudes, group interests and managerial devices which have thus far blocked efforts to institutionalize more participatory workplace relationships via the brigade or team form of work organization.

Since the introduction and extension of the brigade system is official state policy, we can hardly expect to find open expressions of opposition to the idea of brigades as basic units of work organization. What we do find, however, is that unlike the literature on brigades we have thus far reviewed (Levykov, et al.), which stresses the participatory opportunities of these units as their principal advantage, there is also a "conservative" strain in some of the economic and sociological literature which focuses on the alleged dangers of excessive work-team autonomy. Such writings obviously serve the ends of those management groups for whom worker participation is more to be feared than encouraged. Thus an old-line labor economist (S. Shkurko), writing in *Voprosy ekonomiki* in 1980, poses the question of "optimizing the boundaries of brigades' production independence" mainly in order to warn against applying the principle of self-management to brigade activity. The principle to follow is that "the interests of brigades must be subordinate to the interests of the work collective as a whole."[69] More specifically, Shkurko's concern is that following an increase in work teams' productivity and wages, they may resist—become "uninterested in"—upward revisions in output norms and the introduction of new technology. The principle of work-team autonomy must not be permitted to reach the point where brigades could become instruments of collective resistance to management's efforts to speed up the pace of work. Thus the importance of affirming the familiar theme of managerial prerogatives, albeit in somewhat extreme form: ". . . the administration must retain the absolute right to introduce changes designed to intensify production," accompanied, of course, by "discussions" of the proposed changes with brigade members and efforts to "involve" them in their implementation.[70] It should come as no surprise that Shkurko cites with approval what he calls the "usual" practice of having a foreman and Party, Komsomol and union representatives as members of brigade councils.

Similar expressions of the "low-trust syndrome" have appeared in the sociological literature on work teams. Thus for V. G. Britvin the activities of work brigades, whatever their advantages over individual work organization, should not be regarded as the "equivalent of the communist organization of work." One of their afflictions is that they are too often guided by "narrow group interests" and "group egoism." The precise nature of these deficiencies is not spelled out, but the general context suggests a concern that the sense of group solidarity fostered by excessive work-team autonomy may create problems for enterprise managers. "We may observe cases of protectionism and the incorrect distribution of wages" (excessively egalitarian distributions?—M. Y.). In what can only be characterized as a most un-Marxian concern, the author points to the difficulty of fostering "individual competition" or "emulation" within work brigades.[71] Apparently work-group pressure can be directed not only at "loafers"—a common justification for the brigade system—but at potential "rate-busters" as well.

It is highly unlikely that these warnings against permitting undue enlargement of work-team decision-making have fallen on deaf ears. Indeed, they have undoubtedly served to legitimate the attitudes already widespread among enterprise managers, especially lower-level supervisors, that the extension of the brigade system can be assimilated without any significant redistribution of traditional managerial authority to work teams. This is suggested by Table 6.2, which shows the views of a sample of managerial personnel (in eight plants in the Dnepropetrovsk region in 1981) on the proper location of decision-making authority over various work-brigade activities. It should be stressed that these managers were drawn from plants in which the brigade system was already in effect. What is striking here is that in not a single area of brigade functioning shown in the table did a majority of sampled managers regard the brigade itself (the brigade leader) as the appropriate source of managerial authority. This applied not only to decisions bearing on the introduction of new technology, where such attitudes might be expected, but also to decisions on the distribution of team members' job tasks and earnings, areas which the "official" guidelines on brigade functioning specify as being within the competence of the brigade itself. The prevailing view was that all such decisions were the proper responsibility of the foreman or the "administration" (upper-level managers). Moreover, a common feeling among the manager-respondents was that any "additional rights" of brigades ("additional" to what, one wonders) required an "intensification of educational work" and "monitoring" (*kontrol'*) over brigade activities—both functions presumably to be implemented by managerial staffs. It is worth noting, however, that most of the respondents were lower-level supervisors (foremen) who must have regarded genuine work-team autonomy as a direct threat to their authority, while shop chiefs seemed somewhat more tolerant, although hardly enthusiastic, about the enhancement of work-team decision-making powers. In one of those rare explicit references to an issue which all participants must have known was at stake here, the issue of power, the author of the Dnepropetrovsk study noted:

> . . . it is precisely lower-level line managers who particularly complain about their excessive work load and scarcity of time, but . . . they don't take the risk of shifting some of their obligations to brigades. They must be concerned with losing power.[72]

Although the particular study whose findings we have just reviewed was concerned with the attitudes of managerial personnel, there is no

---

Table 6.2

Views of Line Supervisors and Engineering-Technical Personnel on the Appropriate Source of Managerial Authority under the Brigade Form of Work Organization, Dnepropetrovsk, 1981[*]

| | Who should perform managerial functions (in %)? | | | |
Managerial functions	brigade leader	foreman	the "administration"	total
Planning the work assignment	13.4	41.1	45.5	100.0
Preparing work orders used for wage calculations	30.9	62.2	6.9	100.0
Daily distribution of job tasks	46.5	51.0	2.5	100.0
Providing the necessary equipment	27.5	39.3	33.2	100.0
Providing the necessary raw materials and components	10.6	35.9	53.5	100.0
Introducing new technology	15.1	30.4	54.5	100.0
Distribution of premium funds	32.1	46.7	21.2	100.0
Educating members of the collective	31.7	50.0	18.3	100.0
Planning and norm-setting	9.3	33.0	57.7	100.0

Source: P. G. Klivets, ''Conditions of Introduction of Brigade Methods of Work,'' *Sotsiologicheskie issledovaniia*, 1983, No. 3, p. 102.

[*]The study was conducted in eight plants of the Dnepropetrovsk region, and the sample included 515 line managers and engineering-technical personnel. We have excluded some of the managerial functions listed in our source on the grounds that their meaning is nebulous or they repeat functions already cited.

scarcity of evidence that actual practices typically reflect precisely such attitudes. A common theme in the increasing number of studies of work-team functioning which began to appear in the early 1980s was the purely "formal" nature of much of brigade organization (barring, of course, "model" cases like Kaluga and a few others). That is, responding to pressure from ministerial authorities to report "successes" in the transition to the brigade system, plant management would frequently create brigades "on paper," with these units consisting simply of "mechanical sums of workers" but without significant changes in work organization or devolution of managerial authority to work teams. Thus a study published in *EKO* in 1982 reported that more than half of all brigades were "based on individual work and individual forms of wage organization."[73] In other words, workers continued to be assigned individual output norms and piece rates by managerial representatives, directly contrary to the principle of a "single assignment" for the work-group as a whole, which members then distribute among themselves. Nor do managers' methods of reconciling the formalities of brigade organization with the retention of traditional managerial authority seem to require very sophisticated subterfuge: "Often the administration itself, without the participation of the collective, establishes for it the mode of distribution of wages, determines the magnitude of coefficients of work participation for brigade members and grants the brigade council only the right to ratify the decision."[74] It is clear that such procedures are by no means unusual. They undoubtedly help explain why almost half of the workers sampled in a 1980 study at Moscow and Perm industrial plants indicated either that managers "for the most part" do not consider the views of brigade members (22.5%) or do so "by no means always" (23.4%), and why less than 40% of the workers questioned in a 1981 study at a Urals machine-building combine expressed "satisfaction" with the activities of the brigade councils.[75]

The losing but continuing struggle to implement the reformist elements in the work-team system is apparent not only in the results of these empirical studies by economists and sociologists. It also appears in the less "scientific" form of polemical writings by representatives of the participatory current directed against the purely "formal" adoption of work-brigade organization. Soviet workers may lack their own public "voice," but their individual "voices" may be clearly heard in the writings of those sociologists and journalists who have sought to transform worker participation from an empty slogan into a genuine public issue. Here is a small sample of workers' expressions of disillusionment with the typical implementation of the work-team system, drawn from articles by Kaidalov and Levykov, expressions which these writers obviously regard as broadly representative of workers' reactions:

> The brigade system won't work. The bosses [nachal'stvo] won't permit it.

> The bookkeeping department, the bosses, somehow divide up [the work team's—M. Y.] earnings.

> The brigade leaders' council so far has done nothing.

> There is no council of brigade leaders in the shop. The foreman and his assistant get together and fix the coefficients of work participation . . . and we sign—a pure formality. . . . Nothing has changed . . . decisions, as before, are made only by the factory chiefs [nachal'niki].[76]

For some work reformers these signs of failure of the brigade system to lead to workplace democratization are largely the consequence of managerial groups' successful resistance to relinquishing their authority. In this view the responsibility for discrediting the brigade system rests with those "bureaucrats" who "for the sake of the stability of their own position . . . are engendering for all of society something unstable, not genuine, something that unravels in people's hearts and minds."[77] It would surely be simplistic, however, to conclude that the only source of resistance to work reorganization through semiautonomous work teams stems from the power considerations of "managers" and "bureaucrats." There are also marked "intraclass" differences in workers' responses to the prospects of the brigade system. It would be naïve to assume that all strata of a fragmented working class, long unaccustomed to making uncontrolled "collective" decisions, are equally enthusiastic about (or interested in) opportunities for worker involvement in management decisions through the brigade mechanism. This is a theme to which we return in our concluding comments. We raise it here not to deny that underlying issues of the distribution of authority and conflicts of interests between managers and workers are involved but to suggest what may perhaps be obvious—that the prospects for work reform should not be regarded as depending only on a "class" confrontation between a homogeneous group of privileged managers on the one hand and workers united in their eagerness for work democratization on the other.

One thing is clear. The "Kaluga variant," both in its original locale and in a few other plants, may be more than simply the product of a Soviet journalist's imagination; but for the most part the brigade system remains a facade behind which—in the words of one of the workers cited above—"decisions, as before, are made only by the factory chiefs." While the ideas embodied in the participatory current have continued to receive a public hearing, the substance of worker participation remains largely dormant thus far. Why?

7
Some Concluding Observations

There is a striking disproportion between the richness of the material contained in the writings of Soviet proponents of work reform and the poverty of the measures undertaken to implement reformist policies. What is impressive about the reformist literature, however, is not only its continuing and increasingly urgent appeal for worker participation and "democratization" of management but also the rare glimpses it affords of prevailing worker-manager relations and workers' perceptions of their position in the enterprise. It may be true, as Lane and O'Dell have argued, that there is "a greater unity" between managers and workers in Soviet industrial plants "than is the case in Western states." But at the very least some of the evidence in the Soviet reformist literature raises questions about the degree of this "unity" and casts some doubt on their view of Soviet workers as approximating the model of an "incorporated" or "integrated" working class.[1] Let us recall some of this evidence: the markedly differing reactions of workers and managers to the prospect of "elections" of managerial personnel (Table 6.1), the observations of Levykov's "advanced" worker (in connection with the election issue) that managers don't trust workers and that "the workers' environment is a kind of 'darkness' " for them, workers' readiness to reveal their sense of absence of genuine participatory opportunities to inquiring sociologists (Table 5.2), the feelings expressed by some workers that "the bosses" or "authorities" (*nachal'stvo*) will not permit work reorganization based on autonomous work teams, the continuing expressions of egalitarian sentiments by some strata in the face of long-standing official denunciations of egalitarianism. While some of this evidence is impressionistic and perhaps not altogether "representative," taken as a whole it suggests a working class conscious of its subordinate status, with a sense of distinct group interests and traditions which set it apart from its superiors (the *nachal'stvo*) at the workplace.

As for the direct appeals for workplace democratization in the literature of the participatory current, although we have relied heavily on "journalistic" sources, it is well to recall the extensive support such appeals have received in the writings of Soviet management specialists, sociologists and economists. Soviet readers have been informed of successful work reform experiments in the West. The principle of one-man management has been modified to stress the dominance of "collegiality" over "dictatorial methods" and the "positive" role of certain workplace conflicts has been explicitly recognized (Kaidalov and Suimenko). A set of operational indicators of worker participation has been formulated in the Soviet literature on organization theory (Prigozhin). Empirical studies by industrial sociologists have demonstrated that workers' opportunities for "on-the-job independence" improve both job performance and work attitudes (Tikhonov and Alekseev). The country's leading scholar of work attitudes has linked workers' growing indifference to their job tasks and deteriorating work discipline to the unmet need for "democratization of production" (Iadov). Similar views may be found in leading channels of economic opinion.[2] The reports of distinguished social scientists on some of the bolder "experiments" in norm-free work teams in agriculture[3] and semiautonomous work brigades in industry (the "Kaluga variant")[4] have invariably been positive, as have the reports of managers in the few plants affected by "elections" of lower-level supervisors.[5]

Why, then, in the face of all this evidence, all these explicit or implicit appeals for work reform from respectable sources "within" the system, have the authorities been unable or unwilling to institutionalize even moderately persuasive mechanisms of worker participation? The question appears more insistent and intriguing when we recall the enormous powers (including, presumably, the power to institute reforms) concentrated in the hands of central authorities and the increasing costs of standing pat—perhaps best reflected in steadily declining rates of growth of labor productivity (from 6.8% per annum in 1966–70, to 4.6% in 1971–75, to slightly more than 3% in 1976–80, to 2–3% in the early 1980s). There are obviously a variety of ways of explaining this congealed state of affairs. Our view of the principal obstacles to work reform and the creation of a participatory work environment focuses on three factors:

a) Perhaps the major obstacle involves the danger of possible "spillover effects" of workplace democratization, particularly on the political sphere. A classic general formulation of the issue in the Western literature (apparently without explicit application intended to the Soviet case) is that of Almond and Verba:

> . . . if in most social situations the individual finds himself subservient to some authority figure, it is likely that he will expect such an authority relationship in the political sphere. On the other hand, if outside the political sphere he has opportunities to participate in a wide range of social decisions, he will probably expect to be able to participate in political decisions as well.[6]

The presumably healthy "dynamic repercussions" of workplace democratization on the wider political sphere (i.e., the former's promotion of a "democratic polity") are a recurring theme in the writings of Western advocates of worker participation. Thus for Michael Poole "workers' participation in decision-making at workplace level is an important basis for extending democracy within society as a whole." For Carole Pateman "the democratization of the workplace is a necessary basis for the diffusion of participatory political orientations throughout the population." It provides a "training ground . . . for participation in democratic political life."[7]

This is not the place for a full assessment of the validity of these views, but they obviously have some bearing on Soviet sources of resistance to worker participation. The justifications for workplace democratization cited here from the writings of Poole and Pateman are not only unlikely to be invoked in the Soviet Union; they are also precisely among the reasons why those groups whose powers rest on their political status are likely to resist such democratization, or at least be unenthusiastic about its prospects. Consider, for example, the recurring proposal expressed in the literature of the participatory current to extend experiments in the election of lower-level managerial personnel. Any decision to implement it would have to be taken by political authorities. If the elections were designed to create a sense of genuine workers' voice in choice of supervisors at the workplace, rather than as an idle expression of the usual unanimity, how long would it be before pressures were generated to extend the process? Why confront such an incongruity?

The dilemma of advocates of managerial elections is illustrated by the differences in tone and substance of their argument, depending on the place of publication. Thus a writer in a relatively "liberal" economics publication (*EKO*) can wonder why there is only a single candidate per foreman's vacancy confronting worker-electors in a Riga plant's experimental election, and why the "final list" of candidates is selected by plant management. But in the pages of *Pravda* the same writer, once again appealing for workers' participation in selecting lower-level managers, must reassure political authorities that the Party's traditional role is not endangered by the process of "competitive selection." Here the Riga plant's managerial selection process is presented as being "skillfully guided by the Party committee," with the Party (along with management and the trade union) "carefully examining" the list of proposed candidates and of course exercising its usual "policing" (*kontrol'*) function.[8] This kind of "election" the Party can apparently tolerate (although only on an "experimental" basis thus far), but one wonders how "participatory" the resulting process can be.

All this is not to suggest that any conceivable participatory mechanism at the workplace, including some form of genuine elections, is inherently incompatible with an authoritarian political system. The case of Yugoslavia is surely evidence to the contrary. But unlike the Yugoslavs, there are no signs that the Soviet party is prepared to consider the kind of moderation in its intrusive "leading role," either at economic enterprises or elsewhere, that would make such participatory mechanisms credible.

b) It is difficult to imagine how some of the proposed work reform measures can take root in the absence of more far-reaching reforms in the economic planning system as a whole. There is no need to repeat here the familiar litany of long-standing Soviet planning inefficiencies, but some of them must be seen as formidable obstacles to the introduction of credible worker-participation practices. To illustrate, consider the hypothetical case of a plant which introduces the work-brigade system in its ideal participatory version, with decisions on the distribution of job tasks and brigade earnings in the hands of work-team members. Suppose the expectations of work reformers are justified, and the results include significant increases in labor productivity and the plant's output. What will follow? Almost certainly the plant's production plan will be raised, its wage bill may be cut and pressures will be created to increase brigade output norms and reduce collective piece rates. It would not take long for workers to learn what has long been familiar to managers. In Alec Nove's words, "it will seem dangerous to overfulfill the plan by too much, as the authorities might then fix an impossibly ambitious goal for the next plan period."[9] In other words, planning and ministerial authorities may be expected to act in accordance with the familiar principle of planning "according to the achieved basis" (*ot dostignutogo*), increasing the plans of successful enterprises, thereby removing the "advantages of doing better." Nor is this sheer irrationality on the part of planning authorities since they have good reason to suspect that enterprises with unusually high rates of plan overfulfillment have been "concealing reserves." This, of course, is precisely the kind of planning practice that reinforces the tendency to conceal productive potential, not only by managers but also by workers fearful of increases in output norms and associated cuts in piece rates. Hence the continuing appeal by work reformers for both "stable" or "fixed" plans and norms. The demoralizing effects of these prevailing planning procedures are graphically portrayed by two of these reformers (Kaidalov and Suimenko):

> Many directors . . . fear not only collective forms [of work organi-zation—M. Y.] but innovations generally which could sharply raise the enterprise's potential. The consequences are hidden reserves, listless work, a lazy and disjointed style of life of the collective which sickens all—the director, specialists and workers.[10]

The other element in the planning system that tends to compromise worker-participation mechanisms (and is also related to management's habit of "concealing reserves") is the chronic failure of planning authorities to coordinate enterprises' supply plans (for inputs of materi-als, components and equipment) with their output plans. The unreliability of supplies of inputs to producers has familiar conse-quences:[11] overapplication for inputs, attempts to secure easily attain-able production plans in anticipation of possible breakdowns in flows of inputs, work stoppages when such breakdowns do occur, "storming" (*shturmovshchina*) at the end of the plan period to offset supply shortages at the beginning. This is hardly an environment con-ducive to stable mechanisms of worker participation, and evidence of widespread dissatisfaction among work-team members with supply breakdowns and the need for "storming" is readily at hand.[12] Workers must surely be aware that enhanced work-team autonomy can have little meaning in these circumstances.

There is no need on the basis of these chronic problems to regard the Soviet planning system as simply a set of chaotic and contradictory directives, but it is clear that the prospects for work reform seem dim in the absence of more fundamental economic reforms.

c) Managers' hostility to proposals for "elections" and lower-level supervisors' resistance to sharing authority with semiautonomous work teams are, of course, precisely the reactions to be expected from groups holding privileged positions at the workplace. After all, one of the advantages claimed for such work teams is that they would permit sizable reductions in managerial staffs.[13] As for elections—even in Soviet circumstances—why add the principle of managers' "accountability" to subordinates to the already onerous accountability to superiors? Besides, since some advocates of the election idea have already questioned the "experimental" practice of a single candidate per vacancy, who knows where the electoral process might lead?

But the attitudes and values of some strata of Soviet workers may be no less an obstacle to participatory work reform than the self-interested "protective" responses of managers. True, some 60–90% of workers sampled in sociologists' surveys have reacted positively to the prospects of participation in managerial decisions (see Chapter 5). But there may be a world of difference between such survey responses and workers' actual readiness and willingness to respond positively to measures introduced in the name of work democratization. Concern expressed in Soviet discussions that workers may not be sufficiently "mature" or that they "are not prepared" to participate[14] cannot be dismissed only as subterfuge by opponents of work reform. Moreover, how important, in terms of their relative status and "closeness" to management, were the residual 10–40% of surveyed workers who did not seem particularly interested in new participatory opportunities? Let us consider some of the reasons for workers' skepticism, indifference or resistance to work reform.

Like any innovation at the workplace, the shift to allegedly "self-managing" work brigades appears to workers as a management initiative, not as a response to their own collectively formulated demands— there are no channels for the latter. This is as true of the "Kaluga variant" as of the more common, strictly "formal" cases of brigade organization. Although theoretically based on "voluntary" principles, "brigades are frequently created under considerable pressure from management."[15] This alone must operate as a signal to some workers that brigade organization is simply another management "campaign" designed to do no more than heighten work intensity; and like other such "campaigns," it will soon pass. Even when plant directors introduce the brigade system not merely as a response to ministerial directives requiring yet another "success indicator" (a certain proportion of their work force "covered" by brigades) but do so with the objective of improving job performance by redesigning work to permit increased worker initiative, independence and responsibility, workers' reactions may be either disbelieving or indifferent. Why? Their earlier experience both in and outside the workplace, the whole process of socialization of youth, has made workers skeptical of appeals to such qualities, especially in the context of decisions on collective affairs like work organization. Here is the way the country's leading investigator of workers' attitudes poses the problem:

> From their childhood years our future citizens suffer from an underloading [*nedogruzka*] of responsibility. Moreover, young people who attempt to be independent (through self-management in schools, detachments, at youth sections of workshops), who are prepared and desire to assume a share of responsibility, instead of receiving support are too often slapped down [*poluchaiut po rukam*].[16]

Nor can we assume that a system of work organization which promises not only to enhance workers' roles in enterprise decisions but also to speed up the pace of work and subject "loafers" to group (brigade) pressure will be welcomed by all but a small group of malingerers. A large number of workers have undoubtedly grown accustomed to a predictable work rhythm characterized by recurring cycles of prolonged relaxed activity followed by occasional end-of-month "storming." Such a work rhythm is readily compatible with the increasingly "instrumental" work orientations noted by Iadov among young Leningraders in the late 1970s.

It would be foolish to speculate excessively on precisely which groups of workers are most and least receptive to the prospects of work reorganization and enhanced participatory opportunities. But it is important to recognize that some strata have a stake in prevailing workplace relationships. A demographic and occupational "profile" of a group of workers who expressed their opposition to being shifted to the work-team system (as usual to an inquiring sociologist/economist, not through any organization of their own) suggests the existence of a version of a "labor aristocracy" with such a stake. Work-team opponents tended to be older workers (with an average age of 41.2 compared to an average of 30 years for all workers at the investigated enterprise—a radio manufacturing plant in Irkutsk). As a rule they were highly skilled, with earnings averaging 295 rubles per month, compared to a plantwide average of 228 rubles. Their length of service at the plant (12 years) was substantially in excess of the average, and their educational level (less than 8 years of schooling) was below that of most workers. They had established "good relations with foremen and other supervisors'' and thus were able to obtain ''minimum tasks'' for themselves on the ''most profitable jobs''—i.e., they were ahead of the pack in the scramble for ''loose'' norms and high piece rates. In return, they were ready to ''rescue'' foremen in emergency situations when the shop's plan was in danger.[17] Little wonder that these workers were uninterested in the transition to self-managing work teams where their earnings would depend on the output of the team as a whole. We do not suggest that weighty conclusions can be drawn from such fragmentary reports,[18] but it is clear that ''conservative forces'' on the issue of work reform are not confined to ''bureaucrats'' and managers. Some portions of a divided working class have obviously found their niche in the network of privilege.

These are among the continuing and formidable obstacles blocking work reform. They help explain why some recent manifestations of the participatory current seem like echoes of earlier discussions and experiments. But the principal ''message'' of the increasing number of voices of reform also appears more convincing and urgent than ever: that the problems of the Soviet workplace are rooted in the ''social organization'' of work and the need for ''democratization of production'' (Iadov) rather than in technological backwardness. Those with political power have thus far exhibited an incapacity or unwillingness to act effectively on this proposition. The risks of stagnation apparently seem preferable to the risks and inevitable conflicts of destabilizing reform.

Table A-1

Soviet Studies of Work Satisfaction

Year	Scope of sample	Response categories in %						
		highly satisfied	more satisfied than dissatisfied	total satisfied	more dissatisfied than satisfied	highly dissatisfied	total dissatisfied	other
1. 1962–64	2,665 workers up to age 30 in Leningrad industrial enterprises	16.0	24.9	40.9	11.4	4.7	16.1	43.3
2. 1965–66	5,000 workers, engineers, technicians and employees up to age 28 in 6 plants of auto and tractor industry	21.0	28.0	49.0	16.0	13.0	29.0	22.0
3. 1965	2,083 engineering-technical personnel at 21 enterprises and design bureaus in Ufa, Sterlitamaka and Salavata			73.2			26.8	
4. 1966	833 industrial workers in Perm			51.2			13.2	35.6
5. 1965, 1967, 1970	2,696 engineering-technical personnel in industrial enterprises and research organizations in Leningrad	21.2	41.6	62.8	21.8	5.5	27.3	9.9
6. 1970	218 engineers in design and research organizations in Leningrad	21.6	57.8	79.4	11.5	1.7	13.2	7.4
7. 1971–72	Approximately 3,000 workers at Kishinev Tractor Plant			48.7			21.3	30.0
8. 1972	878 workers at the Volga Automobile Plant	31.4	17.3	48.7	19.0	3.3	22.3	29.0

9. 1972	37% of workers up to age 28 in Angarsk Oil-Chemical Combine			46.1			29.5	24.4
10. 1972	Workers in Kazakhstan industrial enterprises:							
	Dzhezhazgansk Mining and Metallurgical Combine			63.7			13.0	23.4
	Alma-Ata Cotton Textile Combine			56.9			16.7	26.4
	Semipalatinsk Meat-Packing Combine			59.3			22.6	18.1
11. 1973	Workers, engineering-technical personnel and employees in three building-materials plants in Uzbekistan, total			60.1			12.5	27.4
	workers			58.0			13.2	28.7
	engineering-technical personnel and employees			70.3			9.5	20.2
12. 1972–74	Workers in oil industry:							
	Glavtiumenneftgas Association	50.2	20.5	70.7	14.8	7.5	22.3	7.0
	Sakhalinneft Association	25.8	31.1	56.9	20.8	12.1	32.9	10.2
13. 1970–74	Individuals employed in variety of jobs (from unskilled workers to managerial personnel) in ship repair plant and port, Odessa	31.8	27.3	59.1	7.6	2.6	10.2	29.5
14. 1974	385 workers in four enterprises of automobile industry:							
	201 workers in nonautomated jobs	16.6	51.8	68.4	4.0	0.5	4.5	27.1
	184 workers in automated jobs	16.2	69.0	85.2	2.2	0.0	2.2	12.5

Table A-1 (continued)

Soviet Studies of Work Satisfaction

		Response categories in %						
Year	Scope of sample	highly satisfied	more satisfied than dissatisfied	total satisfied	more dissatisfied than satisfied	highly dissatisfied	total dissatisfied	other
15. 1975	4,000 urban residents in Moldavia employed in variety of jobs (from unskilled workers to managerial personnel)			63.5			14.0	22.5
16. 1976	1,534 workers up to age 30 in Leningrad industrial enterprises			40.2			22.0	37.8
17. 1977	1,500 workers, engineers, technicians, teachers, medical and film personnel to age 30 in three Latvian cities			67			33	
18. 1979	2,000 workers, employees, and engineering-technical personnel employed in Gorky region							
	workers			71.6			5.9	22.5
	engineering-technical personnel			66.0			6.4	27.6

1. A. G. Zdravomyslov and V. A. Iadov, "The Influence of Differences in the Content and Character of Work on the Attitude toward Work," in G. E. Glezerman and V. G. Afanas'ev, eds., *Opyt*, Moscow, 1965, p. 161. The "other" category here includes the "indifferent" and those giving "indeterminate or contradictory" answers.
2. L. Ananich and L. Bliakhman, "Are You Satisfied with Your Work," *Molodoi kommunist*, 1967, No. 1, p. 86. The figures refer to satisfaction with "specialty" rather than with "job." The "other" category refers to the "indifferent."
3. Osipov and Shchepanskii, p. 242.

4. N. F. Naumova and Sliusarianskii, p. 142. The "other" category includes 9.6% "indifferent," 25.1% "indeterminate," and 0.9% "no answer."

5. S. A. Kugel and O. M. Nikandrov, *Molodye inzhenery*, Moscow, 1971, p. 152. The "other" category includes the "indifferent" and those who "cannot answer."

6. V. A. Iadov, ed., *Sotsial'no-psikhologicheskii portret inzhenera*, 1977, p. 146. The "other" category applies to those who gave "no answer."

7. Akademiia nauk Moldavskoi SSR, otdel filosofii i prava, *Sotsial'naia aktivnost' rabotnikov promyshlennogo predpriiatiia*, Kishinev, 1973, p. 42. This study was based on a sample of "more than 3,300" persons drawn from all occupational groups. We assume approximately 3,000 were manual workers (*rabochie*). The "other" category here refers to those in the whole sample with a "neutral" attitude toward work ("at least 30%"). The 21.3% "dissatisfied" is derived as a residual.

8. I. E. Stoliarova in *Sotsiologicheskie issledovaniia*, 1975, No. 2, p. 143. The "other" category here includes 15.3% "indifferent" and 13.7% with "contradictory" attitudes.

9. Prokhvatilov and Kirdziuk, pp. 259–60. The figure shown for "satisfied" applies to those with a "positive attitude" toward their work; that for the "dissatisfied" applies to those with a "negative attitude." The "other" category applies to those with an "indeterminate" attitude.

10. Akademiia nauk Kazakhskoi SSR, Institut ekonomiki, *Sotsial'no-ekonomichekie voprosy razvitiia Kazakhstana v period razvitogo sotsializma*, Alma-Ata, 1977, p. 92. The respondents in these studies were divided into three categories: those who "liked" their jobs, did "not like" them and the "indifferent."

11. V. I. Soldatova and A. S. Chamkin, *Proizvodstvennyi kollektiv i voprosy kommunisticheskogo vospitaniia*, Tashkent, 1979, pp. 121, 124–25. The figures for workers are calculated as simple averages of the figures shown in this source for workers in unskilled, "low content" and "high content" work.

12. A. N. Mal'kov and V. D. Pivovarov, "The Structure of Labor Turnover at Enterprises of the Oil Industry," *Sotsiologicheskie issledovaniia*, 1979, No. 2, p. 80. The "other" category applies to those with a "neutral" attitude.

13. I. M. Popova, p. 151. These figures were derived as simple averages of those shown in this source for employees whose work was graded "high," "average" and "low" in quality. These grades are shown for each of the job satisfaction categories. The "other" category applies to employees whose answers were "contradictory" or who found it "difficult to answer."

14. Akademiia nauk SSSR, Institut mezhdunarodnogo rabochego dvizheniia, *Rabochii klass v usloviiakh nauchno-tekhnicheskoi revoliutsii*, Moscow, 1979, p. 145. The "other" category applies to those who were "partly satisfied, partly not."

15. Iu. V. Arutiunian, *Opyt etnosotsiologicheskogo issledovaniia obraza zhizni*, Moscow, 1980, p. 54. The "other" category applies to those who "did not answer."

16. Calculated from A. A. Kissel', "The Value-Normative Aspect of Work Attitudes," *Sotsiologicheskie issledovaniia*, 1984, no. 1, p. 53. The "other" category applies to those who were "indifferent" and those whose attitudes were "indeterminate."

17. G. Mints and I. Chechetina, *Molodezh' v zerkale sotsiologii*, Riga, 1980, p. 17. This source cites "about two-thirds" as satisfied and one-third as not.

18. Akademiia nauk SSSR, Institut sotsiologicheskikh issledovanii, *Sovetskaia sotsiologiia*, vol. 2, Moscow, 1982, p. 21.

Notes

Chapter 1

1. Akademiia nauk SSSR, Institut mezhdunarodnogo rabochego dvizheniia, *Sotsial'noe razvitie rabochego klassa SSSR*, Moscow, 1977, pp. 22-23.

2. L. Bliakhman, "A Social Portrait of the Modern Young Worker," *Sotsialisticheskii trud*, 1979, No. 10, p. 63.

3. Akademiia nauk SSSR, pp. 21-22.

4. E. G. Antosenkov and Z. V. Kuprianov, *Tendentsii v tekuchesti rabochikh kadrov*, Novosibirsk, 1977, p. 26; L. Bliakhman, *Molodoi rabochii 70kh godov: sotsial'nyi portret*, Moscow, 1977, p. 53. On the need to develop the elementary habits of an industrial culture, see L. A. Gordon and A. K. Nazimova, "The Production Potential of the Soviet Working Class: Trends and Problems of Development," *Voprosy filosofii*, 1980, No. 11, pp. 36-39.

5. A. G. Zdravomyslov, V. P. Rozhin and V. A. Iadov, *Chelovek i ego rabota*, Moscow, 1967, pp. 281-83, 304-5 (cited henceforth as Zdravomyslov and Iadov, *Chelovek*). For an English translation of this volume, see *Man and His Work*, translated and edited by Stephen P. Dunn, White Plains, New York: International Arts and Sciences Press, Inc., 1970. This also appeared in *Soviet Sociology*, Vol. IX, No. 1-2.

6. For example, V. P. Kochikian, *Planirovanie sotsial'nogo razvitiia kollektivov predpriiatii v otrasliakh mashinostroeniia*, Moscow, 1976, p. 101; O. I. Shkaratan, O. V. Stakanova and O. V. Filippova, "Features of Social Growth of the Soviet Worker (Materials From a Study of Leningrad Workers, 1918-77)," *Sotsiologicheskie issledovaniia*, 1977, No. 4, p. 40.

7. V. Kostakov, "The Effectiveness of Labor and Education," *Ekonomicheskaia gazeta*, 1980, No. 33, p. 10.

8. F. R. Filippov, *Vseobshchee srednee obrazovanie v SSSR*, Moscow, 1976, p. 63, reports that the number of secondary school graduates in 1975 was 88% of the number beginning first grade ten or eleven years earlier. The comparable figure for 1965 was 45%.

9. L. Bliakhman in *Sotsialisticheskii trud*, 1979, No. 10, p. 64.

10. The figures for purely manual jobs are from Akademiia obshchestvennykh nauk pri TsK KPSS, *Sotsial'noekonomicheskie problemy nauchno-tekhnicheskoi revoliutsii*, Moscow, 1976, pp. 198-200; V. Moskovich and V. Anan'ev, "The Occupational-Skill Structure of Workers," *Voprosy ekonomiki*, 1979, No. 6, p. 63; V. G. Aseev and O. I. Shkaratan, *Sotsial'nye normativi i sotsial'noe planirovanie*, Moscow, 1984, p. 8. The Iadov statement appeared in *Znanie—sila*, 1979, No. 10.

11. A partial listing of these studies and their findings appears in M. Kh.

Titma, *Vybor professii kak sotsial'naia problema*, Moscow, 1975, pp. 112–13.

12. M. N. Rutkevich, editor, *Zhiznennye plany molodezhi*, Sverdkovsk, 1966, p. 35. For a more recent formulation of the tendency of secondary school graduates to regard their initial jobs mainly as "trampolines for springing to a VUZ," see V. P. Kochikian, p. 105.

13. F. R. Filippov, "The Role of the Higher School in Changing the Social Structure of Soviet Society," *Sotsiologicheskie issledovaniia*, 1977, No. 2, p. 48.

14. V. Churbanov, "The Young Worker and Low-Content Work," *Molodoi kommunist*, 1972, No. 6, p. 66.

15. G. Slutskii and G. Shestakova, "The Conveyor: Pro and Con," *Molodoi kommunist*, 1972, No. 10, pp. 57–58; N. A. Aitov, "Some Debatable Questions in the Study of the Soviet Intelligentsia," *Sotsiologicheskie issledovaniia*, 1979, No. 3, p. 33.

16. G. Slutskii and G. Shestakova, p. 57.

17. Iu. E. Duberman, *Sotsiologicheskie issledovaniia na neftegazo-dobyvaiushchikh predpriiatiiakh tatarii*, Al'metevsk, 1976, pp. 13–15; G. Slutskii and G. Shestakova, pp. 57–58.

18. "Man and His Work, Fifteen Years Later," *Znanie—sila*, 1979, No. 10. This is a report of an interview with V. A. Iadov.

19. "The Modern Plant and Its Workers," *Znanie—sila*, 1980, No. 2, p. 3. This is a report of an interview with S. T. Gur'ianov.

20. Ibid., p. 4.

21. Holland Hunter, "Soviet Economic Problems and Alternative Policy Responses," in U.S. Congress, Joint Economic Committee, *Soviet Economy in a Time of Change* (Washington, D.C., U.S. Government Printing Office, 1979), p. 25.

22. Murray Feshbach, "The Structure and Composition of the Industrial Labor Force," in Arcadius Kahan and Blair Ruble, editors, *Industrial Labor in the U.S.S.R.* (New York: Pergamon Press, 1979), p. 4.

23. Interview with V. A. Iadov, *Znanie—sila*, 1979, No. 10; L. A. Kostin, "Labor Productivity at the Present Stage," *EKO*, 1980, No. 12, p. 64; Joint Economic Committee, *Soviet Economy in the 1980s: Problems and Prospects*, Part 2 (Washington, U.S. Government Printing Office, 1983), p. 335.

24. This section draws mainly on the following: N. A. Aitov, *Nauchno-tekhnicheskaia revoliutsiia i sotsial'noe planirovanie*, Moscow, 1978; N. I. Lapin, E. M. Korzheva and N. F. Naumova, *Teoriia i praktika sotsial'nogo planirovaniie*, Moscow, 1975; G. N. Cherkasov and G. G. Zaitsev, *Sotsiologiia i nauchnaia organizatsiia truda*, Leningrad, 1973; D. A. Kerimov, A. S. Pashkov and M. N. Rutkevich, editors, *Planirovanie sotsial'nogo razvitiia*, Moscow, 1976.

25. N. A. Aitov, p. 107.

26. N. I. Lapin et al., p. 109; T. Zaslavskaia, in *Znanie—sila*, 1982, No. 2, p. 10.

27. N. I. Lapin et al., pp. 131–37.

28. N. A. Aitov, p. 112.

29. Ibid., p. 113.

30. N. I. Lapin et al., p. 137.

31. Robert Blauner, *Alienation and Freedom* (Chicago and London: University of Chicago Press, 1973); Melvin L. Kohn, "Occupational Structure and Alienation," *American Journal of Sociology*, July, 1976, pp. 111–30.

32. Murray Yanowitch, "Alienation and the Young Marx in Soviet Thought," *Slavic Review*, March, 1967, pp. 29–53.

33. A. A. Zvorykin, *Filosofiia i nauchno-tekhnichekii progress*, Moscow, 1965, pp. 35–38.

34. Zdravomyslov and Iadov, *Chelovek*, pp. 21–27, 131.

Chapter 2

1. This discussion draws mainly on Zdravomyslov and Iadov, *Chelovek*, pp. 98–152; A. G. Zdravomyslov and V. A. Iadov, "The Influence of Differences in the Content and Character of Work on the Attitude toward Work," in G. E. Glezerman and V. G. Afanas'ev, editors, *Opyt i metodika konkretnykh sotsiologicheskikh issledovanii*, Moscow, 1965, pp. 144–96 (cited henceforth as *Opyt*).

2. Zdravomyslov and Iadov, *Opyt*, pp. 159–60.

3. For an illustration, see A. A. Prokhvatilov and G. V. Kirdziuk, "On Some Special Features of Young Workers' Attitudes toward Work at the Angarsk Oil-Chemical Combine," Angarskii gorodskoi komitet KPSS, *Aktual'nye problemy sotsial'nogo planirovaniia*, Irkutsk, 1975, p. 258.

4. Zdravomyslov and Iadov, *Chelovek*, pp. 151-52.

5. Ibid., pp. 138–39.

6. A. A. Murutar and P. A. Vikhalemm, "Some Problems of a Comprehensive Investigation of Satisfaction in a Factory Collective," Tartuskii gosudarstvennyi universitet, *Trudy po sotsiologii*, II, Tartu, 1972, p. 152; Zdravomyslov and Iadov, *Chelovek*, p. 128; N. F. Naumova, "Labor and the Mode of Life," in V. I. Dobrynina, compiler, *Sovetskii obraz zhizhi: sevodnia i zavtra*, Moscow, 1976, p. 115.

7. V. A. Iadov, "Orientation—Creative Work," in G. M. Gusev et al., editors, *Obshchestvo i molodezh'*, Moscow, 1968, pp. 130–31; Zdravomyslov and Iadov, *Chelovek*, p. 128.

8. Murutar and Vikhalemm, p. 141.

9. A Velichko and V. Podmarkov, *Sotsiolog na predpriiatii*, Moscow, 1976, p. 136.

10. N. F. Naumova, p. 113.

11. Ibid., p. 114.

12. Murutar and Vikhalemm, p. 143; I. M. Popova, *Stimulirovanie trudovoi deiatel'nosti kak sposob upravleniia*, Kiev, 1976, p. 139.

13. V. A. Iadov and A. A. Kissel', "Work Satisfaction: An Analysis of Empirical Generalizations and an Attempt at Their Theoretical Interpretation," *Sotsiologicheskie issledovaniia*, 1974, No. 1, pp. 84–86.

14. Jack Barbash, *Job Satisfaction Attitudes Surveys* (Paris: Organization for Economic Cooperation and Development, 1976), p. 22.

15. We exclude from consideration here those surveys which seem to reflect very special circumstances, for example, an 88% job dissatisfaction rate reported for workers in the Belorusneft Combine of the oil industry (A. N. Mal'kov and V. D. Pivovarev, "The Structure of Labor Turnover at Enterprises of the Oil Industry," *Sotsiologicheskie issledovaniia*, 1979, No. 2, p. 80). Similarly, we ignore reports of unbelievably "happy" workers, such as one study which reported that only 1% of respondents disliked their jobs (N. M. Blinov, *Trudovaia deiatel'nost kak osnova sotsialisticheskogo obraza zhizni*, Moscow, 1979, p. 59). We also exclude from consideration those studies in which essentially nothing is revealed about survey procedures and respondents except the proportions "satisfied" and "dissatisfied."

16. George Strauss, "Is There a Blue-Collar Revolt against Work," in James O'Toole, editor, *Work and the Quality of Life* (Cambridge, Mass.: MIT Press, 1976), p. 53.

17. Akademiia nauk Kazakhskoi SSR, Institut filosofii i prava, *Nauchno-tekhnicheskaia revoliutsiia i dukhovnyi mir cheloveka*, Alma-Ata, 1979, pp. 326–29.

18. A Kazakhstan study cites a figure of 12–15% as typical for the share of the "indifferent" and 5–6% for the dissatisfied (ibid., p. 327). Almost all of the studies at our disposal suggest that the latter figure is an understatement.

19. Ibid., p. 328.

20. Murutar and Vikhalemm, pp. 155-56.

21. This appears with particular clarity in comparisons of the proportion of respondents expressing job dissatisfaction and those who express a desire to change jobs. The latter group commonly encompasses one-third to one-half of respondents even where the former is one-fifth or less. For examples see Akademiia nauk SSSR, Institut mezhdunarodnogo rabochego dvizheniia, *Rabochii klass v usloviiakh nauchno-tekhnicheskoi revoliutsii*, Moscow, 1979, pp. 145-46; Akademiia nauk Moldavskoi SSR, otdel filosofii i prava, *Sotsial'naia aktivnost' rabotnikov promyshlennogo predpriiatiia*, Kishinev, 1973, p. 42.

22. Arne L. Kalleberg and Larry J. Griffin, "Positional Sources of Inequality in Job Satisfaction," *Sociology of Work and Occupations*, November 1978, p. 373.

23. See ibid., pp. 371-400.

24. At least one Soviet study has found no essential difference between the job satisfaction rates of engineers, technicians and foremen on the one hand and workers on the other (M. I. Zaitseva, "Creative Work in the Value Structure of Engineering-Technical Personnel," in Akademiia nauk SSSR, *Sotsial'nye issledovaniia*, Issue 3, Moscow, 1970, p. 161.

25. Iadov, "Orientation," pp. 132-33.

26. Akademiia nauk Moldavskoi SSR, pp. 44-46.

27. Zdravomyslov and Iadov, *Chelovek*, p. 180.

28. V. A. Iadov and A. G. Zdravomyslov, "The Attitude of Young Workers toward Their Work," in G. V. Osipov and Ia. Shchepanskii, editors, *Sotsial'nye problemy truda i proizvodstva*, Moscow, 1969, p. 126.

29. Zdravomyslov and Iadov, *Chelovek*, p. 181.

30. Akademia nauk Moldavskoi SSR, p. 186; Akademiia nauk SSSR, Institut mezhdunarodnogo, p. 170.

31. Iadov, "Orientation," pp. 133-35; Zdravomyslov and Iadov, *Chelovek*, pp. 196-98.

32. M. I. Zaitseva, p. 165; the Perm study is reported in N. F. Naumova and M. A. Sliusarianskii, "Work Satisfaction and Some Characteristics of the Personality," Akademiia nauk SSSR, *Sotsial'nye issledovaniia*, Issue 3, Moscow, 1970, pp. 145-60.

33. I. M. Popova, p. 172.

34. It is quite possible that this high "vote" for wages in workers' conceptions of a "good job" reflects the limited options offered them in surveys such as those shown in Table 2.7. But "importance ratings" of job attributes by workers also show adequate wages ranking higher than such elements of job content as variety in work, independence, responsibility, the need to learn something new, opportunity to develop one's abilities (Akademiia nauk SSR, Institut mezhdunarodnogo, p. 153).

35. I. M. Popova, p. 176.

36. V. A. Iadov, "Man at Work," *Komsomolskaia pravda*, February 9, 1978.

37. Interview with V. A. Iadov in *Znanie—sila*, 1979, No. 10.

38. V. A. Iadov, "The Attitude toward Work: A Conceptual Model and Actual Tendencies," *Sotsiologicheskie issledovaniia*, 1983, No. 3, p.58.

39. Ibid., p. 59.

40. A. Zdravomyslov, "The Social Sphere: Urgent Problems," *Kommunist*, 1981, No. 16, p. 62; G. Mints and I. Chechetina, *Molodezh' v zerkale sotsiologii*, Riga, 1980, pp. 74-75.

41. Of the five occupational groups into which the Leningrad workers sampled in both 1962 and 1976 were classified, work satisfaction increased in one, decreased in another and remained essentially unchanged in the remaining three. See A. A. Kissel' in *Sotsiologicheskie issledovaniia*, 1984, No. 1, p. 53. As if confirming that work satisfaction for the sample as a whole failed to increase, Iadov notes in *Sotsiologicheskie issledovaniia*, 1983, No. 3, p. 60, that "absolute indices of

satisfaction," tend to be stable "within the limits of a given culture."

42. Interview with V. A. Iadov in *Znanie—sila*, 1979, No. 10. On the deterioration of discipline and widespread worker indifference, see the interview with Iadov and his colleagues in M. Levin, "Youth and Work," *EKO*, 1983, No. 8, pp. 115–16, 118. The increased proportion of workers reporting a "neutral" attitude toward their speciality (rather than "satisfied" or "dissatisfied") may also be a sign of growing indifference to work activity. See G. Cherkasov and V. Veretennikov, "Social Factors in the Growth of Labor Productivity," *Sotsialisticheskii trud*, 1981, No. 3, p. 105.

43. A partial exception was the study by two Estonian sociologists who sought to elicit their subjects' reactions to the question of whether there was "a conformity of interests between workers and management." There is no evidence that this interesting theme has been pursued further thus far. Murutar and Vikhalemm, p. 160.

44. This section draws mainly on Zdravomyslov and Iadov, *Opyt*, pp. 151–55.

45. A. V. Tikhonov, "The Influence of the Worker's Production Independence on Work Attitudes," *Sotsiologicheskie issledovaniia*, 1976, No. 1, p. 32.

46. Ibid., pp. 35–36.

47. Ibid., p. 44.

48. G. N. Cherkasov and Ia. Kogut, editors, *Sotsial'nye problemy upravleniia trudovymi kollektivami*, Moscow, 1978, pp. 108–9, 219. This is the source of the reference to "social and organizational constraints." See also A. K. Nazimova, "The Social Potential of the Socialist Work Collective," *Rabochii klass i sovremennyi mir*, 1981, No. 1, p. 53. Iadov's acceptance of the importance of job autonomy appears in the first of these sources (pp. 108–9).

Chapter 3

1. U.S. Department of Labor Manpower Research Monograph No. 30, *Job Satisfaction: Is There a Trend?* (Washington, D.C.: U.S. Government Printing Office, 1974), p. 10.

2. See, for example, Alastair McAuley, *Women's Work and Wages in the Soviet Union* (London: George Allen and Unwin, 1981), chaps. 2 and 5; V. G. Podmarkov, editor, *Sotsial'nye problemy proizvodstva*, Moscow, 1979, pp. 198–203.

3. Among women workers below the age of 25 in the Taganrog study, 42% were in the lowest two grades of a six-grade wage scale, while the comparable figure for men was only 14%. E. B. Gruzdeva and E. S. Chertikhina, "Soviet Women: Problems of Work and Everyday Life," *Rabochii klass i sovremennyi mir*, 1982, No. 6, p. 113.

4. McAuley, p. 130.

5. Zdravomyslov and Iadov, *Chelovek*, pp. 158–62; Akademiia nauk Kazakhskoi SSR, Institut ekonomiki, *Upravlenie sotsial'nym razvitiem proizvodstvennykh kollektivov*, Alma-Ata, 1975, pp. 154–55.

6. Zdravomyslov and Iadov, *Chelovek*, pp. 142; Akademiia nauk Kazakhskoi SSR, Institut filosofii i prava, p. 275.

7. In four such studies (in the Kazakh, Kirghiz and Latvian republics and the city of Volgograd) the job satisfaction rates were higher for men than for women. See Akademiia nauk Kazakhskoi SSR, Institut ekonomiki, p. 154; N. V. Nastavshev, p. 89; S. Bekkhodzhaeva, *Sotsial'no-ekonomicheskie problemy truda zhenshchin v narodnom khoziaistve Kirgizi*, Frunze, 1978, p. 170; G. Mints and L. Chechetina, *Molodezh' v zerkale sotsiologii*, Riga, 1980, p. 18. In an Uzbekistan study the opposite was the case. V. I. Soldatova and A. S. Chamkin, *Proizvodstvennyi kollektiv i voprosy kommunisticheskogo vospitaniia*, Tashkent, 1979, p. 131.

8. N. F. Naumova, p. 114.

9. Zdravomyslov and Iadov, *Chelovek*, pp. 162, 215, 230, 263.

10. Osipov and Shchepanskii, p. 424.

11. Kharchev and Golod, pp. 45–49; Osipov and Schchepanskii, p. 441.

12. This discussion is based largely on Kharchev and Golod, pp. 161–70.

13. Zdravomyslov and Iadov, *Chelovek*, p. 311.

14. For an illustration of this approach, see I. E. Stoliarova in *Sotsiologicheskie issledovaniia*, 1975, No. 2., pp. 148–49.

15. M. V. Nastavshev, p. 90.

16. *Komsomolskaia pravda*, February 9, 1978.

17. N. M. Shishkan, *Sotsial'no-ekonomicheskie problemy zhenskogo truda*, Moscow, 1980, pp. 111-12.

18. McAuley, pp. 26, 207.

19. This paragraph draws on Mints and Chechetina, pp. 18, 56–59.

20. L. A. Gordon and A. K. Nazimova in *Voprosy filosofii*, 1980, No. 11, pp. 37–38.

21. Prokhvatilov and Kirdziuk, p. 260; Akademiia nauk Ukrainskoi SSR, Institut ekonomiki, Odesskoe otdelenie, *Problemy sotsial'nogo regulirovaniia na promyshlennykh predpriiatiiakh*, Kiev, 1973, p. 86.

22. Prokhvatilov and Kirdziuk, p. 265.

23. U.S. Department of Labor, Manpower Research Monograph No. 30, p. 12.

24. Ibid.

25. Akademiia nauk Ukrainskoi SSR, p. 86.

26. See Table 2.1 for the results of the initial Leningrad study, the Angarsk Oil-Chemical Combine study and the report on "mixed occupational groups" in the auto and tractor industry. For a more recent example, see Iu. E. Volkov and Iu. S. Loshkarev, *Trudovoe vospitanie molodezhi*, Moscow, 1976, p. 28.

27. Gordon and Nazimova, pp. 36–37.

28. Harold J. Noah, editor and translator, *The Economics of Education in the U.S.S.R.* (New York, Washington, London: Frederick A. Praeger, Inc., 1969), p. IX.

29. Noah, p. 101; S. G. Strumilin, "The Economic Significance of National Education," in E. A. G. Robinson and J. E. Vaizey, editors, *The Economics of Education* (New York: St. Martin's Press, 1966), pp. 290, 298–300. The latter is a translation of an article Strumilin originally published in 1925.

30. S. G. Strumilin, "The Effectiveness of Education in the USSR," *Narodnoe obrazovanie*, 1962, No. 6, pp. 35–36.

31. A. Zvorykin, *Nauka, proizvodstva, trud*, Moscow, 1965, p. 149.

32. We rely here on a slightly revised version of Harold J. Noah's translation (Noah, pp. 108-11) of an article by I. I. Kaplan in V. A. Zhamin, editor, *Aktual'nye voprosy ekonomiki narodnogo obrazovaniia*, Moscow, 1965, pp. 88–91.

33. L. G. Istomin, "Some Problems of Managing Social and Economic Factors in the Effectiveness of Labor," *Izvestiia sibirskogo otdeleniia, Akademii nauk SSSR, seriia obshchestvennykh nauk*, January 1981, p. 150.

34. V. A. Sidorov, "The Effectiveness of Labor and the Quality of Training of Workers," *EKO*, 1981, No. 1, p. 150.

35. V. A. Zhamin, *Sotsial'no-ekonomicheskie problemy obrazovaniia i nauki v razvitom sotsialisticheskom obshchestve*, Moscow, 1979, pp. 129–30.

36. This quotation from an article by V. N. Shubkin and A. G. Aganbegian in a volume (not available to us) published in 1964 (*Kolichestvennye metody v sotsiologicheskikh issledovaniiakh*, p. 16) is cited in Zdravomyslov and Iadov, *Chelovek*, p. 282.

37. V. N. Shubkin, "Some Questions of Adapting Youth to Work," in Akademiia nauk SSSR, *Sotsial'nye issledovaniia*, Moscow, 1965, p. 133.

38. V. N. Shubkin, p. 132; V. A. Kalmyk, "A Multifactor Model of the Formation of Workers' Skills," in A. G. Aganbegian, G. V. Osipov and V. N. Shubkin, editors, *Kolichestvennye methody v sotsiologii*, Moscow, 1966, pp. 302, 305, 313.

39. N. A. Aitov, "Workers' Education and Their Work," *Voprosy filosofii*, 1966, No. 11, pp. 26-27.

40. Zdravomyslov and Iadov, *Chelovek*, pp. 119, 277, 280.

41. Ibid., p. 283; V. N. Shubkin, p. 132.

42. L. Bliakhman in *Sotsialisticheskii trud*, 1979, No. 10, pp. 64-65; R. A. Zlotnikov, *Dukhovnye potrebnosti sovetskogo rabochego*, Saratov, 1975, pp. 117-18.

43. Akademiia nauk Kazakhskoi SSR, Institut ekonomiki, *Upravlenie sotsial'nym razvitiem proizvodstvennykh kollektivov*, Alma-Ata, 1975, p. 81.

44. L. Bliakhman, "A Surplus of Education or an Inability to Utilize It," *Molodoi kommunist*, 1972, No. 11.

45. Zdravomyslov and Iadov, *Chelovek*, pp. 304-5.

46. L. Kogan, "Necessity or Luxury," *Ural*, 1968, No. 6, p. 147; N. A. Aitov, *Tekhnicheskii progress i dvizhenie rabochikh kadrov*, Moscow, 1972, pp. 65-66; A. Tashbulatova, "Youth and Unskilled Labor," *Molodoi kommunist*, 1972, No. 6, p. 61.

47. V. Churbanov, "The Young Worker and Low-Content Work, *Molodoi kommunist*, 1972, No. 6, p. 66.

48. Tashbulatova, pp. 59, 62.

49. Churbanov, pp. 65, 69.

50. G. Slutskii and G. Shestakova, "The Conveyor, For and Against," *Molodoi kommunist*, 1972, No. 10, p. 58.

51. Slutskii and Shestakova, p. 57.

52. Churbanov, p. 65; Interview with O. Shkaratan, *Molodoi kommunist*, 1973, No. 1, p. 67.

53. Interview with S. P. Neprintsev, *Molodoi kommunist*, 1972, No. 8, p. 72.

54. V. Krevnevich, "The Diploma of Today's Worker," *Molodoi kommunist*, 1973, No. 4, p. 80.

55. Krevnevich, pp. 83-84.

56. Akademiia nauk Ukrainskoi SSR, p. 88.

57. Ibid., p. 92.

58. Ibid., p. 92.

59. Krevnevich, p. 83; Interview with S. P. Neprintsev, *Molodoi kommunist*, 1972, No. 8, p. 71; for "official" figures, see V. A. Zhamin, *Sotsial'no-ekonomicheskie problemy obrazovaniia i nauki v razvitom sotsialisticheskom obshchestve*, Moscow, 1979, p. 50.

60. O. I. Shkaratan, O. S. Stakanova and O. V. Filippova, "Characteristics of Social Growth of the Soviet Worker," *Sotsiologicheskie issledovaniia*, 1977, No. 4, p. 40.

61. O. I. Shkaratan, *Promyshlennoe predpriiatie*, Moscow, 1979, p. 143.

62. L. A. Gordon, E. V. Klopov and B. B. Komarovskii, "Current Tendencies in the Dynamics of the Social Structure of a Developed Socialist Society," *Rabochii klass i sovremennyi mir*, 1981, No. 3, pp. 22-23; T. A. Babushkina, V. S. Dudin and E. A. Zenkovich, "Social Problems of Creating New Replacements for the Working Class," *Rabochii klass i sovremennyi mir*, 1981, No. 3, pp. 46-47.

63. Interview with V. A. Iadov, *Znanie—sila*, 1979, No. 10.

Chapter 4

1. For a recent example see O. I. Shkaratan et al. in *Sotsiologicheskie issledovaniia*, 1977, No. 4, p. 40.

2. N. Ottenberg, "Changes in Workers' Occupational Structure and Their Training Requirements," in D. I. Valentei, editor, *Obrazovatel'naia i sotsial'no-professional'naia struktura naseleniia SSSR*, Moscow, 1975, p. 57.

3. Shakaratan et al., p. 39.

4. Slesarev, p. 159.

5. F. Panachin, "New Horizons of the Soviet School," *Narodnoe obrazovanie*, 1981, No. 1, p. 2.

6. E. Zhiltsov, "Improving the Integrated Planning of Education and Training of Cadres," *Ekonomicheskie nauki*, 1980, No. 1, p. 66.

7. Zhiltsov, p. 66. See also I. S. Bolotin, "The Impact of the Demographic Situation on the Secondary and Higher School," *Sotsiologicheskie issledovaniia*, 1979, No. 4, pp. 127-218.

8. For evidence of the adaptive process, see V. Shubkin, *Nachalo puti*, Moscow, 1979, pp. 55-56. For evidence of continuing difficulties in this process, see G. Kulagin, "Does the Educational System Correspond to the Needs of the Economy," *Sotsialisticheskii trud*, 1980, No. 1, p. 89; editorial in *Ekonomika i organizatsiia promyshlennogo proizvodstva*, 1981, No. 5, p. 14 (cited henceforth as *EKO*).

9. V. Churbanov in *Molodoi kommunist*, 1972, No. 6, p. 71.

10. For rejection of the proposal, see the articles by G. Slutskii and G. Shestakova, in *Molodoi kommunist*, 1972, No. 10, p. 56, and L. Bliakhman in the same source, 1972, No. 11, p. 71. For evidence of occasional above-normal vacation periods, see A. A. Prokhorov, "Searches and Results," *EKO*, 1979, No. 7, p. 64.

11. See, for example, B. N. Kolodizh, "Work Discipline and Turnover," *EKO*, 1980, No. 5, p. 126.

12. N. Karpukhin, "New Forms of Work Organization: A Means of Intensifying the Exploitation of Working People," *Sotsialisticheskii trud*, 1977, No. 2., pp. 121-27; M. Moshenskii, "The Doctrine of 'Humanization of Work' and Current Methods of Exploitation," ibid., 1977, No. 4, pp. 111-12; M. Kapralova, "Peculiarities of Applying New Forms of Work Organization in the FRG," ibid., 1979, No. 4, pp. 115-19; A. Nikiforova, "The Conflict of Interests and Social Aims of Working People and Monopolies in the Sphere of Work Organization," ibid., 1979, No. 10, pp. 107-14; M. Moshenskii, "The Theory of 'Quality of Work Life' and Its Role in the Economics and Sociology of Modern Capitalism," ibid., 1981, No. 9, pp. 105-14; I. I. Dakhno and M. N. Kapralova, "The Volvo Experiment," *EKO*, 1980, No. 4, pp. 172-84.

13. Moshenskii in *Sotsialisticheskii trud*, 1977, No. 2, p. 117.

14. Dakhno and Kapralova, p. 184.

15. Ibid., pp. 183-84.

16. Nikiforova, p. 113.

17. G. Slutskii and A. Molchanov, "New Elements in Work Organization on Assembly Jobs," *Sotsialisticheskii trud*, 1970, No. 5, p. 100; Slutskii and Shestakova, p. 60; V. Kononov, "Aspects of Progress: Technical and Social," *Molodoi kommunist*, 1972, No. 12, p. 80.

18. For a recent example, see V. M. Tarasenko and V. Ia. Kvitko, "Mechanization: Not Only Positive Features," *EKO*, 1980, No. 6, pp. 160-61.

19. G. V. Khalpakhchiev, "The Consumer Gains, Production Gains," *EKO*, 1979, No. 1, pp. 107-8. In this case the description of conveyor work applies to shoe production.

20. B. P. Kutyrev, "Monotony and the Conveyor," *EKO*, 1979, No. 7, p. 52a.

21. V. A. Skripov, "Who Will Help the Plant Sociologist?" *EKO*, No. 3, p. 107.

22. For example, Khalpakhchiev, pp. 106-14; Kutyrev, p. 50.

23. Dakhno and Kapralova, p. 183; for an earlier example, see Slutskii and Shestakova, p. 60.

24. The phrase is from ibid., p. 58.

25. V. Markov, "The Payment of Labor and the Occupational-Skill Composition of Cadres," *Sotsialisticheskii trud*, 1980, No. 1, pp. 104-5.

26. From "Editorial: Social Progress and the Program to Raise Public Welfare," *EKO*, 1981, No. 5, p. 14.

27. This paragraph is based on V. Z. Rogovin, *Sotsial'naia politika v razvitom sotsialisticheskom obshchestve*, Moscow, 1980, pp. 48, 51, 54-55.

28. Cherkasov and Kogut, pp. 216-17.

29. *Znanie—sila*, 1979, No. 10.

30. Z. I. Pruts, R. M. Sultanova and M. I. Talalai, *Sozdanie postoiannykh kadrov na predpriiatiiakh*, Moscow, 1980, p. 67.

31. O. V. Stakanova, "On the Structure of Work Potential," *Sotsiologicheskie issledovaniia*, 1981, No. 2, p. 77; Soldatova and Chamkin, p. 116.

32. *Znanie—sila*, 1979, No. 10.

33. I. A. Oblomskaia, *Razvitia obshchestvennogo truda v usloviiakh zrelogo sotsializma*, Moscow, 1980, pp. 150-51.

34. V. N. Pukhov, "Social Problems of Automation and the Role of Trade Unions in Their Solution," *Rabochii klass i sovremennyi mir*, 1979, No. 5, pp. 125-26.

35. Kutyrev, p. 45. An editorial note preceding this article (p. 43) makes the interesting point that "to eliminate monotony on the conveyor is necessary, but to do so we must reject the conveyor itself."

36. Pukhov, p. 126.

37. Ibid., p. 126.

38. V. Mokriak and V. Savich, "What Lies behind the Announcement of Departure," *Molodoi kommunist*, 1973, No. 2., p. 87. The appeal for a system that would be "equal and clear" appears in ibid., 1972, No. 11, p. 74.

39. Akademiia nauk SSR, Sibirskoe otdelenie, *Sotsial'no-ekonomicheskie problemy truda na promyshlennom predpriiatii*, Novosibirsk, 1979, p. 208.

40. L. N. Kogan, editor, *Sotsial'nye rezervy trudovogo kollektiva*, Moscow, 1978, pp. 227-29.

41. This paragraph draws on the following: Kogan, pp. 227-31; Pruts et al., pp. 138-40; Pukhov, p. 127.

42. Pukhov, p. 127.

43. A. Dovba and A. Andrianov, "The Brigade, the Basic Form of Work Organization," *Sotsialisticheskii trud*, 1981, No. 5, p. 92. Essentially the same argument appears in A. E. Kogut, editor, *Effektivnost' brigadnoi organizatsii truda*, Leningrad, 1980, p. 11.

44. V. V. Postal'nyi, "A Steady and Persistent Extension," *EKO*, 1980, No. 4, p. 38.

45. B. P. Zhdanov, "The Volga Experiment in Prikam'e," *EKO*, 1976, No. 6, p. 71.

46. Postal'nyi, p. 51.

47. N. Safronov, Ia. Shagalov and A. Shirov, "Reserves for Increasing Labor Productivity in Soviet Industry," *Sotsialisticheskii trud*, 1983, No. 7, p. 13; S. Shkurko, "New Forms of Brigade Organization and Stimulation of Labor," *Voprosy ekonomiki*, 1980, No. 10, p. 27.

48. V. V. Novikov and V. S. Dunin, "Designing Labor Processes against Monotony," *EKO*, 1979, No. 7, p. 55.

49. This paragraph draws mainly on: "The *Vazovskii* Original Version," *EKO*, 1980, No. 4, pp. 76-81; Dovba and Andrianov, pp. 93-97; Shkurko, p. 36; N. Lobanov, L. Grigor'eva and G. Silant'eva, "What Does the Experience of Lenin-

grad Enterprises Show," *Sotsialisticheskii trud*, 1981, No. 5, p. 81; G. Kulagin, "A Very Necessary Variant," *Nash sovremennik*, 1982, No. 5, pp. 168–72.

50. Shkaratan et al., p. 41.

51. A. Pavlov and E. Gavrilenko, "A Choice between Two Evils or a Third Path," *Literaturnaia gazeta*, March 17, 1982.

52. Shkurko, pp. 34–35.

53. V. G. Britvin, "The Production-Technical Environment of the Enterprise and Worker Behavior," *Sotsiologicheskie issledovaniia*, 1982, No. 2, p. 143.

Chapter 5

1. V. Kokashinskii, "An Experiment with Puzzles," *Molodoi kommunist*, 1974, No. 3, pp. 95–98; Edward L. Deci, "Work—Who Does Not Like It and Why," *Psychology Today*, August 1972, pp. 57–58, 92. All quotations in the discussion which follows are drawn from these two sources.

2. Murray Yanowitch, *Social and Economic Inequality in the Soviet Union* (White Plains: M. E.Sharpe, Inc., 1977), ch. 5.

3. Ibid., pp. 137–40.

4. D. P. Kaidalov and E. I. Suimenko, *Psikhologiia edinonachaliia i kollegial'nosti*, Moscow, 1979, p. 172.

5. Ibid., pp. 15–16.

6. Ibid., p. 171. It is not clear how the authors can reconcile this with their statement (p. 173) that collegiality must remain "subordinate to" one-man management.

7. Ibid., p. 174.

8. Ibid., p. 158.

9. Ibid., p. 202. The 15% figure is cited in this source on p. 211.

10. E. S. Kuzmin and A. L. Sventsitskii, editors, *Promyshlennaia sotsial'naia psikhologiia*, Leningrad, 1982, p. 121; Leningradskii ordena Lenina i ordena trudovogo krasnogo znameni gosudarstvennyi universitet imeni A. A. Zhdanova, *Chelovek i obshchestvo*, Isssue 17, Leningrad, 1978, p. 102.

11. Even here the authors qualify this remark by immediately reminding the reader that "frictions" may develop when managers pursue a "correct course, but not all members of the collective recognize this." Our discussion of production conflicts and all direct quotations are drawn from Kaidalov and Suimenko, pp. 202–11.

12. A. K. Orlov, *Sovetskii rabochii i upravlenie proizvodstvom*, Moscow, 1978. There are some cases in the management literature in which Soviet writers have openly acknowledged the "contradiction" between one-man management with its "subordination of people to the requirements of the plan, the blueprint . . . the strict divisions of labor . . ." on the one hand and "the natural striving of a literate, cultured . . . person for independent creativity, his unwillingness to blindly follow outside directives" on the other. See G. A. Kulagin, "A Director's Every-day Life," *EKO*, 1983, No. 3, p. 125.

13. N. I. Lapin et al., pp. 142–46; E. S. Kuzmin and A. L. Sventsitskii, pp. 13–14.

14. A. I. Prigozhin, *Sotsiologiia organizatsii*, Moscow, 1980. The two reviews appear in *Sotsiologicheskie issledovaniia*, 1981, No. 3, pp. 214–19.

15. A. I. Prigozhin, p. 53.

16. Ibid., p. 56.

17. Ibid., p. 57.

18. See the review by L. N. Suvorov in *Sotsiologicheskie issledovania*, 1981, No. 3, pp. 216–19.

19. A. I. Prigozhin, p. 59.

20. This section draws on ibid., pp. 208–14.

21. Prigozhin normally refers to participation by *rabotniki*, i.e., working people, rather than *rabochie* (workers). The former implies enterprise personnel drawn from all occupational groups rather than the more narrowly defined "workers." While we occasionally refer to "worker" participation in our discussion of Prigozhin's views, his reference is normally to "working people" (*rabotniki*).

22. A. K. Nazimova, "The Social Potential of the Socialist Work Collective," *Rabochii klass i sovremennyi mir*, 1981, No. 1, p. 53.

23. O. Shkaratan, "What Kind of Worker Is Needed in Production," *Znanie—sila*, 1982, No. 10, p. 14.

24. Ibid.

25. L. A. Gordon and A. K. Nazimova, "The Social-Occupational Structure of Current Soviet Society; Typology and Statistics," *Rabochii klass i sovremennyi mir*, 1983, No. 2, pp. 65, 72.

26. V. N. Shubkin and G. A. Cherednichenko, "Social Problems of Choice of Occupation," *Rabochii klass i sovremennyi mir*, 1978, No. 2, p. 123.

27. L. A. Gordon and A. N. Nazimova, p. 73.

28. A. K. Nazimova, p. 57.

29. V. A. Smirnov, *Sotsial'naia aktivnost' sovetskikh rabochikh*, Moscow, 1979, pp. 161–62.

30. Akademiia nauk SSSR, Institut mechdunarodnogo rabochego dvizeniia, *Rabochii klass v usloviiakh naucho-tekhnichekoi revoliutsii*, Moscow, 1979, p. 236.

31. Ibid., p. 238.

32. Carole Pateman, *Participation and Democratic Theory* (London: Cambridge University Press, 1980), p. 68.

33. A. K. Nazimova, pp. 55, 57.

34. A. Orlov, "Participation of Working People in the Management of Production and Indicators of Its Effectiveness," *Sotsialisticheskii trud*, 1978, No. 5, p. 132.

35. Akademiia nauk SSSR, Institut mezhdunarodnogo rabochego dvizheniia, p. 226.

36. G. N. Cherakasov and Ia. Kogut, *Sotsial'nye problemy upravleniia trudovym kollektivami*, Moscow, 1978, pp. 134–35.

37. A. K. Orlov, "Problems of Improving the Organization of Managerial Activity of Working People at Enterprises," in *Organizatsiia upravleniia*, Moscow, 1979, p. 202; A. K. Orlov, *Sovetskii rabochii*, p. 89.

38. Akademiia nauk SSSR, Institut mezhdunarodnogo rabochego dvizheniia, p. 225; "Problems of Social Planning and Educational Work," *Kommunist*, 1982, No. 2, p. 53; Akademiia nauk SSSR, Institut sotsiologicheskikh issledovanii, *Formirovanie sotsial'noi odnorodnosti sotsialisticheskogo obshchestva*, Moscow, 1981, p. 39; T. T. Timofeev, editor, *Sotsial'no-ekonomicheskie problemy truda i byta rabochego klassa*, Moscow, 1979, p. 101; A. K. Nazimova, p. 59.

39. Ibid., p. 59; A. K. Orlov in *Sotsialisticheskii trud*, 1978, No. 5, p. 138.

40. Akademiia nauk SSSR, Institut sotsiologicheskikh issledovanii, *Formirovanie*, p. 40. This conclusion was supported by the author's finding that "the relative number of workers affirming the necessity to extend the sphere of involvement of workers . . . in participation in various types of management activity was 2.5 times higher than the proportion of workers believing that workers were being sufficiently involved in such participation." The same point is made by Nazimova, who refers to "a definite gap" between the "strong orientation of workers to participate in management and their satisfaction with the actual state of affairs . . . ." A. K. Nazimova, p. 59.

41. We draw here on our article "Pressures for More 'Participatory' Forms of

Economic Organization in the Soviet Union," *Economic Analysis and Workers' Management*, 1978, Nos. 3–4, pp. 405–6. The article by N. Alekseev, "The Interrelationship of Social Factors Determining Work Attitudes," originally appeared in *Sotsiologicheskie issledovaniia*, 1975, No. 3, pp. 112–21.

42. Ibid., pp. 119–20.

43. We draw here on our article in *Economic Analysis and Workers' Management*, 1978, Nos. 3–4, pp. 406–7. The article by A. V. Tikhonov, "The Influence of the Worker's Production Independence on Work Attitudes," originally appeared in *Sotsiologicheskie issledovaniia*, 1976, No. 1, pp. 31–44. Both the Alekseev and Tikhonov articles have been translated in M. Yanowitch, editor, *Soviet Work Attitudes* (White Plains: M. E. Sharpe, Inc., 1979), pp. 81–126.

44. A.V. Tikhonov, p. 32.

45. Ibid., p. 33.

46. Ibid., pp. 42, 44.

47. Alan Fox, *Beyond Contract: Work, Power and Trust Relations* (London: Faber and Faber Limited, 1975), ch. 1; Melvin L. Kohn, *Class and Conformity* (Chicago and London: the University of Chicago Press, 2nd ed., 1977), pp. xxxxiv–xxxxv.

48. G. N. Cherakasov and Ia. Kogut, pp. 108–9, 219; O. I. Shkaratan, "The Effectiveness of Work and Attitudes toward Work," *Sotsiologicheskie issledovaniia*, 1982, No. 1, p. 23.

Chapter 6

1. See W. Teckenberg's comments in a book review in *Soviet Studies*, July 1981, p. 462.

2. Ia. S. Kapeliush, *Obshchestvennoe mnenie o vybornosti na proizvodstve*, Information Bulletin No. 39 (54) of the Institute of Concrete Social Research of the Academy of Sciences of the USSR, Moscow, 1969. Portions of this study have been translated in M. Yanowitch, editor, *Soviet Work Attitudes*, pp. 60–80. We draw here, in part, on our article in *Economic Analysis and Workers' Management*, 1978, Nos. 3–4, pp. 411–14.

3. Kapeliush, pp. 4–5, 105. According to the author, reports of the experiments and/or readers' reactions appeared in at least the following: *Komsomol'skaia pravda*, September 24 and October 8, 1966, and May 12 and June 24, 1967; in *Izvestia*, July 16, 1967; in *Literaturnaia gazeta*, October 4, 1967. The report on the Krasnoiarsk experiment is reproduced in Kapeliush, pp. 98–105.

4. Kapeliush, p. 6

5. Ibid., p. 14.

6. Ibid., p. 16.

7. See M. Yanowitch in *Economic Analysis and Workers' Management*, 1978, Nos. 3–4.

8. Kapeliush, p. 59. Among ordinary workers the proportion agreeing that elections would dilute one-man management was 29%. The comparable figure for workers who were deputies of soviets was 19%. These figures should be compared with those showing the proportions opposed to elections of managers in our Table 6.1.

9. Ibid., p. 27.

10. Ibid., pp. 4, 26–27.

11. Ibid., p. 26.

12. Ibid., p. 26.

13. V. G. Afanas'ev, *Nauchnoe upravlenie obshchestvom*, 2nd ed., Moscow, 1973, pp. 264–65.

14. G. Popov and G. Dzhavadov, *Kadry upravleniia sotsialisticheskim obshchestvennym proizvodstvom*, Moscow, 1974, cited by A. Levykov in *Novy mir*, 1980, No. 5, p. 220.

15. We rely here on *Literaturnaia gazeta*, November 3, 1976; O. I. Kosenko, "The Collective Chooses a Leader," *EKO*, 1977, No. 1, pp. 89–95 (referred to henceforth as *EKO*); A. Levykov, "What Remains for People," *Novy mir*, 1980, No. 5, pp. 220-21.

16. O. I. Kosenko, p. 95.

17. *Literaturnaia gazeta*, November 3, 1976.

18. A. Levykov, *Kaluzhskii variant*, Moscow, 1980, p. 242.

19. O. I. Kosenko, p. 94.

20. Ibid., p. 95. It is noteworthy that the director of the Riga plant also stressed the limited impact of the experiment, perhaps with a view to "protecting" it rather than to urge its radicalization: "No radical changes occurred in the course of the elections of foremen simply because there were no worthy competitors for many of them . . ." (cited in ibid., p. 95).

21. "A Word in Favor of the Experiment," *Literaturnaia gazeta*, August 31, 1977.

22. V. Mikheev, "Social Psychology and Management," *Pod znamenem leninizma*, 1974, No. 17, p. 58, cited in Kaidalov and Suimenko. p. 168.

23. Ibid., p. 169.

24. A. Levykov, *Kaluzhskii*, pp. 225–26.

25. Ibid., p. 235.

26. The next several paragraphs draw on ibid., pp. 246–48.

27. For illustrations, see A. A. Miasnikov, "The Work Force and Labor Time: Reserves Are Utilized Weakly," *EKO*, 1980, No. 7, pp. 80–81; F. M. Rudich, "Combining One-Man Management and Collegiality in the Management of Socialist Production," *Sotsiologicheskie issledovaniia*, 1981, No. 3, pp. 67–68; M. Sonin, "Notes on Labor Discipline," *EKO*, 1981, No. 5, p. 73; A. M. Kurennoi, *Aktivnaia zhiznennaia pozitsiia sovetskogo rabochego*, Moscow, 1983, p. 62.

28. G. Kulagin, "A Very Necessary Variant," *Nash sovremennik*, 1982, No. 5, p. 171.

29. Ibid., pp. 171–72.

30. Kulagin was not prepared to go further than elections of brigade leaders and foremen at "leading enterprises in the form of an experiment," something that was already in effect.

31. O. Kosenko, "Taking Account of the Collective's Opinion," *Pravda*, April 5, 1983. A 1980 article in *EKO* had noted with approval that experiments in elections and "competition" to fill lower-level managerial positions "had been and were being conducted at tens of enterprises in industry and construction at Krasnoiarsk, Alma-Ata, Frunze, Riga, Lvov and other cities." See A. A. Miasnikov, p. 80.

32. There is some ambiguity on this score in the *Pravda* account. At the preliminary stage of the selection process, apparently "one or more persons" may be presented as candidates for a given managerial vacancy, with "every worker of the enterprise" having the right to submit names of candidates. But there is also a reference to a "final listing" (*utochnennykh spiskov*) of candidates, which suggests that the number of these per vacancy might be pared to the usual one prior to the formal voting process. As in earlier accounts, it is clear that the "personnel department" and the plant's "social organizations" play a decisive role in drawing up the list of candidates. An essentially similar description of the Riga plant's procedures appears in an editorial article, "The Work Collective and Discipline," *Kommunist*, 1983, No. 14, p. 7.

33. S. Shkurko in *Voprosy ekonomiki*, 1980, No. 10, pp. 27–28; supplement to

Ekonomicheskaia gazeta ("Collective Forms of Work Organization. Brigade Economic Accounting"), 1983, No. 37. Our estimate of one-third as the maximum proportion of workers in brigades in the late 1970s is based on Shkurko's statement that "at the present time" (i.e., 1980) 20–40% of workers "in most branches" were organized in work brigades.

34. N. Lobanov, L. Grigor'eva and G. Silant'eva, "What Does the Experience of Leningrad Enterprises Show?" *Sotsialisticheskii trud*, 1981, No. 12, p. 81.

35. I. Shapiro, "The Development of the Brigade Form of Organization and Stimulation of Labor," *Planovoe khoziaistvo*, 1983, No. 7, p. 100.

36. G. Kulagin, p. 169.

37. For examples of such criticism, see: ibid., p. 168; B. P. Zhdanov, "The Volga Experiment in Prikam'e," *EKO*, 1976, No. 6, pp. 70–71; A. Levykov, pp. 105–9.

38. G. Slesinger, "A Composite Approach to the Introduction of the Scientific Organization of Labor: A Guarantee of Increased Effectiveness," *Sotsialisticheskii trud*, 1982, No. 5, p. 37.

39. G. Kulagin, p. 169.

40. B. P. Zhdanov, p. 72.

41. *Ekonomicheskaia gazeta* (supplement), 1983, No. 37. This and the following two paragraphs also draw on B. N. Gavrilov, "Foreman and Brigade Leader," *Ekonomicheskaia gazeta*, 1983, No. 12, p. 6; L. N. Kogan and A. V. Merenkov, "Composite Brigades: Opinions, Assessments and Experience of Introduction," *Sotsiologicheskie issledovaniia*, 1983, No. 1, p. 89; Iu. Baryshnikov, "The Economic Mechanism and Management of Labor," *Ekonomicheskie nauki*, 1981, No. 6, p. 91; I. Shapiro, pp. 99–106; S. Shkurko, pp. 26–36; R. Batkaev and M. Veller, "Collective Forms of Organization and Payment of Labor," *Voprosy ekonomiki*, 1980, No. 1, pp. 60–70.

42. B. N. Gavrilov, p. 6. The author, at the time of this statement, was deputy chairman of the State Committee on Labor.

43. A. K. Osipov, "Brigade Forms of Work Organization: Conditions of Effective Application," *EKO*, 1981, No. 8, p. 82.

44. T. G. Cummings and Edmond S. Molloy, *Improving Productivity and the Quality of Work Life* (New York and London: Praeger, 1977), p. 21.

45. A. K. Osipov, p. 77; "The Composite System of VAZ" (no author), *EKO*, 1981, No. 8, p. 14; I. Shapiro, p. 102; B. N. Gavrilov, p. 6.

46. *Ekonomicheskaia gazeta* (supplement), 1983, No. 37, p. 7; S. Shkurko, p. 36.

47. D. Kaidalov and E. Suimenko, "Is It Winning? It Will Win!" *Literaturnaia gazeta*, March 17, 1982.

48. A. Levykov, p. 189. As usual, Levykov speaks here through the people he has interviewed or from whom he has received letters.

49. Ibid., pp. 266–67.

50. For a more detailed account of this experiment, see M. Yanowitch, *Social and Economic Inequality*, pp. 156–61.

51. V. I. Vladimirov, "Problems and Prospects of Socioeconomic Development of the Countryside," *Sotsiologicheskie issledovaniia*, 1974, No. 1, p. 186.

52. A. Levykov, p. 193.

53. A. Rzhevuskii, "The Management of Production on the Basis of the Brigade Organization of Labor," *Sotsialisticheskii trud*, 1979, No. 11, p. 35.

54. A. Levykov, p. 368.

55. Ibid., pp. 34–35.

56. Ibid., p. 29.

57. Ibid., p. 132.

58. Ibid., p. 50.

59. This section draws largely on ibid., pp. 36, 45, 51, 222–23, 342–43, 360.

60. Foremen do have the right to "monitor" the "coefficients of work participation" set by the brigade council for its members which serve as a basis for sharing the brigade's wage pool. See A. A. Rzhevuskii, "What Are Labor Economists Working on and What Are They Accomplishing," *Sotsialisticheskii trud*, 1978, No. 3, p. 44.

61. A. Levykov, pp. 273, 390.

62. A. Levykov, "The Kaluga Variant," *Literaturnaia gazeta*, 1978, No. 19.

63. A. Pavlov and E. Gavrilenko, "A Choice of Two Evils or a Third Path," *Literaturnaia gazeta*, 1982, March 17, 1982.

64. D. Kaidalov and E. Suimenko in *Literaturnaia gazeta*, March 17, 1982. For other illustrations of pro-egalitarian sentiments, see V. V. Postol'nyi, "A Steady and Persistent Extension," *EKO*, 1980, No. 4, p. 38; Iu. V. Boitsov, "The New, But Don't Forget the Old," *EKO*, 1980, No. 4, p. 44.

65. M. Levin, "Youth and Work," *EKO*, 1983, No. 8, p. 114. This is a report of an interview with V. Iadov, A. N. Alekseev and A. A. Zhdanov. This section also draws on V. Iadov, "Attitudes toward Work: A Conceptual Model and Actual Tendencies," *Sotsiologicheskie issledovaniia*, 1983, No. 3, pp. 58–60.

66. M. Levin, p. 118.

67. Ibid., pp. 124–25.

68. Ibid., p. 125.

69. S. Shkurko, p. 34.

70. Ibid., p. 35.

71. V. G. Britvin, p. 143.

72. P. G. Klivets, "Conditions of Introduction of Brigade Methods of Work," *Sotsiologicheskie issledovaniia*, 1983, No. 3, p. 102.

73. A. A. Gorel'skii, "What Is Brigade Economic Accounting," *EKO*, 1982, No. 7, 122.

74. Ibid., p. 125.

75. A. N. Komozin, "Workers' Assessments of Different Aspects of the Brigade Method," *Sotsiologicheskie issledovaniia*, 1982, No. 3, p. 114; L. N. Kogan and A. V. Merenkov, "Composite Brigades: Opinions, Assessments and the Experience of Their Introduction," *Sotsiologicheskie issledovaniia*, 1983, No. 1, p. 89.

76. D. Kaidalov and E. Suimenko in *Literaturnaia gazeta*, March 17, 1982; A. Levykov, "Firmness," *Literaturnaia gazeta*, March 2, 1983.

77. Ibid.

Chapter 7

1. David Lane and Felicity O'Dell, *The Soviet Industrial Worker* (New York: St. Martin's Press, 1978), pp. 21, 50.

2. ". . . it should be stressed that such forms of democratization of production as the election of managerial personnel, and their more extensive accountability and removability in accordance with the will of the collective, the redistribution of the functions of management and their increasing transfer to the collectives themselves, the strengthening of work brigades and their legal consolidation, the decisive granting of greater independence and responsibility to youth—all of these in the most direct fashion operate to strengthen both labor and planning discipline." See the editorial, "Filling the Struggle for Discipline with Greater Content," *EKO*, 1983, No. 9, p. 13.

3. See V. Perevedentsev, "For All and for Each," *Nash sovremennik*, 1974, No. 1, pp. 141–42.

4. V. A Iadov in *Sotsiologicheskie issledovaniia*, 1983, No. 3, p. 58.

5. I. Dizhbit in *Literaturnaia gazeta*, November 3, 1976.

6. G. A. Almond and S. Verba, *The Civic Culture* (Boston: Little Brown and Co., 1965), pp. 271-72, cited in Carole Pateman, *Participation and Democratic Theory* (Cambridge: Cambridge University Press, 1970), p. 47.

7. Michael Poole, *Workers' Participation in Industry* (London: Routledge and Kegan Paul, rev. ed., 1978), p. 29; Carole Pateman, "The Civic Culture: A Philosophic Critique," in G. A. Almond and S. Verba, editors, *The Civic Culture Revisited* (Boston and Toronto: Little, Brown and Company, 1980), p. 89.

8. Compare O. Kosenko in *EKO*, 1977, No. 1, pp. 94-95, and in *Pravda*, April 5, 1983.

9. Alec Nove, *The Soviet Economic System* (London: George Allen and Unwin Ltd., 1977), p. 103.

10. D. Kaidalov and E. Suimenko in *Literaturnaia gazeta*, March 17, 1982.

11. Alec Nove, p. 102.

12. A. N. Komozin, p. 113; L. N. Kogan and A. V. Merenkov, p. 90.

13. A. Sarno et al., "Some Aspects of Establishing Brigade Work Organization," *Sotsiologicheskie issledovaniia*, 1983, No. 2, p. 101.

14. D. Kaidalov and E. Suimenko in *Literaturnaia gazeta*, March 17, 1982; A. A. Gorel'skii, "What Is Brigade Economic Accounting?" *EKO*, 1982, No. 7, p. 125.

15. V. V. Bronshtein, "Building Blocks on the Way to the Brigade Organization of Work," *EKO*, 1982, No. 7, p. 135.

16. M. Levin in *EKO*, 1983, No. 8, pp. 126-27.

17. V. V. Bronshtein, pp. 136-37.

18. For other reports of the resistance of "individualists" to the work-team principle, see *EKO*, 1980, No. 4, pp. 59-68.

Bibliography

Afanas'ev, V. G. *Nauchnoe upravlenie obshchestvom.* 2nd ed. Moscow, 1973.
Aitov, N. A. *Nauchno-tekhnicheskaia revoliutsiia i sotsial'noe planirovanie.* Moscow, 1978.
————. "Some Debatable Questions in the Study of the Soviet Intelligentsia." *Sotsiologicheskie issledovaniia,* 3, 1979.
————. *Tekhnicheskii progress i dvihzenie rabochikh kadrov.* Moscow, 1972.
————. "Workers' Education and Their Work." *Voprosy filosofii,* 11, 1966.
Akademiia nauk Kazakhskoi SSR, Institut ekonomiki. *Sotsial'no-ekonomicheskie voprosy razvitiia Kazakhstana v period razvitogo sotsializma.* Alma-Ata, 1977.
————. *Upravlenie sotsial'nym razvitiem proizvodstvennykh kollektivov.* Alma-Ata, 1975.
Akademiia nauk Kazakhskoi SSSR, Institut filosofii i prava. *Naucho-tekhnicheskaia revoliutsiia i dukhovnyi mir cheloveka.* Alma-Ata, 1979.
Akademiia nauk Moldavskoi SSSR, otdel filosofii i prava. *Sotsial'naia aktivnost' rabotnikov promyshlennogo predpriiatiia.* Kishinev, 1973.
Akademiia nauk SSSR, Institut istorii SSSR. *Sotsial'nyi oblik rabochei molodezhi.* Moscow, 1980.
————, Institut mezhdunarodnogo rabochego dvizheniia. *Rabochii klass v usloviiakh nauchno-tekhnicheskoi revoliutsii.* Moscow, 1979.
————. *Sotsial'noe razvitie rabochego klassa SSSR.* Moscow, 1977.
Akademiia nauk SSSR, Institut sotsial'no-ekonomicheskikh problem. *Sotsial'nye faktory povysheniia effektivnosti truda.* Leningrad, 1981.
Akademiia nauk SSSR, Institut sotsiologicheskikh issledovanii. *Formirovanie sotsial'noi odnorodnosti sotsialisticheskogo obshchestva.* Moscow, 1981.
————. *Sovetskaia sotsiologiia,* Vol. 2. Moscow, 1982.
Akademiia Nauk SSSR, Sibirskoe otdelenie. *Sotsial'no-ekonomicheskie problemy truda na promyshlennom predpriiatii.* Novosibirsk, 1979.
Akademiia nauk Ukrainskoi SSR, Institut ekonomiki, Odesskoe otdelenie. *Problemy sotsial'nogo regulirovaniia na promyshlennykh predpriiatiiakh.* Kiev, 1973.
Akademiia obshchestvennykh nauk pri TsK KPSS. *Sotsial'no-ekonomicheskie problemy nauchno-tekhnicheskoi revoliutsii.* Moscow, 1976.
Alekseev, N. "The Interrelationship of Social Factors Determining Work Attitudes." *Sotsiologicheskie issledovaniia,* 3, 1975.
Ananich, L., and Bliakhman, L. "Are You Satisfied with Your Work?" *Molodoi kommunist,* 1, 1967.
Antosenkov, E. G., and Kuprianov, Z. V. *Tendentsii v tekuchesti rabochikh kadrov.* Novosibirsk, 1977.
Arutiunian, Iu. V. *Opyt etnosotsiologicheskogo issledovaniia obraza zhizni.* Moscow, 1980.
Aseev, V. G., and Shkaratan, O. I. *Sotsial'nye normativi i sotsial'noe planirovanie.* Moscow, 1984.
Babushkina, T. A.; Dudin, V. S.; and Zenkovich, E. A. "Social Problems of Creating New Replacements for the Working Class." *Rabochii klass i sovremennyi mir,* 3, 1981.
Barbash, J. *Job Satisfaction Attitudes Surveys.* Paris: Organization for Economic Cooperation and Development, 1976.

Baryshnikov, Iu. "The Economic Mechanism and Management of Labor." *Ekonomicheskie nauki*, 6, 1981.

Batkaev, R., and Veller, M. "Collective Forms of Organization and Payment of Labor." *Voprosy ekonomiki*, 1, 1980.

Bekkhodzhaeva, S. *Sotsial'no-ekonomicheskie problemy truda zhenshchin v narodnom khoziaistve Kirgizii.* Frunze, 1978.

Blauner, R. *Alienation and Freedom.* Chicago and London: University of Chicago Press, 1973.

Bliakhman, L. *Molodoi rabochii 70kh godov; sotsial'nyi portret.* Moscow, 1977.

———. "A Social Portrait of the Modern Young Worker." *Sotsialisticheskii trud*, 10, 1979.

———. "A Surplus of Education or an Inability to Utilize It." *Molodoi kommunist*, 11, 1972.

Blinov, N. M. *Trudovaia deiatel'nost' kak osnova sotsialisticheskogo obraze zhizni.* Moscow, 1979.

Boitsov, Iu. V. "The New, but Don't Forget the Old." *EKO*, 4, 1980.

Bolotin, I. S. "The Impact of the Demographic Situation on the Secondary and Higher School." *Sotsiologicheskie issledovaniia*, 4, 1979.

Britvin, V. G. "The Production-Technical Environment of the Enterprise and Worker Behavior." *Sotsiologicheskie issledovaniia*, 2, 1982.

Bronshtein, V. V. "Building Blocks on the Way to the Brigade Organization of Work." *EKO*, 7, 1982.

Cherkasov, G. N., and Kogut, Ia., eds. *Sotsial'nye problemy upravleniia trudovymi kollektivami.* Moscow, 1978.

Cherkasov, G. N., and Veretennikov, V. "Social Factors in the Growth of Labor Productivity." *Sotsialisticheskii trud*, 3, 1981.

Cherkasov, G. N., and Zaitsev, G. G. *Sotsiologiia i nauchnaia organizatsiia truda.* Leningrad, 1973.

Churbanov, V. "The Young Worker and Low-Content Work." *Molodoi kommunist*, 6, 1972.

Cummings, T. G., and Molloy, E. S. *Improving Productivity and the Quality of Work Life.* New York and London: Praeger, 1977.

Dakhno, I. I., and Kapralova, M. N. "The Volvo Experiment." *EKO*, 4, 1980.

Deci, E. L. "Work—Who Does Not Like It and Why." *Psychology Today*, August, 1972.

Dizhbit, I. "Workers Select the Foreman," *Literaturnaia gazeta*, 44, 1976.

Dovba, A., and Andrianov, A. "The Brigade, the Basic Form of Work Organization." *Sotsialisticheskii trud*, 5, 1981.

Duberman, Iu. E. *Sotsiologicheskie issledovaniia na neftegazodobyvaiushchikh predpriiatiakh tatarii.* Al'metevsk, 1976.

Editorial. "Filling the Struggle for Discipline with Greater Content." *EKO*, 9, 1983.

Editorial. "Social Progress and the Program of Raising Living Standards." *EKO*, 5, 1981.

Editorial. "The Work Collective and Discipline." *Kommunist*, 14, 1983.

Feshbach, M. "The Structure and Composition of the Industrial Labor Force," in A. Kahan and B. Ruble, eds., *Industrial Labor in the U.S.S.R.* New York: Pergamon Press, 1979.

Filippov, F. R. "Children in the Country of Developed Socialism." *Sotsiologicheskie issledovaniia*, 4, 1979.

———. "The Role of the Higher School in Changing the Social Structure of Soviet Society." *Sotsiologicheskie issledovaniia*, 2, 1977.

———. *Vseobshchee srednee obrazovanie v SSSR.* Moscow, 1976.

Fox, A. *Beyond Contract: Work, Power and Trust Relations.* London: Faber and Faber Limited, 1975.

Gavrilov, B. N. "Foreman and Brigade Leader." *Ekonomicheskaia gazeta*, 12, 1983.

Gordon, L. A.; Klopov, E. V.; and Komarovskii, B. B. "Current Tendencies in the Dynamics of the Social Structure of a Developed Socialist Society." *Rabochii klass i sovremennyi mir*, 3, 1981.

Gordon, L. A., and Nazimova, A. K. "The Production Potential of the Soviet Working Class: Trends and Problems of Development." *Voprosy filosofii*, 11, 1980.

———. "The Social-Occupational Structure of Current Soviet Society: Typology and Statistics." *Rabochii klass i sovremennyi mir*, 2, 1983.

Gorel'skii, A. A. "What Is Brigade Economic Accounting?" *EKO*, 7, 1982.

Gruzdeva, E. B., and Chertikhina, E. S. "Soviet Women: Problems of Work and Everyday

Life." *Rabochii klass i sovremennyi mir*, 6, 1982.

Gur'ianov, S. T. Interview. *Znanie—sila*, 2, 1980.

Hunter, H. "Soviet Economic Problems and Alternative Policy Responses," in U.S. Congress, Joint Economic Committee. *Soviet Economy in a Time of Change*. Washington, D.C.: U.S. Government Printing Office, 1979.

Iadov, V. A. Interview. *Znanie—sila*, 10, 1979.

————. "Orientation—Creative Work," in G. M. Gusev et al., eds., *Obshchestvo i molodezh'*. Moscow, 1968.

————. "The Attitude toward Work: A Conceptual Model and Actual Tendencies." *Sotsiologicheskie issledovaniia*, 3, 1983.

————. "Man at Work." *Komsomolskaia pravda*, February 9, 1978.

————, ed. *Sotsial'no-psikhologicheskii portret inzhenera*. Moscow, 1977.

————, and Kissel', A. A. "Work Satisfaction: An Analysis of Empirical Generalizations and an Attempt at Their Theoretical Interpretation." *Sotsiologicheskie issledovaniia*, 1, 1974.

————, and Zdravomyslov, A. G. "The Attitude of Young Workers toward Their Work," in G. V. Osipov and Ia. Shchepanskii, eds., *Sotsial'nye problemy truda i proizvodstva*, Moscow, 1969.

Istomin, L. G. "Some Problems of Managing Social and Economic Factors in the Effectiveness of Labor." *Izvestiia sibirskogo otdeleniia, Akademii nauk SSSR, seriia obshchestvennykh nauk*, January 1981.

Joint Economic Committee. *Soviet Economy in the 1980's: Problems and Prospects*, Part 2. Washington, D.C: U.S. Government Printing Office, 1983.

Kaidalov, D., and Suimenko, E. "Is It Winning? It Will Win!" *Literaturnaia gazeta*, March 17, 1982.

————. *Psikhologiia edinonachaliia i kollegial'nosti*, Moscow, 1979.

Kalleberg, A. L., and Griffin, L. J. "Positional Sources of Inequality in Job Satisfaction." *Sociology of Work and Occupations*, November 1978.

Kalmyk, V. A. "A Multifactor Model of the Formation of Workers' Skills," in A. G. Aganbegian, G. V. Osipov, and V. N. Shubkin, eds., *Kolichestvennye metody v sotsiologii*, Moscow, 1966.

Kapeliush, Ia. S. *Obshchestvennoe mnenie o vybornosti na proizvodstve*. Information Bulletin No. 39 (54) of the Institute of Concrete Social Research of the Academy of Sciences of the USSR. Moscow, 1969.

————. "A Word in Favor of the Experiment." *Literaturnaia gazeta*, August 31, 1977.

Kapralova, M. "Peculiarities of Applying New Forms of Work Organization in the FRG." *Sotsialisticheskii trud*, 4, 1979.

Karpukhin, N. "New Forms of Work Organization: A Means of Intensifying the Exploitation of Working People." *Sotsialisticheskii trud*, 2, 1977.

Kerimov, D. A.; Pashkov, A. S.; and Rutkevich, M. N., eds. *Planirovanie sotsial'nogo razvitiia*. Moscow, 1976.

Khalpakhchiev, G. V. "The Consumer Gains, Production Gains." *EKO*, 1, 1979.

Kharchev, A. G., and Golod, S. I. *Professional'naia rabota zhenshchin i sem'ia*. Leningrad, 1971.

Klivets, P. G. "Conditions of Introduction of Brigade Methods of Work." *Sotsiologicheskie issledovaniia*, 3, 1983.

Kochikian, V. P. *Planirovanie sotsial'nogo razvitiia kollektivov predpriiatii v otrasliakh mashinostroeniia*. Moscow, 1976.

Kogan, L. N. "Necessity or Luxury." *Ural*, 6, 1968.

————, ed. *Sotsial'nye reservy trudovogo kollektiva*. Moscow, 1978.

————, and Merenkov, A. V. "Composite Brigades: Opinions, Assessments and Experience of Introduction." *Sotsiologicheskie issledovaniia*, 1, 1983.

Kogut, A. E., ed. *Effektivnost' brigadnoi organizatsii truda*. Leningrad, 1980.

Kohn, M. L. *Class and Conformity*. Chicago and London: The University of Chicago Press, 2nd ed., 1977.

————. "Occupational Structure and Alienation." *American Journal of Sociology*, July, 1976.

Kokashinskii, V. "An Experiment with Puzzles." *Molodoi kommunist*, 3, 1974.

Kolodizh, B. N. "Work Discipline and Turnover." *EKO*, 5, 1980.

Komozin, A. N. "Workers' Assessments of Different Aspects of the Brigade Method."

Sotsiologicheskie issledovaniia, 3, 1982.

Kononov, V. "Aspects of Progress: Technical and Social." *Molodoi kommunist*, 12, 1972.

Kosenko. O. "Considering the Opinion of the Collective." *Pravda*, April 5, 1983.

————. "The Collective Selects the Leader." *EKO*, 1, 1977.

Kostakov, V. "The Effectiveness of Labor and Education." *Ekonomicheskaia gazeta*, 33, 1980.

Kostin, L. A. "Labor Productivity at the Present Stage." *EKO*, 12, 1980.

Krevnevich, V. "The Diploma of Today's Worker." *Molodoi kommunist*, 4, 1973.

Kugel, S. A., and Nikandrov, O. M. *Molodye inzhenery*. Moscow, 1971.

Kulagin, G. "A Very Necessary Variant." *Nash sovremennik*, 5, 1982.

————. "A Director's Every-Day Life." *EKO*, 3, 1983.

————. "Does the Educational System Correspond to the Needs of the Economy?" *Sotsialisticheskii trud*, 1, 1980.

Kurennoi, A. M. *Aktivnaia zhiznennaia pozitsiia sovetskogo rabochego*. Moscow, 1983.

Kutyrev, B. P. "Monotony and the Conveyor." *EKO*, 7, 1979.

Kuzmin, E. S., and Sventsitskii, A. L., eds. *Promyshlennaia sotsial'naia psikhologiia*. Leningrad, 1982.

Lane, D., and O'Dell, F. *The Soviet Industrial Worker*. New York: St. Martin's Press, 1978.

Lapin, N. I.; Korhzeva, E. M.; and Naumova, N. F. *Teoriia i praktika sotsial'nogo planirovaniia*. Moscow, 1975.

Leningradskii ordena Lenina i ordena trudovogo krasnogo znameni gosudarstvennyi universitet imeni A. A. Zhdanova. *Chelovek i obshchestvo*, XVII. Leningrad, 1978.

Lepp, M. "The Attitude toward Work in the Light of Sociological Studies." *Kommunist Estonii*, 6, 1966.

Levin, M. "Youth and Work." *EKO*, 8, 1983.

Levykov, A. "Firmness." *Literaturnaia gazeta*, March 2, 1983.

————. *Kaluzhskii variant*. Moscow, 1980.

————. "The Kaluga Variant." *Literaturnaia gazeta*, 19, 1978.

————. "What Remains for People?" *Novyi mir*, 5, 1980.

Lobanov, N.; Grigor'eva, L.; and Silant'eva, G. "What Does the Experience of Leningrad Enterprises Show?" *Sotsialisticheskii trud*, 5, 1981.

McAuley, A. *Women's Work and Wages in the Soviet Union*. London: George Allen and Unwin, 1981.

Mal'kov, A. N., and Pivovarev, V. D. "The Structure of Labor Turnover at Enterprises of the Oil Industry." *Sotsiologicheskie issledovaniia*, 2, 1979.

Markov, V. "The Payment of Labor and the Occupational-Skill Composition of Cadres." *Sotsialisticheskii trud*, 1, 1980.

Miasnikov, A. A. "The Work Force and Labor Time: Reserves are Utilized Weakly." *EKO*, 7, 1980.

Mints, G., and Chechetina, I. *Molodezh' v zerkale sotsiologii*. Riga, 1980.

Mokriak, V., and Savich, V. "What Lies behind the Announcement of Departure?" *Molodoi kommunist*, 2, 1973.

Moshenskii, M. "The Doctrine of 'Humanization of Work' and Current Methods of Exploitation." *Sotsialisticheskii trud*, 4, 1977.

————. "The Theory of 'Quality of Work Life' and Its Role in the Economics and Sociology of Modern Capitalism." *Sotsialisticheskii trud*, 9, 1981.

Moskovich, V., and Anan'ev, V. "The Occupational-Skill Structure of Workers." *Voprosy ekonomiki*, 6, 1979.

Murutar, A. A., and Vikhalemm, P. A. "Some Problems of a Comprehensive Investigation of Satisfaction in a Factory Collective," in Tartuskii gosudarstvennyi universitet. *Trudy po sotsiologii*, II. Tartu, 1972.

Nastavshev, N. V. "The Attitude toward Work and Some Characteristics of the Personality," in V. S. Rakhmanin et al., eds. *Lichnost' i problemy kommunisticheskogo vospitaniia*. Voronezh, 1973.

Naumova, N. F. "Labor and the Mode of Life," in V. I. Dobrynina, comp. *Sovetskii obraz zhiznii: sevodnia i zavtra*. Moscow, 1976.

———— and Sliusarianskii, M. A. "Work Satisfaction and Some Characteristics of the Personality," in Akademiia nauk SSSR, *Sotsial'nye issledovaniia*, 3, Moscow, 1970.

Nazimova, A. K. "The Social Potential of the Socialist Work Collective." *Rabochii klass i sovremennyi mir*, 1, 1981.

Neprintsev, S. P. Interview. *Molodoi kommunist*, 8, 1972.

Nikiforova, A. "The Conflict of Interests and Social Aims of Working People and Monopolies in the Sphere of Work Organization." *Sotsialisticheskii trud*, 10, 1979.

Noah, H. J., ed. *The Economics of Education in the USSR*. New York, Washington, London: Frederick A. Praeger, 1969.

No author. "The Composite System of VAZ." *EKO*, 8, 1981.

No author. "Problems of Social Planning and Educational Work." *Kommunist*, 2, 1982.

No author. "The Vazovskii Original Version." *EKO*, 4, 1980.

Nove, A. *The Soviet Economic System*. London: George Allen and Unwin, 1977.

Novikov, V. V., and Dunin, V. S. "Designing Labor Processes against Monotony." *EKO*, 7, 1979.

Oblomskaia, I. A. *Razvitia obshchestvennogo truda v usloviiakh zrelogo sotsializma*. Moscow, 1980.

Orlov, A. "Participation of Working People in the Management of Production and Indicators of Its Effectiveness." *Sotsialisticheskii trud*, 5, 1978.

————. *Sovetskii rabochii i upravlenie proizvodstvom*. Moscow, 1978.

Osipov, A. K. "Brigade Forms of Work Organization: Conditions of Effective Application." *EKO*, 8, 1981.

Osipov, G. V., and Shchepanskii, Ia. *Sotsial'nye problemy truda i proizvodstva*. Moscow and Warsaw, 1969.

Ottenberg, N. "Changes in Workers' Occupational Structure and Their Training Requirements," in D. I. Valentei, ed. *Obrazovatel'naia i sotsial'no-professional'naia struktura naseleniia SSSR*, Moscow, 1975.

Panachin, F. "New Horizons of the Soviet School." *Narodnoe obrazovanie*, 1, 1981.

Pateman, C. "The Civic Culture: A Philosophic Critique," in G. A. Almond and S. Verba, eds. *The Civic Culture Revisited*. Boston and Toronto: Little, Brown and Company, 1980.

————. *Participation and Democratic Theory*. Cambridge: Cambridge University Press, 1970.

Pavlov, A., and Gavrilenko, E. "A Choice between Two Evils or a Third Path." *Literaturnaia gazeta*, March 17, 1982.

Perevedentsev, V. I. "For All and for Each." *Nash sovremennik*, 1, 1974.

Podmarkov, V. G., ed. *Sotsial'nye problemy proizvodstva*. Moscow, 1979.

Poole, M. *Workers' Participation in Industry*. London: Routledge and Kegan Paul, rev. ed., 1978.

Popova, I. M. *Stimulirovanie trudovoi deiatel'nosti kak sposob upravleniia*. Kiev, 1976.

Postal'nyi, V. V. "A Steady and Persistent Extension." *EKO*, 4, 1980.

Prigozhin, A. I. *Sotsiologiia organizatsii*. Moscow, 1980.

Prokhorov, A. A. "Searches and Results." *EKO*, 7, 1979.

Prokhvatilov, A. A., and Kirdziuk, G. V. "On Some Special Features of Young Workers' Attitudes toward Work at the Angarsk Oil-Chemical Combine," in Angarskii gorodskoi komitet KPSS, *Aktual'nye problemy sotsial'nogo planirovaniia*. Irkutsk, 1975.

Pruts, Z. I.; Sultanova, R. M.; and Talalai, M. I. *Sozdanie postoiannykh kadrov na predpriiatiiakh*. Moscow, 1980.

Pukhov, V. N. "Social Problems of Automation and the Role of Trade Unions in Their Solution." *Rabochii klass i sovremennyi mir*, 5, 1979.

Quinn, R. P., and Staines, G. L. *The 1977 Quality of Employment Survey*. Ann Arbor, Mich.: The University of Michigan Survey Research Center, 1978.

Rogovin, V. Z. *Sotsial'naia politika v razvitom sotsialisticheskom obshchestve*. Moscow, 1980.

Rudich, F. M. "Combining One-Man Management and Collegiality in the Management of Socialist Production." *Sotsiologicheskie issledovaniia*, 3, 1981.

Rutkevich, M. N., ed. *Zhiznennye plany molodezhi*. Sverdlovsk, 1966.

Rzhevuskii, A. "The Management of Production on the Basis of the Brigade Organization of Labor." *Sotsialisticheskii trud*, 11, 1979.

————. "What Are Labor Economists Working on and What Are They Accomplishing?" *Sotsialisticheskii trud*, 3, 1978.

Safronov, N.; Shagalov, Ia.; and Shirov, A. "Reserves for Increasing Labor Productivity in Soviet Industry." *Sotsialisticheskii trud*, 7, 1983.

Sarno, A., et al. "Some Aspects of Establishing Brigade Work Organization" *Sotsiologicheskie issledovaniia*, 2, 1983.

Seniavskii, S. L., and Tel'pukhovskii, V. B. *Rabochii klass SSSR (1938-1965 gg.)*. Moscow, 1971.

Shapiro, I. "The Development of the Brigade Form of Organization and Stimulation of Labor." *Planovoe khoziaistvo*, 7, 1983.

Shishkan, N. M. *Sotsial'no-ekonomicheskie problemy zhenskogo truda*. Moscow, 1980.

Shkaratan, O. I. "The Effectiveness of Work and Attitudes toward Work." *Sotsiologicheskie issledovaniia*, 1, 1982.

————. Interview. *Molodoi kommunist*, 1, 1973.

————. *Promyshlennoe predpriiatie*. Moscow, 1979.

————. "What Kind of Worker Is Needed in Production?" *Znanie—sila*, 10, 1982.

————; Stakanova, O. V.; and Filippova, O. V. "Features of Social Growth of the Soviet Worker (Materials from a Study of Leningrad Workers, 1918-77)." *Sotsiologicheskie issledovaniia*, 4, 1977.

Shkurko, S. "New Forms of Brigade Organization and Stimulation of Labor." *Voprosy ekonomiki*, 10, 1980.

Shubkin, V. N. "Some Questions of Adapting Youth to Work," in Akademiia nauk SSSR, *Sotsial'nye issledovaniia*, Moscow, 1965.

————. *Nachalo puti*. Moscow, 1979.

————, and Cherednichenko, G. A. "Social Problems of Choice of Occupation." *Rabochii klass i sovremennyi mir*, 2, 1978.

Sidorov, V. A. "The Effectiveness of Labor and the Quality of Training of Workers." *EKO*, 1, 1981.

Skripov, V. A. "Who Will Help the Plant Sociologist?" *EKO*, 3, 1979.

Slesarev, G. A. *Rastet rabochii klass*. Moscow, 1976.

Slesinger, G. "A Composite Approach to the Introduction of the Scientific Organization of Labor: A Guarantee of Increased Effectiveness." *Sotsialisticheskii trud*, 5, 1982.

Slutskii, G., and Molchanov, A. "New Elements in Work Organization on Assembly Jobs." *Sotsialisticheskii trud*, 5, 1970.

Slutskii, G., and Shestakova, G. "The Conveyor: Pro and Con." *Molodoi kommunist*, 10, 1972.

Smirnov, V. A. *Sotsial'naia aktivnost' sovetskikh rabochikh*. Moscow, 1979.

Soldatova, V. I., and Chamkin, A. S. *Proizvodstvennyi kollektiv i voprosy kommunisticheskogo vospitaniia*. Tashkent, 1979.

Sonin, M. "Notes on Labor Discipline." *EKO*, 5, 1981.

Stakanova, O. V. "On the Structure of Work Potential." *Sotsiologicheskie issledovaniia*, 2, 1981.

Stoliarova, I. E. "Some Social Indicators of the Development of a Collective (VAZ and Leningrad Enterprises)." *Sotsiologicheskie issledovaniia*, 2, 1975.

Strauss, G. "Is There a Blue-Collar Revolt against Work," in J. O'Toole, ed. *Work and the Quality of Life*. Cambridge, Mass.: MIT Press, 1976.

Strumilin, S. G. "The Economic Significance of National Education," in E. A. G. Robinson and J. E. Vaizey, eds. *The Economics of Education*. New York: St. Martin's Press, 1966.

————. "The Effectiveness of Education in the USSR." *Narodnoe obrazovanie*, 6, 1962.

Supplement to *Ekonomicheskaia gazeta* ("Collective Forms of Work Organization. Brigade Economic Accounting."), 37, 1983.

Tarasenko, V. M., and Kvitko, V. Ia. "Mechanization: Not Only Positive Features." *EKO*, 6, 1980.

Tashbulatova, A. "Youth and Unskilled Labor." *Molodoi kommunist*, 6, 1972.

Tikhonov, A. V. "The Influence of the Worker's Production Independence on Work Attitudes." *Sotsiologicheskie issledovaniia*, 1, 1976.

Timofeev, T. T., ed. *Sotsial'no-ekonomicheskie problemy truda i byta rabochego klassa*. Moscow, 1979.

Titma, M. Kh. *Vybor professii kak sotsial'naia problema*. Moscow, 1975.

Tsentral'noe statisticheskoe upravlenie SSSR. *Narodnoe khoziaistvo SSSR* (for 1974, 1977, and 1980). Moscow, 1975, 1978, 1981.

————. *Narodnoe obrazovanie, nauka i kul'tura v SSSR*. Moscow, 1977.

U.S. Department of Labor Manpower Research Monograph No. 30. *Job Satisfaction: Is There a Trend?* Washington, D.C.: U.S. Government Printing Office, 1974.

Velichko, A., and Podmarkov, V. *Sotsiolog na predpriiatii*. Moscow, 1976.

Vladimirov, V. I. "Problems and Prospects of Socioeconomic Development of the

Countryside." *Sotsiologicheskie issledovaniia*, 1, 1974.

Volkov, Iu. E., and Loshkarev, Iu. S. *Trudovoe vospitanie molodezhi*. Moscow, 1976.

Yanowitch, M. "Alienation and the Young Marx in Soviet Thought." *Slavic Review*, March, 1967.

—————. "Pressures for More 'Participatory' Forms of Economic Organization in the Soviet Union." *Economic Analysis and Workers' Management*, 3-4, 1978.

—————. *Social and Economic Inequality in the Soviet Union*. White Plains, N.Y.: M. E. Sharpe, Inc., 1977.

—————, ed. *Soviet Work Attitudes*. White Plains, N.Y.: M. E. Sharpe, Inc., 1979.

Zaitseva, M. I. "Creative Work in the Value Structure of Engineering-Technical Personnel, " in Akademiia nauk SSSR, *Sotsial'nye issledovaniia*, 3, Moscow, 1970.

Zaslavskaia, T. Interview. *Znanie—sila*, 2, 1982.

Zdravomyslov, A. G. "The Social Sphere: Urgent Problems." *Kommunist*, 16, 1981.

—————, and Iadov, V. A. "The Influence of Differences in the Content and Character of Work on the Attitude toward Work," in G. E. Glezerman and V. G. Afanas'ev, eds. *Opyt i metodika konkretnykh sotsiologicheskikh issledovanii*. Moscow 1965.

—————; Rozhin, V. P.; and Iadov, V. A. *Chelovek i ego rabota*. Moscow, 1967. For an English translation of this volume, see *Man and His Work*, translated and edited by Stephen P. Dunn, White Plains, N.Y.: International Arts and Sciences Press, Inc., 1970, which also appeared in *Soviet Sociology*, Vol. IX, No. 1-2.

Zhamin, V. A. *Sotsial'no-ekonomicheskie problemy obrazovaniia i nauki v razvitom sotsialisticheskom obshchestve*. Moscow, 1979.

Zhdanov, B. P. "The Volga Experiment in Prikam'e." *EKO*, 6, 1976.

Zhiltsov, E. "Improving the Integrated Planning of Education and Training of Cadres." *Ekonomicheskie nauki*, 1, 1980.

Zlotnikov, R. A. *Dukhovnye potrebnosti sovetskogo rabochego*. Saratov, 1975.

Zvorykin, A. A. *Filosofiia i nauchno-tekhnicheskii progress*. Moscow, 1965.

—————. *Nauka, proizvodstva, trud*. Moscow, 1965.

Index